MOST
DANGEROUS

DANIEL ELLSBERG AND THE SECRET HISTORY OF THE VIETNAM WAR

MOST DANGEROUS

DANIEL ELLSBERG AND THE SECRET HISTORY OF THE VIETNAM WAR

STEVE SHEINKIN

ROARING BROOK PRESS   SQUARE FISH   NEW YORK

**SQUARE
FISH**

An imprint of Macmillan Publishing Group, LLC
120 Broadway, New York, NY 10271
mackids.com

Our books may be purchased in bulk for promotional, educational, or business
use. Please contact your local bookseller or the Macmillan Corporate and
Premium Sales Department at (800) 221-7945 ext. 5442 or by email at
MacmillanSpecialMarkets@macmillan.com.

Library of Congress Cataloging-in-Publication Data

Sheinkin, Steve.
    Most dangerous / Steve Sheinkin.
        pages cm
    Summary: "The story of Daniel Ellsberg and his decision to steal and publish
secret documents about America's involvement in the Vietnam War"—Provided
by publisher.
    Audience: Ages 10 to 14.
    Includes bibliographical references and index.
    ISBN 978-1-250-18083-4 (paperback)—ISBN 978-1-59643-953-5 (e-book)
    1. Ellsberg, Daniel—Juvenile literature. 2. Pentagon Papers—Juvenile literature.
3. Whistle blowing—United States—History—20th century—Juvenile literature.
4. Rand Corporation—Employees—Biography—Juvenile literature. 5. Vietnam
War, 1961–1975—United States—Juvenile literature. 6. United States—Foreign
relations—Vietnam—Juvenile literature. 7. Vietnam—Foreign relations—United
States—Juvenile literature. 8. United States—Politics and government—
1969–1974—Juvenile literature. I. Title.
    CT275.E38518S54 2015
    959.704'3092—dc23

                                                                        2014040761

Originally published in the United States by Roaring Brook Press
First Square Fish edition, 2019
Square Fish logo designed by Filomena Tuosto

10 9 8 7 6 5 4 3 2 1

AR: 6.7 / LEXILE: 890L

In memory of Lynn and Jill

Daniel Ellsberg is the most dangerous man in America.
He must be stopped at all costs.
—Henry Kissinger

CAST OF CHARACTERS

DANIEL ELLSBERG'S FAMILY, FRIENDS, AND ASSOCIATES

Carol Cummings Ellsberg's first wife

Patricia (Marx) Ellsberg Ellsberg's second wife and partner in activism

Robert Ellsberg Ellsberg's son with Carol Cummings

Mary Ellsberg Ellsberg's daughter with Carol Cummings

Dr. Lewis Fielding Ellsberg's psychiatrist

Randy Kehler antiwar activist who influenced Ellsberg

Tony Russo a former colleague from the Rand Corporation
and co-conspirator in copying the Pentagon Papers

Harry Rowen Ellsberg's boss at Rand

Lynda Sinay let Ellsberg and Russo use
her Xerox machine to copy Pentagon Papers

John Paul Vann retired Army colonel
who showed Ellsberg around Vietnam

Howard Zinn Boston University professor and antiwar activist

PRESIDENTS AND THEIR STAFFS

Harry S. Truman U.S. President from 1945–1953, supported
France's bid to retake Vietnam in 1945

Dwight D. Eisenhower U.S. President from 1953–1961, opposed elections in
Vietnam in an effort to block Communists from taking power

John Fitzgerald Kennedy U.S. President from 1961–1963, increased the number
of American troops in Vietnam from a few hundred to more than 16,000

Lyndon Baines Johnson U.S. President from 1963–1969

Claudia "Lady Bird" Johnson First Lady

Hubert Humphrey Vice President

Dean Rusk Secretary of State

Robert McNamara Secretary of Defense

John McNaughton Assistant Secretary of Defense

McGeorge Bundy National Security Advisor

PRESIDENTS AND THEIR STAFFS *(cont'd)*

Walt Rostow National Security Advisor
John McCone CIA Director
Bob Komer aide to President Johnson
Richard Nixon U.S. President from 1969–1974
Pat Nixon First Lady
Tricia Nixon older daughter of Richard and Pat Nixon
Julie Nixon younger daughter of Richard and Pat Nixon
Gerald Ford Nixon's Vice President, 1973–74
Bob Haldeman Nixon's White House Chief of Staff
John Mitchell Attorney General, later Nixon's campaign manager
Henry Kissinger National Security Advisor, later Secretary of State
Mort Halperin National Security Council staff member
Melvin Laird Secretary of Defense
Ron Ziegler White House Press Secretary
Erwin Griswold Solicitor General
Charles Colson White House Counsel
John Dean White House Counsel
John Ehrlichman Assistant to the President for Domestic Affairs

THE PLUMBERS

Egil Krogh White House aide, head of
Special Investigations Unit, also known as "the Plumbers"
G. Gordon Liddy formerly of the FBI
Howard Hunt formerly of the CIA
David Young of Kissinger's staff
Kathy Chenow Plumbers' secretary
"Steve" specialist with the CIA's technical services
Bernard Barker recruited by Plumbers to break into
Dr. Fielding's office and the Watergate
Felipe DeDiego and **Eugenio Martinez** anti-communists
working with Barker
James McCord former CIA technician who
worked with the Plumbers

U.S. MILITARY PERSONNEL

General Earle Wheeler Chairman of the Joint Chiefs of Staff, 1964–1970

John McConnell Air Force Chief of Staff

General William Westmoreland Commander of U.S. military operations in Vietnam, 1964–1968

Admiral Ulysses Sharp Commander-in-Chief of U.S. Pacific fleet, 1963–1964

Captain John Herrick Commodore of the USS *Maddox* and *Turner Joy*

Commander James Stockdale pilot in the Gulf of Tonkin, prisoner of war (POW)

Lieutenant Everett Alvarez pilot, first American POW in Vietnam

Lieutenant Philip Caputo one of the first marines to fight in Vietnam, later a journalist

John McCain prisoner of war at the Hanoi Hilton, later U.S. Senator

John Kerry first Vietnam veteran to speak against the war in Congress, later presidential candidate and Secretary of State to President Barack Obama

General Victor Krulak U.S. Marines, demonstrated the flaws in General Westmoreland's attrition strategy

U.S. CONGRESS

Senator Wayne Morse (D-OR), early objector to American involvement in Vietnam, cast the sole opposing vote against the Gulf of Tonkin Resolution

Senator William Fulbright (D-AR), helped steer the Gulf of Tonkin Resolution, later regretted his participation and considered releasing the Pentagon Papers

Norvil Jones, aide to Senator Fulbright

Senator Barry Goldwater (R-AZ), ran against Johnson for president in 1964

Senator Everett Dirksen (R-IL), powerful senator, friend to Lyndon Johnson

Senator George McGovern (D-SD), antiwar senator, later presidential candidate, considered taking the Pentagon Papers public

Senator Mike Gravel (D-AK), read sections of the Papers into public record

IN VIETNAM

Ho Chi Minh (Nguyen Tat Thanh) President, North Vietnam

Nguyen Van Thieu President, South Vietnam

IN VIETNAM *(cont'd)*

Le Duc Tho North Vietnamese negotiator
Bui Diem South Vietnamese Ambassador to the United States

THE PRESS

The New York Times
Neil Sheehan Reporter, broke Pentagon Papers story
Abe Rosenthal Managing Editor
James Goodale General Counsel
Hedrick Smith Reporter, worked with Sheehan on Pentagon Papers
Arthur Sulzberger Publisher
Louis Loeb attorney for the *New York Times*

The Washington Post
Katherine Graham Publisher
Ben Bradlee Executive Editor
Ben Bagdikian Assistant Managing Editor

The Boston Globe
Thomas Winship Publisher
Tom Oliphant Reporter

CBS News
Gordon Manning Vice President
Walter Cronkite Anchor

THE COURTROOM

Matthew Byrne Presiding Judge in the case against Daniel Ellsberg
Murray Gurfein Presiding Judge in case against the *New York Times*
Alexander Bickel and **Floyd Abrams** Attorneys,
defended the *New York Times* in Pentagon Papers case
Charlie Nesson Defense Lawyer for Daniel Ellsberg
David Nissen Chief Prosecutor in the case against Daniel Ellsberg

CONTENTS

PROLOGUE
FEASIBILITY STUDY

THEY CAME TO CALIFORNIA TO RUIN A MAN. Not to kill him, not literally. But the next best thing.

On a summer day in 1971, two men in wigs and glasses strolled along a sunny sidewalk in Los Angeles. One had a black mustache and walked with a limp. The other carried a camera on a strap over his shoulder.

They stopped in front of a three-story building of brick and glass. The man with the mustache posed beside the entryway, smiling like a tourist while his friend snapped a series of surveillance shots. They quickly repeated the process in front of alternative entry and escape points—low windows and the door in the back.

As they headed to their hotel, the mustached man's limp grew increasingly pronounced and by the time they reached the lobby, he was struggling to keep up. After shutting the door of their shared room, he yanked off his shoe, causing a heel-shaped hunk of lead to drop to the carpet. He pulled off his wig and glasses. The mustache stayed on; that part was real. This was G. Gordon Liddy, former agent of the Federal Bureau of Investigation.

The photographer, a retired Central Intelligence Agency agent named Howard Hunt, sat down to take notes. All that remained was to visit the target building under operating conditions. That is, at night.

Hunt and Liddy were part of a secret team working directly for the president of the United States. The focus of their mission was a man named Daniel Ellsberg. Ellsberg was all over the TV news that summer, and his blue eyes blazed from the covers of magazines. The press was calling him brilliant, intense, unpredictable. Some said he was a hero; some said the exact opposite. The president considered Ellsberg a traitor. At a White House meeting, the president's top foreign policy advisor put it bluntly: "Daniel Ellsberg is the most dangerous man in America. He must be stopped at all costs."

Precisely what Hunt and Liddy were planning to do.

After dark the operatives got back into their disguises. Liddy refused to put the lead hunk into his shoe—the limp-inducing device was part of his cover, designed to distract passersby from his face, but it was just too painful. He did, however, plan to try out a different piece of espionage equipment loaned to him by the CIA, a tobacco pouch with a miniature camera hidden in the bottom, and a hole for the camera lens.

They walked out into the warm summer night. It was just a few blocks to the building. The front door was not locked. Liddy pulled the tobacco pouch and a pipe from his pocket, and stuck the pipe in his mouth.

"Let's go," he said.

They climbed the stairs to the second floor and started down the dark hall toward the office of a psychiatrist named Lewis Fielding. A woman stepped out of a different office, holding cleaning supplies. Hunt thought she looked Mexican American.

"Señora," Hunt began, "somos doctores y amigos de Doctor Fielding."

The woman, Maria Martinez, seemed unconvinced these visitors were really doctors and Fielding's friends.

Hunt continued in Spanish. "With your permission, we would like to go into his office for a moment and leave for him something he has been expecting."

She hesitated.

"Please, we promise not to take anything."

Shrugging, she said, "Very well, caballeros."

Martinez unlocked Fielding's door and flicked on a light in the small reception room. Liddy entered with his tobacco pouch. Martinez stood by the door, expecting him to drop off his delivery and come right out. He didn't come out.

"What's he doing in there?" she asked.

"Writing a message to the doctor," Hunt said.

She took a step into the office just as Liddy strode out.

"Well, I left it," he said.

Hunt thanked the woman and tipped her. Liddy snapped a few photos with his tobacco pouch as they walked toward the exit.

"Did you have time to get any shots?" Hunt asked.

"A few, but Jesus, I kept thinking she was going to charge in on me!"

Anyway, it all looked fine, Liddy reported when they got outside. The filing cabinets had locks, but they were child's play. If the information they needed was in those files, it was there for the taking.

The men drove to the airport to catch the red-eye back to Washington. They could report to the White House with confidence that the operation to destroy Daniel Ellsberg was most definitely feasible.

PART I

INSIDER

COLD WARRIOR

WHAT COULD DANIEL ELLSBERG possibly have done to provoke such wrath—to be seen as such a threat? The story begins twenty-six years earlier, as World War II came to an end and the Cold War began. Ellsberg was just starting ninth grade at a prep school near Detroit, Michigan.

He did not, at that time, appear particularly dangerous.

"Kind of a nerd," is how one classmate described him.

"Very intense," another recalled. "Very studious and very interested in a lot of things."

A scrawny teen with dark curly hair, Dan was shy and quiet and had the unusual habit of walking around campus in a double-breasted suit, carrying his books and papers in a black briefcase. To classmates, he seemed obsessed with absorbing information and new ideas. But Dan did make an effort to branch out, landing

Daniel Ellsberg, age 16

the role of a wisecracking detective in the school play. He joined the bowling and rifle clubs. He gave soccer a try.

"I was terrible at soccer," he recalled.

Like many of his peers, Ellsberg was riveted by the rise of the Cold War. The global rivalry between the United States and the Soviet Union intensified quickly during Ellsberg's high school years, as Soviet ruler Joseph Stalin installed communist dictatorships in the countries of Eastern Europe, violently crushing calls for freedom in any land under his control. Ellsberg admired President Harry Truman's response—a commitment to supporting democracies and containing Soviet influence from spreading further.

"I had become," Ellsberg later said, "along with many other Americans, a cold warrior." In 1949 the Soviets tested their first atomic bomb, using plans stolen by spies from American labs. That same year Communists took power in China, the world's most populous nation. Then, with Soviet and Chinese backing, communist North Korea invaded democratic South Korea in 1950. In the Korean War, U.S. forces helped push back the invasion, but at a cost of more than thirty-six thousand American lives. The Cold War was clearly going to be a long and bitter fight. Daniel Ellsberg wanted in.

After graduating third in his class from Harvard University, Ellsberg stunned friends and professors alike by applying for officer's training with the Marine Corps. "I didn't seem the type," he later conceded. "My interests were almost entirely intellectual, and I wasn't any kind of athlete." But those recruiting posters—the ones asking men if they were tough enough to be a Marine—called to him.

Marine Lieutenant Daniel Ellsberg, 1954

Ellsberg willed his way through a training course filled with jocks and tough guys, and he served with pride as a marine lieutenant. He then returned to Harvard and earned his PhD in economics. Questions of risk and decision making particularly intrigued him. "To act reasonably, one must judge actions by their consequences," Ellsberg wrote in his doctoral thesis. "But what if their consequences are uncertain?"

How should one act when consequences are uncertain? That question would become a major theme in Ellsberg's life.

In the summer of 1964, Daniel Ellsberg was thirty-three, lean and fit, with blue eyes and brown hair cut short. As an analyst for the Rand Corporation, a think tank focused on military and international issues, he had been granted permission to conduct research at the Pentagon, home of the United States Department of Defense. He spent his days in a borrowed office, working on a study of recent international crises that he hoped would be useful to government policymakers.

One day in mid-July, he was at his desk, reading and taking notes, when Assistant Secretary of Defense John McNaughton dropped by. McNaughton knew Ellsberg's reputation as one of the brightest young thinkers in the field of crisis decision making. He wanted to discuss a trouble spot of increasing concern to the United States: a mountainous, heavily forested country winding more than a thousand miles along the coast of Southeast Asia. He wanted to discuss Vietnam.

Ellsberg was no expert, but on its surface the conflict there looked simple. There were two Vietnams in 1964. North Vietnam had a communist government, allied with the Soviet Union and China. North Vietnam's ruler, Ho Chi Minh, was waging war to unite the country under one government—his. The United States, committed to stopping the further spread of communism, backed the government of South Vietnam; it was corrupt and unpopular, but firmly non-communist. About twenty thousand American soldiers were stationed in South Vietnam, arming and training the military. This was a clear-cut Cold War showdown.

At that time, no one knew where events in Vietnam were headed. John McNaughton was the secretary of defense's main assistant on Vietnam policy. He needed help. He wanted Ellsberg on his staff.

Ellsberg was tempted, but hesitant. He liked working on projects of his own choosing, at his own pace. And he doubted he'd make a good aide to McNaughton, or anyone else for that matter. As he later confessed, "I'm not very organized."

McNaughton argued that Ellsberg could learn only so much from the study of historical cases. Here was a chance to see a real international crisis unfold as it happened—and from the inside.

"Vietnam is one crisis after another," McNaughton said. "It's one long crisis."

That clinched it. Ellsberg took the job.

And in the two weeks between that interview and Ellsberg's start date at the Pentagon, violence in Vietnam pushed the country closer to open war.

On the last night of July, South Vietnamese sailors on patrol boats fired missiles at radar stations in North Vietnam. On August 2, North Vietnamese forces spotted the American destroyer *Maddox* cruising in the Gulf of Tonkin, off the coast of North Vietnam. Three North Vietnamese boats sped up and fired torpedoes at the *Maddox*. None hit the ship.

President Lyndon Johnson ordered the *Maddox* to continue patrolling in the Tonkin Gulf. He ordered a second American destroyer, the *Turner Joy*, to join the *Maddox*. If there was another attack, Johnson intended to respond with force.

On August 3, South Vietnamese boats again hit targets in the North.

As the sun set on August 4, Captain John Herrick continued cruising aboard the *Maddox* in the Tonkin Gulf. The night was stormy and "completely dark," Herrick recalled, "ink black." He expected to come under attack at any moment.

Night in the Gulf of Tonkin was morning on the east coast of the United States. Daniel Ellsberg parked his white Triumph Spitfire convertible in the sprawling parking lot of the Pentagon. He got out of his car and joined the streams of men and women walking toward the massive five-sided building. This was the first day of his new job.

Ellsberg climbed the stairs to the third floor and walked down the hall to John McNaughton's office. It was a large suite with windows looking out across the Potomac River to the Washington Monument and the Capitol dome. McNaughton's secretary kept watch from a desk just outside the boss's private room. Other assistants sat in cubicles. Ellsberg entered his tiny workspace—"a cubbyhole," he called it—barely big enough for a desk and chair, a bookcase, and two safes for classified files. There was a little window with a view of Washington. He sat down and began reading through a pile of papers.

He did not have long to wait for the crisis his boss had promised. "My very first day on the job," he later said, "all hell broke loose."

DAY ONE

A FEW MINUTES AFTER eleven in the morning, a courier charged into John McNaughton's suite with a Flash priority cable for McNaughton. The secretary said her boss was down the hall, meeting with Secretary of Defense Robert McNamara. She told the courier to give the top priority cable to the new assistant. Ellsberg stepped out of his office and took the paper.

With one glance he knew why the courier had been running.

The cable was from Captain Herrick, commodore of the *Maddox* and *Turner Joy*. The American destroyers were under attack in the Gulf of Tonkin. Enemy speedboats had fired two torpedoes, both misses. The Americans were blasting back at the smaller craft.

Ten minutes later, the courier hurried in again with a second cable.

"Am under continuous torpedo attack," Herrick reported.

August 2, 1964. North Vietnamese torpedo boats attack the USS *Maddox* in the Gulf of Tonkin.

Then, a few minutes later: "Torpedoes missed. Another fired at us. Four torpedoes in water."

The battle was taking place on the other side of the world, in the dark. But Herrick's Flash messages made Ellsberg feel almost as if he were watching the action unfold.

His instinct was to hit back, and hit hard.

"We're going to really strike these guys," Ellsberg said, slamming fist into palm. "You can't attack an American ship on the high seas, and anybody that does has to pay for it."

Down the hall, Secretary of Defense Robert McNamara was reading the same cables. Given the rising tensions in the Gulf of

Tonkin, McNamara had been anticipating trouble. He knew he could handle it.

With his deep, decisive voice, slicked-back hair, and round rimless glasses, McNamara strode the halls of the Pentagon exuding confidence. President John Kennedy, who had appointed him secretary of defense in 1961, called McNamara the smartest man he'd ever met. Formerly a Harvard Business School professor and president of the Ford Motor Company, McNamara had a passion for statistics and organizational charts, and firm faith that no problem was too complex to be solved by the skillful application of logic, intelligence, and American firepower.

He picked up the phone and dialed the president.

"Yes, Bob," Lyndon Johnson answered.

"Mr. President, we just had word," McNamara began. "The destroyer is under torpedo attack."

"Where are these torpedoes coming from?"

"Well, we don't know, presumably from these unidentified craft," the secretary explained, referring to the enemy boats in Herrick's cable.

Johnson wanted to know if American planes from nearby aircraft carriers were in the air supporting the ships.

"Presumably," McNamara replied. He hadn't had time to find out. McNamara suggested that he, Secretary of State Dean Rusk, and National Security Advisor McGeorge Bundy head over to the White House.

"Okay, you get them," Johnson agreed, "then you come over here."

★ ★ ★

While McNamara crossed the Potomac into Washington, the action in the Gulf of Tonkin continued. As Johnson had hoped, several American planes were already in the air above the Gulf. First on the scene was one of the most experienced fighter pilots in the Navy, forty-year-old Commander James Stockdale.

It was a lousy night for flying, with low clouds and driving rain. Stockdale nosed his Crusader down to just a thousand feet above the water. Lightning flashes lit momentary glimpses of the two American destroyers. Between flashes, the churning white water of the ships' wakes was clearly visible against the black sea. Stockdale watched the ships swerving to avoid torpedoes. He saw the orange blasts of gunfire from the American ships.

But he couldn't see any enemy boats.

Stockdale was flying in and out of rain clouds, but he knew his view was much better than the one from the decks of the destroyers, where sailors were looking through rain and the spray from crashing waves. "I had the best seat in the house from which to detect boats," he later explained, "if there were any."

And yet the panicky radio reports from the *Maddox* kept coming. "We think there is a boat closing on us from astern."

"I have to press in," Stockdale shouted aloud in the cockpit. "I've got to see him, I've got to see him!"

He dove even lower, arcing behind the ships and squinting through his gun sight. He fired a rocket at the spot the enemy boats were reported to have been seen. The rocket disappeared

17

into the sea. He was so low now that saltwater spray was splattering his windshield.

"Now calm down and think, Jim," he told himself. "There's something wrong out here. Those destroyers are talking about hits, but where are the metal-to-metal sparks? And the boat wakes—where are they? And boat gun flashes?"

Running low on fuel, Stockdale headed back to his carrier, the *Ticonderoga*.

The moment he walked into the pilot's ready room on the ship, a group of intelligence officers began firing questions.

The first was: "What in the hell has been going on out there?"

"Damned if I know," Stockdale said.

"Did you see any boats?"

"Not a one. No boat, no boat wakes, no ricochets off boats, no boat gunfire, no torpedo wakes."

"Have a look at this," an officer said, handing him copies of Captain Herrick's cables to Washington. They contained a lot of the same things he'd been hearing over his cockpit radio. But after the first few reports, Herrick's cables began expressing hints of doubt about whether he was really under attack. The noise his crew was interpreting as that of enemy torpedoes, Herrick suggested, could actually be coming from the American ship's own propeller. And then, on the last page, Herrick spelled it out:

"Review of action makes many reported contacts and torpedoes fired appear doubtful. Freak weather effects on radar and overeager sonar men may have accounted for many reports. No actual visual sightings by *Maddox*. Suggest complete evaluation before any further action taken."

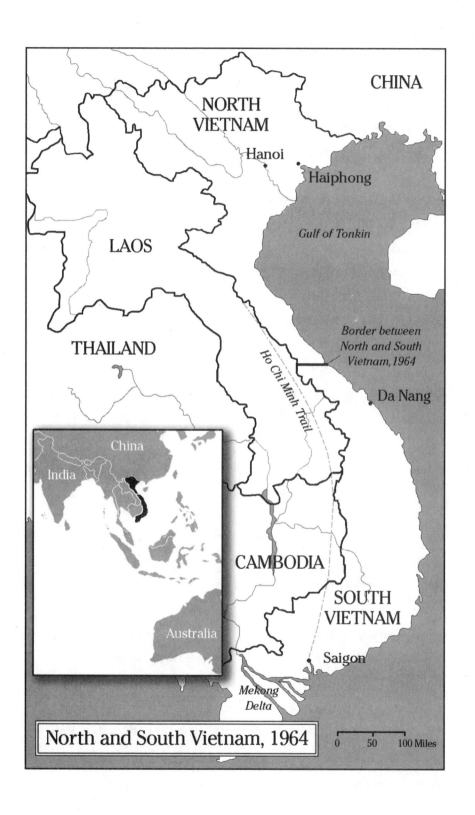

CHINA

NORTH
VIETNAM

Hanoi
Haiphong

LAOS

Gulf of Tonkin

THAILAND

*Border between
North and South
Vietnam, 1964*

Da Nang

Ho Chi Minh Trail

China

India

CAMBODIA

Australia

SOUTH
VIETNAM

Saigon

*Mekong
Delta*

North and South Vietnam, 1964

0   50   100 Miles

Stockdale handed back the paper, walked to his stateroom, and hung his flight gear in his locker. After washing his face he looked at himself in the mirror.

"Boy, you look tired," he thought. "At least you didn't fly into that water. And at least there's a commodore up there in the Gulf who has the guts to blow the whistle on a screwup, and take the heat to set the record straight."

He lay down and switched off his lamp.

"I would have never guessed," Stockdale would say many years later, "that commodores in charge on the scene of action are sometimes not allowed to blow the whistle on a screwup."

It was lunchtime in Washington, D.C. Secretary of Defense Robert McNamara, Secretary of State Dean Rusk, National Security Advisor McGeorge Bundy, and CIA Director John McCone gathered with President Johnson in the second floor dining room of the White House.

The men spread maps and reconnaissance photos of North Vietnam on the table. While Johnson leaned over the table to look, McNamara pointed out potential targets for an American air strike, mainly North Vietnamese torpedo boat bases along the coast.

Johnson approved. He wanted the strike launched as soon as possible. McNamara said it could be under way within a few hours.

"All right," Johnson said. "Let's go."

The White House press officer alerted television networks that President Johnson wanted air time that night to make an important statement on Vietnam. McNamara rushed back to the Pentagon, where he was handed Herrick's "Suggest complete evaluation" cable.

"I wish the hell we had more information about what's going on out there," he said.

He hoped to get conclusive answers from Admiral Ulysses Sharp, commander of the Pacific fleet, who was monitoring the situation from his base in Hawaii.

"The latest dope we have, sir, indicates a little doubt on just exactly what went on," Sharp told McNamara. He thought it possible that mistakes by inexperienced sonar operators could account for the reports of enemy torpedoes.

"There isn't any possibility there was no attack, is there?" McNamara asked.

August 4, 1964. Secretary of Defense Robert McNamara gives a late-night press briefing on events in the Gulf of Tonkin.

"Yes," Sharp said, "I would say that there is a slight possibility."

Later that afternoon McNamara drove back to the White House for a National Security Council meeting.

"Do we know for a fact that the North Vietnamese provocation took place?" one advisor asked.

"We will know definitely in the morning," McNamara replied.

No one suggested waiting.

Retaliation had been ordered, and President Johnson saw no reason to postpone. Privately, he had his doubts about what had really happened in the Gulf of Tonkin. "For all I know, our Navy was shooting at whales out there," he later confided in an aide.

But on the night of August 4, Johnson expressed no hesitation.

In the South China Sea, aboard the aircraft carrier USS *Constellation*, twenty-six-year-old Navy Lieutenant Everett Alvarez zipped up his flight suit. The night before, Alvarez had been one of the pilots looking down on the confusing scene in the Tonkin Gulf. Like Stockdale, he'd come away unconvinced the American destroyers were under attack.

Now, after a few hours of sleep, he was back in his plane. The president's orders for an air strike on North Vietnam had reached the *Constellation*. Alvarez was assigned one of the targets.

Pulling on his flight gloves, he noticed he was still wearing his wedding ring. A stark warning issued by survival school instructors flashed through his mind—*never wear wedding rings into combat*. If a pilot were ever taken prisoner, his captors could use the knowledge that he was married to torment him by inventing stories about his wife.

There was no time to put the ring anywhere. Alvarez climbed up a ladder to the cockpit of his Skyhawk. He put on his helmet and attached his oxygen mask. He tested the radio. Everything was working fine.

"Go get 'em, sir!" a deck crew member shouted. "Good luck."

The crew attached steel cables to the bottom of the plane. Alvarez pushed the throttle forward and his engines thundered. The steel cables stiffened and strained like a drawn archer's bow. Alvarez gave the "all clear" signal. The deck officer flashed a thumbs-up to the pilot, then arced his arm in the air, signaling the catapult crewman to hit his button. Alvarez's Skyhawk catapulted down the deck at two hundred miles per hour, and he was in the air.

Climbing to twenty thousand feet, he rendezvoused with nine other Skyhawks headed for North Vietnam. It was a seventy-minute flight to the target, a small torpedo boat base in the port town of Hon Gai.

"I wasn't scared," Alvarez later said of his first combat mission. "Just a little jittery."

It felt to him like that moment right before a high school track race, when the runners are tensed and waiting for the bang of the starter's gun.

HOSTILE ACTION

IT WAS 11:00 P.M. IN WASHINGTON, D.C. Daniel Ellsberg's first day at the Pentagon was now his first night.

Ellsberg and other staff members were gathered with John McNaughton in his office, reading the latest cables and waiting for the president's announcement. A big TV screen flickered, the volume turned down.

At 11:37, they saw President Johnson's face on the television. Someone turned up the sound.

"My fellow Americans," Johnson began, speaking from a podium in the White House. "As President and Commander-in-Chief, it is my duty to the American people to report that renewed hostile actions against United States ships on the high seas in the Gulf of Tonkin have today required me to order the military forces of the United States to take action in reply."

Johnson told viewers that the North Vietnamese attacks had

been fought off, with no American casualties. "But repeated acts of violence against the Armed Forces of the United States must be met not only with alert defense, but with positive reply," he said. "That reply is being given as I speak to you tonight."

He made clear that the strikes would be limited. For months, Johnson had been assuring Americans that he had no intention of expanding the country's role in Vietnam. As he had put it often, "We seek no wider war."

Now he repeated the pledge. "We Americans know, although others appear to forget, the risks of spreading conflict. We *still* seek no wider war."

The early afternoon skies were blue above the coast of North Vietnam. Alvarez had a clear view of the rocky coast, dotted with islands.

"When we go in, everybody drop back," Commander Bob Nottingham radioed to the other Skyhawk pilots. "Alvie and I'll go in first."

Nottingham began his approach, with Alvarez flying wing just seventy feet back. Diving at five hundred miles per hour, they saw the docks, and tied up there, as the briefers had told them, were four torpedo boats and one bigger patrol ship.

Alvarez fired his rockets as he sped past the target, then began banking to come around again.

"Look out!" another pilot shouted to Alvarez over the radio. "They're shooting at you!"

Alvarez saw black clusters of antiaircraft flak bursting all around his plane. He flipped the switch to arm his 20 mm gun.

"I'm going in again," he told the team.

All ten Skyhawks had taken shots at the targets, and the torpedo boats were on fire. Alvarez sped over the pier again, strafing the bigger ship from barely a hundred feet above the water.

Then he heard a sudden *BOOM* and saw a yellow flash over his left wing.

"The plane shook violently," he later said, "rattling and clanking as if someone had thrown a bucket of nuts and bolts into the engine." All the warning lights in the cockpit came on. Smoke started pouring in.

"I've been hit!" Alvarez shouted over his radio. "I'm on fire and out of control!"

The plane swerved to the left and started falling from the sky.

"I'm getting out! I'll see you guys later!"

Alvarez felt for the ring hanging behind his head and pulled. The plane's canopy shot off and a rocket blasted his seat into the air, the sudden rush of wind nearly knocking him unconscious. He heard the *POP* of his parachute opening. Seconds later he hit the water.

Ripping off his helmet, Alvarez could see that he was a few hundred yards from the coast. Bobbing in the water nearby were several fishing boats, manned by Vietnamese militiamen with rifles. They were moving toward him.

Alvarez thought of his wife. They'd been married just seven months. He took off his wedding ring and let it sink.

August 1964. U.S. Navy pilot Everett
Alvarez is taken prisoner by a North
Vietnamese sailor after being shot down.

Daniel Ellsberg spent the night at the Pentagon monitoring the air strikes. A total of sixty-four American planes hit four North Vietnamese patrol boat bases. Early in the morning on August 5, he went home to his empty apartment.

President Johnson flew to upstate New York that morning to dedicate a new building at Syracuse University. After a brief mention of the building, he turned to the action in Vietnam, emphasizing that the air strikes had been made necessary by the North Vietnamese torpedo boat attacks.

"The attacks were deliberate," Johnson said. "The attacks were unprovoked. The attacks have been answered."

Back in Washington, D.C., later that day, the president focused on next steps. Priority number one was to gain congressional approval for expanded military action in Vietnam, if deemed necessary. Johnson and his aides quickly finalized the language of what became known as the Tonkin Gulf Resolution. Here's the key sentence:

"Congress approves and supports the determination of the President, as Commander-in-Chief, to take all necessary measures to repel any armed attack against the forces of the United States and to prevent further aggression."

Essentially, the resolution was designed to grant the president the power to order further attacks in Vietnam without asking Congress for a formal declaration of war. Johnson submitted it to Congress. House and Senate leaders agreed to hold hearings the next day.

Late that night, Wayne Morse, a senator from Oregon, got a call from a man he knew in the Pentagon. The caller told Morse he wanted to pass on some information, but only on the strictest assurance that the source would never be revealed. Morse agreed.

The secretive caller informed Morse that whatever attacks had taken place on the American destroyers had hardly been, as the president claimed, "unprovoked." Part of the reason the *Maddox* was in the Gulf of Tonkin was to support the recent South Vietnamese raids on the North. American forces, the caller explained, were heavily involved in planning and carrying out those raids. The caller urged Morse to question Secretary McNamara about this.

The next morning, on Capitol Hill, Senator Morse cornered several senators before the joint hearings of the Senate Armed

Services and Foreign Relations Committees began. He was hoping to convince colleagues to join him in asking McNamara some tough questions.

"Hell, Wayne," one told him, "you can't get in a fight with the president at a time when the flags are waving."

The hearings were closed to the public. McNamara urged quick passage of the resolution. The senators seemed supportive—with the exception of Wayne Morse.

"I am unalterably opposed to this course of action which, in my judgment, is an aggressive course of action on the part of the United States," Morse said.

He didn't know about the doubts surrounding the August 4 "attacks" on Americans ships—and McNamara certainly didn't volunteer that information. But Morse definitely suspected that whatever had happened in the Gulf, the Americans were hardly innocent bystanders.

McNamara categorically denied this.

"Our Navy played absolutely no part in, was not associated with, was not aware of any South Vietnamese actions, if there were any," he told the senators. "I want to make that very clear to you." The *Maddox* had been on a routine patrol, he insisted, no different from patrols carried out by American ships every day, all over the world. "I think it is extremely important that you understand this," he lectured. "If there is any misunderstanding on that we should discuss the point at some length."

"I think we should," Morse answered.

"I say this flatly," McNamara shot back. "This is the fact."

McNamara was blatantly misleading Congress, but aside from

Morse, no other senators knew it. Some had misgivings about handing President Johnson what was practically a declaration of war, especially in such a hurry, and with such a vague idea of where things might lead. Still, most saw it as their responsibility to rally around the president.

"Our national honor is at stake," said Senator Richard Russell of Georgia. "We cannot and we will not shrink from defending it."

The committees voted 31–1 in favor of the resolution, with only Morse opposing. The full Senate vote was 88–2. The House approved the Tonkin Gulf Resolution 416–0.

President Johnson's approval rating shot up fourteen percentage points. Eighty-five percent of the public supported Johnson's handling of the crisis. Reelection in November looked certain.

Daniel Ellsberg's reaction was different. Unlike most Americans, he was seeing things from the inside.

He already had serious doubts that American ships had been attacked in the Gulf of Tonkin on the stormy night of August 4. Over the following hours and days, reading classified cables in his Pentagon office, Ellsberg learned the truth about the South Vietnamese attacks on North Vietnam. McNamara had told Congress the United States had "played absolutely no part in" these raids. In fact, they had been top secret operations planned by the CIA. The U.S. Navy provided the Swift boats, machine guns, and training.

"They were entirely U.S. operations," Ellsberg concluded. "Every particular detail of these operations was known and approved by the highest authorities in Washington."

President Johnson and Secretary of Defense McNamara were telling the world that the American destroyers had been on a routine patrol in the Gulf of Tonkin. They declared the ships had definitely been attacked on August 4. They insisted the attacks had been unprovoked.

"Within a day or two," Ellsberg would later say, "I knew that each one of these assurances was false."

But what was he supposed to do with that kind of information?

What he did *not* do was walk away from his new job.

Ellsberg was new to Washington, but he was not naïve. He knew the government did not really function like the neat little charts in some middle-school civics textbook. Yes, Johnson and McNamara were telling Congress and the public only part of the story of recent events in Vietnam. But secrecy was an essential element of military operations, and Ellsberg was not one to blow the whistle. "I really looked down on people who had done that," he said of insiders who leaked secrets. "You shouldn't play the game that way."

In his final analysis, only one point truly mattered—this was the Cold War. Ellsberg's job was to help win it. "We were all cold warriors," he explained. "We couldn't conceive of any alternative to what we were doing."

WELCOME AMERICANS

PERSPECTIVE IS EVERYTHING.

What looked from Washington, D.C., like a distant battlefield of the Cold War, appeared completely different from the vantage point of North Vietnam.

In the late 1800s, long before the start of the Cold War, France took control of Vietnam, Cambodia, and Laos, ruling the three countries as a colony known as French Indochina. This is the world Nguyen Tat Thanh was born into in 1890. Nguyen grew up watching French colonists abusing workers at plantations and mines, ripping out and exporting the country's natural resources. He joined anti-French protests as a teenager. In his twenties he became a communist; communism's promise to redistribute land and wealth among the people seemed an attractive alternative to French oppression. After studying in the Soviet capital of Moscow, he spent much of the 1920s and 1930s traveling through Asia, organizing covert communist groups. When Japan occupied Indochina during World War II, he slipped across the border from China into Vietnam and formed the Viet Minh, a guerrilla force that began battling the invaders. This is when he started calling himself Ho Chi Minh—"Bringer of Light."

And the United States was on his side.

In July 1945, toward the end of World War II, American soldiers parachuted into North Vietnam with orders to find and to help Ho Chi Minh. The Americans were greeted by friendly villagers and a banner reading, "Welcome Americans." The villagers slaughtered a cow and treated their guests to barbecue and beer. It was an auspicious beginning to America's military involvement in Vietnam.

Future North Vietnamese leader Ho Chi Minh (standing, third from left) with U.S. military personnel in 1945, shortly after the end of World War II.

American soldiers worked with the Viet Minh, helping train the troops for the fight against their mutual enemy, Japan. Three weeks later, two American atomic bombs forced Japan to surrender. Ho Chi Minh seized the opportunity to fill the power vacuum left by the Japanese defeat.

On the morning of September 2, more than half a million people crowded into an open square in the city of Hanoi. Homemade banners hung limp in the hot, humid air.

"Vietnam to the Vietnamese"

"Independence or Death"

Soldiers blew on whistles and the crowd quieted as men began walking up the stairs onto a wooden platform in the square. Ho Chi Minh, a frail figure in his mid-fifties, with a wispy gray goatee, stepped toward the microphone.

Seeing him, the crowd began to cry: *"Doc-Lap! Doc-Lap! Doc-Lap!"*—Vietnamese for *independence*. The chant continued for several minutes. Ho listened, smiling, savoring the moment. Then he raised his hands and the square went silent.

"All men are created equal," he began. "The creator has given us certain inviolable rights: the right to life, the right to be free, and the right to achieve happiness."

Ho stopped and asked, "Do you hear me distinctly, fellow countrymen?"

"Yes!" roared the crowd.

"These immortal words," he continued, "are taken from the Declaration of Independence of the United States of America in 1776. In a larger sense, this means that all the people on earth are born equal; all the people have the right to live, to be happy, to be free."

If Ho Chi Minh hoped quoting from the Declaration of Independence would help win him friends in Washington, D.C., he was mistaken. Ho sent a series of messages to President Harry Truman, asking the United States to recognize the independent nation of Vietnam.

Truman never responded. Perspective is everything.

Yes, the United States supported every country's right to self-determination—in theory. In the real world, Ho Chi Minh and his followers were Communists. An independent Vietnam might ally itself with the Soviet Union. Truman's other option was to back France. With World War II over, France wanted its old colony back. French rule in Vietnam would deny power to the Communists.

Which goal was more important: supporting Vietnam's right to independence, or containing the spread of communism?

Containing communism won. Truman agreed to support France's bid to retake its former colony. French forces returned to Hanoi, sparking all-out war between France and the Viet Minh.

The Soviets shipped weapons to Ho Chi Minh; the Americans supplied weapons to the French.

In May 1954, just as Daniel Ellsberg was beginning his Marine training in Virginia, Viet Minh fighters surrounded French forces at a remote military outpost called Dien Bien Phu. The French surrendered on May 7.

"Your rifles had better be clean," Ellsberg's drill sergeant told the men, "because Dien Bien Phu just fell."

But American troops did not go to Vietnam, and neither did Ellsberg. Not yet.

★ ★ ★

The Geneva Accords, which officially ended France's eight-year war in Vietnam, temporarily divided the country into North and South. Ho Chi Minh and his communist allies gained control of North Vietnam, with their capital in Hanoi. Ho consolidated power by arresting anyone suspected of disloyalty to his regime, executing many, and sending thousands more to prison camps.

In South Vietnam, a U.S.-backed leader named Ngo Dinh Diem took power in the capital city of Saigon. Diem was a firm anti-communist, though hardly committed to democracy. In one early referendum on his rule in the South, Diem's agents openly intimidated and beat up voters. Diem claimed to have won a ludicrous 98.2 percent of the vote; in Saigon, he somehow received more votes than there were registered voters.

The Geneva Accords called for a national election in 1956. The plan was for the citizens of both the North and South to choose a single government that would lead a reunited Vietnam.

It never happened. American intelligence agents in Southeast Asia reported to Washington that a national election would almost certainly be won by Ho Chi Minh. Again, the United States faced the possibility of a communist Vietnam. Again, this proved unacceptable.

"You have a row of dominoes set up," said President Dwight Eisenhower. "You knock over the first one, and what will happen to the last one is the certainty that it will go over very quickly."

According to the Domino Theory, which dominated American foreign policy during the Cold War, countries were like dominos standing on end. If one fell to communism, it would knock over the next one, and so on—one country after another would fall into communist hands. Determined not to allow the Vietnamese domino to topple, American agents worked in secret to prevent elections in Vietnam.

The Communists, meanwhile, were busy violating the Geneva Accords themselves. Viet Minh fighters were supposed to have left the South, but thousands stayed behind and helped to form a new guerrilla force calling itself the National Front for the Liberation of South Vietnam. The Americans called them the Viet Cong—short, in Vietnamese, for Vietnamese Communists. When it became clear there would be no national elections, Viet Cong forces launched a guerilla war against Diem's government in South Vietnam. Ho Chi Minh, who was determined to unite Vietnam with or without elections, worked closely with the Viet Cong.

Eisenhower responded by sending weapons and military advisors to South Vietnam. President John Kennedy, elected in 1960, increased the number of American soldiers from a few hundred to over sixteen thousand. When Lyndon Johnson took over after Kennedy was assassinated in 1963, he promised to continue backing South Vietnam.

"Lyndon Johnson," he told his advisors, "is not going down as the president who lost Vietnam."

WIDER WAR

IN THE WEEKS following the Gulf of Tonkin action, Daniel Ellsberg was at the Pentagon twelve hours a day. He was supposed to be at his desk when McNaughton showed up in the morning; some days he didn't quite make it. And not until his boss left for the night could he go home.

This was a lonely time for Ellsberg. He was going through a divorce from his wife of thirteen years, Carol Cummings. Their two young children, Robert and Mary, lived with Cummings in California. To Ellsberg's Pentagon co-workers, it was obvious he was struggling with the break-up of his family. His eyes would tear up anytime he talked about his kids.

"He was sad," one McNaughton staffer remembered. "He was like a scruffy, lost puppy."

The demands of the job, at least, kept his mind occupied. Every morning when Ellsberg walked into his little office in the Pentagon, there were tall stacks of documents waiting on his desk. Most were top secret cables and reports on Vietnam from the U.S. military, the CIA, and other agencies. He would pull a paper off the top of the stack and start reading. If it looked important, he'd set it aside to show to his boss. If not, he'd drop it in the burn bag—a large, brown paper sack standing by his desk. The moment the bag was filled, a secretary would come in and replace it with an empty one. The full bag was hauled to the basement and burned.

"All this was exciting," Ellsberg remembered. "Both the incredible pace and the inside dope make you feel important, fully engaged, on an adrenaline high much of the time. Clearly it was addictive."

Nearly everything he read was stamped with a secret classification such as: "McNaughton Eyes Only" or "Eyes Only of the Secretary," meaning McNaughton's boss, Robert McNamara. Some were marked: "Literally Eyes Only of the Secretary." He read them anyway. McNaughton didn't mind—so long as Ellsberg kept the fact he was seeing this stuff secret.

He learned that the hard way. One day, on the phone with a State Department official named Mike Forrestal, Ellsberg quoted from a cable that had just come in from the American embassy in Saigon. It was stamped "Eyes Only for the Secretary," but Ellsberg suggested that Forrestal read it.

Later that same day, McNaughton called Ellsberg into his office.

"Did you have anything to do with telling Mike Forrestal about the new series from the embassy?" McNaughton asked. He was as upset as Ellsberg had ever seen him.

"He didn't seem to know about it," Ellsberg said, "and it was obvious he needed to see these."

McNaughton tapped his fingers on his desk, staring at his new employee for an uncomfortably long moment.

"I've been told to fire you," he finally said.

Ellsberg's mind raced—*was the document really that secret? Why was one department of government keeping secrets from another? How did they trace it back to me so quickly?*

"Well, you're new on the job," McNaughton said. "My father used to say, 'Every dog gets one bite.' Really, Dan, watch out after this."

"You will stay here."

With those words, a guard shoved Everett Alvarez into room 24 of the Hao Lo prison in Hanoi. After crashing into the Gulf of Tonkin, the American pilot had been pulled from the water by North Vietnamese militiamen. He'd been tied up with rope, interrogated, and driven to this prison.

There was a bed in his cell, a table, and a sharp-edged, rusty bucket for a toilet. A bare bulb hung on a wire from the ceiling. It stayed on, day and night. Rats wriggled under the door, coming and going between his cell and a small, walled courtyard outside.

Twice a day, a guard brought water and, to use the term loosely, food. One day he got a chicken head in grease; another day an animal hoof, a few carrots on the side. Suffering from a miserable mix of dysentery, headaches, and dizziness, Alvarez quickly slipped from 165 pounds to 135.

"I began to fear that I might indeed be trapped for weeks or even months to come," the pilot later wrote. "How much longer would it take for my government to get me out of this hellhole?"

As the weather grew colder, Alvarez heard more truck traffic on the roads outside. At night he heard the city conducting air-raid drills. The prison guards seemed to be growing increasingly edgy.

"We know there's going to be a war," they told Alvarez.

According to the president of the United States, there would be no war.

In campaign speeches that fall, Johnson told voters again and again: "We are not about to send American boys nine or ten thousand miles away from home to do what Asian boys ought to be doing for themselves." The line always got a loud cheer.

And there's no doubt he hoped it was true. In twenty-four years of representing Texas in the House and Senate, Johnson's focus had always been on domestic policy. His talent was for muscling bills through Congress, using what became known in Washington as "The Johnson Treatment," which involved planting his giant frame in front of a fellow legislator, standing nose to nose, and letting loose a stream of stories, statistics, arguments, jokes—until the other guy gave in. As president he envisioned what he called his Great Society—an ambitious set of programs including civil rights legislation and expanded access to quality education and health care. Vietnam was, at best, an unwelcome distraction.

"I don't think it's worth fighting for," Johnson told an aide during the campaign. "What the hell is Vietnam worth to me? What is it worth to this country?"

But he could not ignore Vietnam. The North Vietnamese had begun using a series of forest-covered paths known as the Ho Chi Minh Trail to move soldiers and supplies from North to South. The North Vietnamese and Viet Cong were now working together, and getting more aggressive in their attacks. Advisors warned Johnson that the government of South Vietnam would not survive long without increased U.S. military support.

Senator Barry Goldwater, the Republican candidate for president, blasted Johnson for not doing more to stop the Communists. Goldwater called Johnson "soft on communism," and when asked what he would do if elected, Goldwater suggested he might use atomic bombs on the Ho Chi Minh Trail.

That kind of talk terrified more voters than it won over. Polls showed that a large majority of Americans wanted no part of a war in Vietnam. Lyndon Johnson told them what they wanted to hear. Again and again he declared, "We seek no wider war."

Daniel Ellsberg did not vote in the presidential election of 1964. He was too busy planning a wider war.

On the morning of November 3, Election Day, Johnson's advisors secretly met to discuss how the American military could most effectively come to the aid of South Vietnam. Johnson had known all along that American intervention would be necessary to prevent the fall of the South.

"We all knew that within the government, and not one of us told the press or the public," Ellsberg said later. "It was a well-kept secret by thousands and thousands of people. Including me."

Johnson crushed Goldwater, getting 43 million votes to Goldwater's 27 million. It was the largest margin of victory in American history.

"On the day the electorate, as expected in polls, was voting in unprecedented numbers against bombing North Vietnam or otherwise escalating the war, we were working to set such a policy in motion," Ellsberg recalled. "It didn't matter that much to us what the public thought."

On the morning of January 27, 1965, a week after inauguration day, Johnson and his top foreign policy advisors met to discuss the crisis.

"The time has come for harder choices," National Security Advisor McGeorge Bundy told the group.

Bundy and Robert McNamara presented a memo that laid out the stark reality as they saw it. "Our current policy can lead only to disastrous defeat," they warned. "Bob and I believe that the worst course of action is to continue in this essentially passive role which can lead only to eventual defeat and an invitation to get out in humiliating circumstances."

It was time, Bundy and McNamara urged, to begin bombing North Vietnam.

"Both of us understand the very grave questions presented

by any decision of this sort. We both recognize that the ultimate responsibility is not ours."

"I feel like a hitchhiker caught in a hailstorm on a Texas highway," President Johnson confided to his press secretary. "I can't run. I can't hide. And I can't make it stop."

★ ★ ★

One of Ellsberg's many tasks at the Pentagon was to catalogue assaults carried out by Viet Cong forces in South Vietnam. They were getting increasingly vicious, and they were beginning to target Americans. On February 8, communist guerrillas attacked a U.S. helicopter base, killing eight American advisors. Two days later they struck another American base, killing ten more. Johnson authorized U.S. planes to hit targets in the North, the first American air strikes since the August 5 raids the year before.

Normally, part of Ellsberg's job would be to monitor the American strikes. Instead, McNaughton told him to spend the night gathering grisly details about the recent Viet Cong attacks. Secretary McNamara was going to the White House in the morning, McNaughton explained. McNamara wanted to use the details to help convince the president to begin a sustained bombing campaign against North Vietnam.

Ellsberg felt a moment of doubt.

As a kid during World War II, he'd sat in movie theaters, horrified by newsreel images of the smoking rubble of European cities that had been flattened by German bombs. His school held terrifying air-raid drills, and in each classroom was a large bucket of sand—to be used to extinguish fires sparked by incendiary bombs.

Enemy planes never got anywhere near Detroit. Still, the experience stuck with him. "Nothing else," he later recalled, "seemed so purely, incomprehensibly evil as the deliberate bombing of women and children."

Now he had until early the next morning to gather the stories McNamara wanted. There was no time for qualms. "An order from McNamara," he later said, "was like an order from God."

PATRICIA

ELLSBERG HURRIED DOWN to the war room in the Joint Chiefs
of Staff offices. He found a desk and a phone with a direct line to
the American military headquarters in Vietnam. It was late at night
in Washington, late morning in Saigon. Ellsberg got an American
officer on the line.

"I need blood," he told the colonel.

There was no shortage. The colonel described a recent incident in which a group of Viet Cong fighters had disemboweled a
village chief in front of the entire village. Then they murdered
the chief's wife and children.

"Great! That's what I want to know!" Ellsberg shouted into the
phone. "That's what we need! More of that. Can you find other
stories like that?"

Ellsberg was at the desk all night. At four in the morning, the colonel called with an update—the bodies of two of the American advisors recently killed by the Viet Cong may have been dragged through the streets on chains.

"Good, good, more like that," Ellsberg said, taking notes. "Wow. Jesus! This is it. Anything else? Anything like this anywhere else?"

At six thirty, Ellsberg gathered his papers and raced back to his own office. He wrote up a quick report, handing each sheet to McNaughton's secretary as he finished it. McNaughton stood over the secretary's shoulder, reading as she typed. When she finished the last page, he grabbed the small stack and ran down the hall to McNamara's office.

When McNamara returned from the White House later that morning, he told McNaughton to thank his assistant for a job well done.

Looking back, Ellsberg would say, "That night's work was the worst thing I've ever done."

A few days later, Lyndon Johnson formally approved Operation Rolling Thunder, the sustained bombing of Vietnam.

"Now we're off to bombing these people," Johnson groaned to his secretary of defense. "We're over that hurdle. I don't think anything is going to be as bad as losing, and I don't see any way of winning."

This was Johnson's first major escalation of America's war in Vietnam. He chose not to explain to the American people that the bombing would continue indefinitely.

February 1965. A U.S. warplane bombs targets near Saigon at the beginning of Operation Rolling Thunder, the first major escalation of the Vietnam War.

On February 17, he told the public, "We seek no wider war."

Over the next three and a half years, American planes would drop a daily average of eight hundred tons of bombs on targets in North and South Vietnam. Yet the supplies and soldiers continued flowing from North to South along the Ho Chi Minh Trail.

"The brutal fact is that we have been losing ground at an

increasing rate," McNamara warned in a memo soon after Rolling Thunder began. Bombs alone would never stop the bleeding, the secretary explained. Most of the Ho Chi Minh Trail was covered with dense forest, making it hard to hit from the air. And the Viet Cong's military supplies were mainly coming from factories in the Soviet Union and China. Bombing those targets was not an option, unless the objective was to ignite World War III.

Another alternative was to send in American ground troops.

In early March, General William Westmoreland, commander of American forces in Vietnam, requested that two battalions of marines be sent to Vietnam to help guard the American airfield at Da Nang in central Vietnam.

"I guess we've got no choice," Johnson said, "but it scares the death out of me."

The number of marines was small—about thirty-five hundred. But it was still a major turning point. These were the first American combat troops sent to the Vietnam War.

Ellsberg was in his office at the Pentagon when the orders hit McNaughton's desk.

"Oh my god! We're sending in the marines!" Ellsberg heard his boss shouting from the next room. "That means we'll never get out!"

On the morning of March 8, 1965, hundreds of United States Marines splashed through shallow water up to the beaches of Da Nang, South Vietnam. The scene looked like something out of

March 1965. U.S. Marines come ashore in Da Nang, South Vietnam.

a war movie—only there was no enemy fire. As the marines walked, dripping, onto the sand, local schoolgirls stepped forward and placed garlands of red and yellow flowers over their necks.

The men spent that first day digging foxholes, filling and stacking sandbags to protect their positions. To Philip Caputo, among the marines to arrive that day, the whole thing had the feeling of yet another exercise. The twenty-three-year-old lieutenant got out his binoculars and scanned the landscape beyond the fences of the American base.

Beautiful groves of palm trees and bamboo. Women walking along rice paddies, carrying baskets on long poles balanced on their shoulders. A boy riding a water buffalo.

He thought, "Where is this war we've heard so much about?"

Back in the United States, the antiwar protests began almost immediately.

In April, an organization called Students for a Democratic Society urged members to gather in front of the White House. A twenty-seven-year-old journalist named Patricia Marx packed a bag and flew to Washington. She wanted to be there to cover the first major protest against the Vietnam War.

A slim woman with dark hair, Marx was the host of "Patricia Marx Interviews," a weekly radio show in New York City. The show featured in-depth conversations with prominent figures in politics, science, and the arts. It was a dream job.

"I really loved to learn," Marx recalled. "I loved ideas."

The work took her to Washington often, and on a previous visit she'd actually met Daniel Ellsberg. She had been at a party, and a friend had pointed out some of the more interesting guests.

"Stay away from *him*," the friend warned, gesturing to Ellsberg.

"He's brilliant, but dangerous." Marx took this to mean that the recently single Ellsberg was dating a lot of women.

She and Ellsberg spoke briefly at the party. He asked her for a date. She turned him down.

"I thought Dan was interesting," Patricia remembered of their first meeting, "but it wasn't like love at first sight or anything."

She had not forgotten him, though. Now back in Washington to cover the antiwar rally, Marx decided to invite Ellsberg to a dinner party her sister was hosting. He jumped at the second chance. And the moment he walked into the house, both of their lives changed.

"I opened the door," Marx remembered, "and I hadn't seen him for a year, and I hadn't really connected—and somehow the light hit his blue eyes. I hadn't seen those blue eyes in that way. And he walked in, and I just instantly went, 'Ah!' And I was a goner."

Dan was equally smitten. "I saw that she had marvelous eyes, green and slightly tilted, pointed at the corners," he later said. "I've never gotten over them."

Soon after the party, he called her from his office.

"I have tomorrow off," he said. Washington's famous cherry trees were in bloom. They should see them together, he suggested.

"No," she said. "I'm covering the peace rally for the radio program."

He asked if she could slip away for a quick picnic.

She said no, she'd be doing interviews and taping speeches—but he could come along and hold her tape recorder.

"You can't ask me to go to an antiwar rally on the first day I've

Patricia Marx

had off from the war," he said, "the one day I've had off from the Pentagon in eight months!"

"Well, that's where I'll be. You're welcome to come."

On the day of the protest, April 17, Daniel Ellsberg and Patricia Marx walked together toward the Washington Monument. It was a warm spring morning with bright blue skies, and the cherry trees on the National Mall were bursting with pink blossoms.

Thousands of protesters gathered at the base of the monument, many waving banners with antiwar slogans. When they began marching toward the White House, Marx held up her microphone to catch the antiwar chants. Ellsberg, feeling absurdly out of place, hurried behind with his date's heavy tape machine.

When they reached Lafayette Park, in front of the White House, the crowd was bigger than expected, about twenty-five thousand. It was national news, and there were lots of newspaper photographers and TV cameras. Ellsberg tried to keep his face hidden.

I hope this is not going to be a photo in the Washington Post *tomorrow,* he was thinking. *Because it's going to be a little hard to explain.*

The speeches started, and Ellsberg listened to the protestors' arguments against bombing Vietnam and sending in the marines. When the rally broke up, he headed back to the Pentagon to see how the war was going.

Patricia Marx's friends questioned her harshly. "How can you be going out with somebody who's working on Vietnam?"

She tried to explain that there was more to it than politics. "Despite the fact that he was in the Pentagon and I was against the war," she later said, "I really saw his brilliance and his courage and his integrity."

She agreed to see him again, and the next day, a Sunday, he picked her up in his convertible and they drove out of the city to a park in Maryland. They sat under a blooming cherry tree. Ellsberg pulled out a wicker basket with bread, cheese, and a bottle of wine. After eating and drinking, he leaned his back against the tree trunk. She rested her head in his lap. They talked for a long time. Finally, he bent down to kiss her.

"By the next morning," he remembered, "as I drove on the Rock Creek Parkway toward the Pentagon, I realized I was falling in love."

LIMITED OPERATIONS

ABOUT SIX WEEKS AFTER arriving at Da Nang, Lieutenant Philip Caputo and seven of his men sat in a helicopter, holding their rifles between their knees. Below, the Toy Loan River snaked through lush green hillsides that stretched to the horizon. Caputo wondered how he was supposed to find the enemy out there. This would be his first day of combat.

When the marines had first arrived at Da Nang, the orders had been clear: "The U.S. Marine Force will not, repeat will not, engage in day-to-day actions against the Viet Cong."

That lasted three weeks. With enemy forces advancing, the Joint Chiefs requested permission to broaden the mission from merely guarding the base to engaging in what was described as "limited offensive operations." Johnson agreed.

The chopper landed in a grassy clearing and the men jumped out, ducking to keep their heads below the whirling blades. Other helicopters were landing nearby. Caputo quickly moved his men out of the open space and under the dense forest canopy. In an instant it was dark. As the helicopters lifted off, Caputo gathered his platoon and set out on one of the first American patrols of the Vietnam War.

Their mission was to march to a nearby village and conduct a search for Viet Cong fighters and weapons. Single file, the men walked along a narrow, muddy trail that wound alongside the river. On one side of them was thick forest; on the other was the brown river, and beyond that a tall tangle of elephant grass and bamboo. The only sounds were of the flowing water and creatures in the forest.

"It was not at all a tranquil silence," Caputo recalled.

May 1965. U.S. soldiers on patrol in the Vietnamese jungle.

They marched for an hour. The air was so humid, it felt like walking underwater. As the trail twisted along the river, the patrol began to take on a nightmarish quality that would become all too familiar to soldiers in this war. The men felt surrounded, but did not know by what. There was a constant sense that something violent was about to happen—and the men wished it *would* happen, just to break the unbearable tension.

Suddenly, there was a burst of rifle fire from somewhere in the forest. The men dropped to the wet ground and fired back into the trees. Caputo could feel his heart hammering against the earth beneath him.

Then the enemy firing stopped. Caputo got his men up and they continued the march. This went on all morning—the rapid bursts of gunfire from the dark forest, and then the silence. It took the platoon four hours to cover the three miles from the landing zone to the tiny village they were supposed to search.

There were about twenty thatch huts along the dirt road. A few old men and women, a few mothers with young children. No young men. No weapons.

The return to the landing zone was a repeat of the morning's march, stretches of quiet interrupted by bursts of bullets from unseen enemies. The Americans fired back, but couldn't see if they were hitting anything.

"It was as if the trees were shooting at us," Caputo remembered.

Late that afternoon, in uniforms so sweat soaked they looked black, with shoulders aching under the weight of their packs, the men jumped into helicopters and flew back to camp. They wondered if they had accomplished anything. They suspected they had not.

Daniel Ellsberg saw Patricia Marx almost every night that spring. Early in the morning, he'd drive from the apartment she was renting in Georgetown to work at the Pentagon.

But if Ellsberg's personal life was finally looking up, the situation in Vietnam was getting worse. At his desk, Ellsberg read cables from General Westmoreland warning that communist forces were close to cutting the country in two along the central highlands. The marines at Da Nang were doing well, but there were far too few of them to make a real difference. Without help, the army of South Vietnam could not hold out much longer.

Lyndon Johnson appealed to North Vietnam, offering massive financial aid in exchange for leaving South Vietnam alone. Ho Chi Minh rejected the offer. The United States, he insisted, must stop the bombing and withdraw American troops from the South before any serious negotiation could begin.

The president was annoyed, but understood the reality. "If I were Ho Chi Minh, I would never negotiate," he said privately. Ho's forces were winning—why should he cut a deal?

As the pressure grew, Johnson's angry outbursts became more frequent. In April, at a speech in Philadelphia, Canadian Prime Minister Lester Pearson sparked the president's wrath by gently suggesting the United States might try harder to find a negotiated settlement in Vietnam. When Johnson read this, he asked Pearson to meet him at Camp David, the presidential retreat in rural

Undated photograph of Daniel Ellsberg and President Lyndon Johnson at the White House.

Maryland. The moment Pearson showed up, Johnson gave him "the Treatment," grabbing the startled prime minister by the lapels and shouting, "You don't come here and piss on my rug!"

"Are we sure to win?" Daniel Ellsberg asked an audience of students. "No. But should we quit without trying?"

This was a new part of Ellsberg's job—defending the war on college campuses. He wanted students to understand why it was vital for the United States to fight in Vietnam. "I saw our involvement in the context of a worldwide conflict with communism," he said of his thinking at this time. "A Cold War perspective I shared with most of my fellow officials."

This was also the time that Ellsberg made the unsettling discovery that he was not quite the insider he'd thought he was. There were layers of secrets even he was not permitted to know.

In John McNaughton's office at the Pentagon, there was a special bookcase where McNaughton kept his most sensitive cables and reports in three-ring binders. The bookcase had wheels, and each night, before he left, McNaughton would wheel it into a closet-sized safe and lock the door.

Ellsberg was permitted to enter the office and look in the binders. Most of them. There was one thick binder labeled "Vietnam: McNaughton Eyes Only." Ellsberg disregarded that stamp on documents all the time, but in this case, his boss warned, the papers *really were* off limits.

This was not easy for Ellsberg. He knew the combination to the safe. And he was dying to know what was in that binder. "I want to be the Einstein of political science," he'd told Patricia on one of their early dates. "I want to understand how crises work, how governments react, *everything*."

Night after night, he was alone in McNaughton's suite with access to the prohibited documents. Night after night, he resisted temptation.

On June 7, Secretary of Defense McNamara got the news he had been dreading.

"The conflict in Southeast Asia is in the process of moving to a higher level," General Westmoreland reported. The bombing and marines were not having any noticeable effect on enemy momentum. Westmoreland wanted to increase American troops in Vietnam to 200,000 in 1965, and that was just to prevent catastrophe. Many more would be needed in the near future.

"Of the thousands of cables I received during my seven years in the Defense Department, this one disturbed me the most," McNamara later said. "We could no longer postpone a choice about which path to take."

Should the United States commit to fighting a major ground war in Vietnam? It would prove to be one of the most important debates in American history, and it took place entirely in secret.

"The decision you face now, therefore, is crucial," Assistant Secretary of State George Ball advised in a memo to President Johnson: "Once large numbers of U.S. troops are committed to direct combat they will begin to take heavy casualties in a war they are ill-equipped to fight in a non-cooperative if not downright hostile countryside.

"Once we suffer large casualties we will have started a well-nigh irreversible process. Our involvement will be so great that we cannot—without national humiliation—stop short of achieving our complete objectives. Of the two possibilities I think humiliation would be more likely than the achievement of our objectives—even after we had paid terrible costs."

No one outside of Johnson's inner circle saw this advice. In fact, this was one of the memos in the binder Daniel Ellsberg was ordered not to open.

Neither did the public learn that the Central Intelligence Agency was warning Johnson that even a large American ground force would probably be unable to stop the Communists from eventually taking over in Vietnam. Simply put, the enemy was willing to fight longer and take more losses. "Their staying power," advised the CIA, "is inherently superior."

Robert McNamara agreed that the situation was grim, the options limited. In his own top secret memo to Johnson, he outlined the three remaining alternatives.

Option one: "Cut our losses and withdraw."

This would be humiliating, McNamara warned. It would be damaging to American prestige, because it would be viewed around the world as a defeat for the United States in the Cold War.

Option two: "Continue at about the present level."

This would lead to a continually worsening situation in Vietnam. It wouldn't really eliminate the need to make a decision, because the closer South Vietnam got to collapse, the more pressure there would be on the United States to intervene.

Option three: "Expand promptly and substantially the U.S. military pressure against the Viet Cong."

This would prevent defeat in the short term, but at a substantial cost. McNamara bluntly listed the disadvantages: "risk of escalation, casualties will be high, and may be a long war without victory."

To President Johnson, all three options looked lousy.

"He had no stomach for it, no heart for it," Claudia "Lady Bird" Johnson later said of her husband's feelings about Vietnam. "It wasn't the war he wanted. The one he wanted was on poverty and ignorance and disease, and that was worth putting your life into."

Lady Bird Johnson knew the stress was reaching new heights when the president began pacing the White House halls at night.

Night after night, in dressing gown and slippers, carrying a flashlight, Johnson would walk from his bedroom down to the situation room in the basement. There was nothing he could do at that hour. But it was more peaceful than the nightmares that tormented his sleep.

"I knew from the start that I was bound to be crucified either way I moved," Johnson later said of the awful options remaining. If he committed to war in Vietnam, it would drain resources from the domestic programs he dreamed of crafting. But the alternative—that appeared even more terrifying.

"Losing the Great Society was a terrible thought," he told an aide, "but not so terrible as the thought of being responsible for America's losing a war to the Communists. Nothing could possibly be worse than that."

When he finally went to bed, the nightmares returned.

"Every night when I fell asleep I would see myself tied to the ground in the middle of a long, open space," Johnson later described. "In the distance, I could hear the voices of thousands of people. They were all shouting at me and running toward me: 'Coward! Traitor! Weakling!' They kept coming closer. They began throwing stones. At exactly that moment I would generally wake up, terribly shaken."

DIVING BOARD

DANIEL ELLSBERG WAS WORKING LATE AGAIN. His boss's office was dark, except for a faint light coming from the open safe in the wall. When he finished for the night, Ellsberg rolled McNaughton's special bookcase into the safe.

But he did not shut the door.

"It was too much for me," Ellsberg later confessed.

He pulled out the "McNaughton Eyes Only" binder and opened it. Heart thumping, he flipped through the pages. There were memos in the distinctive typeface used by the White House. There were cables from Vietnam he hadn't seen, minutes from meetings he hadn't known had taken place.

He read a few paragraphs—but stopped himself. He quickly replaced the binder on the bookcase, shut the door, and spun the combination dial to make sure it was locked.

The next day, he changed his mind again.

That night, Ellsberg left the office when his boss did, at about eight o'clock. But he did not go home. He walked down to the Pentagon cafeteria, and lingered over dinner.

The suite was empty when Ellsberg returned. He walked into McNaughton's office and flicked on the light. He went to the safe and turned the dial left and right, stopping at each number of the combination. He pulled the handle of the safe. It wouldn't open.

He tried the numbers again. Still locked. Then a third time. He was absolutely sure of the combination. Someone had changed it. In the last twenty-four hours.

How had McNaughton picked this up so fast? Ellsberg wondered. Had he put the binder back in the wrong place? Had McNaughton used some trick out of a spy novel, like laying a strand of hair over the binder—a strand that would remain in place only so long as the binder was not touched?

The moment Ellsberg walked into the office the next morning, McNaughton's secretary told him the boss wanted to see him immediately.

McNaughton was seated at his desk. He looked up from his work.

"He told me," Ellsberg recalled, "that he had been feeling for some time that I was overqualified for this job." He offered Ellsberg a different job, in a different office. No mention was made of the safe. "He could not have been more cordial as I left his office."

Ellsberg never found out how he'd been caught.

President Johnson sat at the long wooden table in the White House Cabinet Room. Around the table sat his top advisors and military commanders. It was time to make a decision about Vietnam.

"I asked Secretary McNamara to invite you here to counsel with you on these problems and the ways to meet them," the president began. He outlined the three options in McNamara's memo. Turning to the military leaders, he asked, "If we give Westmoreland all he asks for, what are our chances?"

July 21, 1965. President Lyndon Johnson during a National Security meeting on Vietnam.

No one could say for sure.

"If you put in these requested forces and increase air and sea effort, we can at least turn the tide to where we are not losing anymore," commented Air Force Chief of Staff John McConnell.

"Have results of bombing actions been as fruitful and productive as we anticipated?" asked the president.

"No, sir, they haven't been," McConnell replied.

"Doesn't it really mean if we follow Westmoreland's requests we are in a new war?" Johnson asked. "Isn't this going off the diving board?"

"This is a major change in U.S. policy," agreed McNamara. "We have relied on South Vietnam to carry the brunt. Now we would be responsible for satisfactory military outcome."

"The least desirable alternative is getting out," insisted General Harold Johnson, army chief of staff. "The second least is doing what we are doing. Best is to get in and get the job done."

"But I don't know how we are going to get that job done," Johnson said. "Are we starting something that in two or three years we simply can't finish?" The North Vietnamese were vowing to fight for as long as it took to win, Johnson pointed out. Turning to General Johnson, the president asked, "What is your reaction to Ho's statement he is ready to fight for twenty years?"

"I believe it," said the general.

Recent polls, an aide pointed out, showed that the public approved of the American commitment to support South Vietnam.

"But if you make a commitment to jump off a building," President Johnson said, "and you find out how high it is, you may withdraw the commitment."

★ ★ ★

Ellsberg had lost his position in McNaughton's inner circle, but he was still on McNaughton's staff and was one of many gathered in front of the television in the boss's office on the afternoon of July 28. Everyone in the room knew that President Johnson had decided to approve Westmoreland's request for 200,000 troops. They wanted to watch him tell the country.

"We did not choose to be the guardians at the gate, but there is no one else," Johnson said at his midday press conference. "I have asked the commanding general, General Westmoreland, what more he needs to meet this mounting aggression. He has told me. And we will meet his needs. We cannot be defeated by force of arms. We will stand in Vietnam."

The president announced he was increasing the number of American troops in Vietnam to 125,000. More forces would be sent, he said, "as requested."

There was an audible gasp in McNaughton's office. Ellsberg couldn't believe what he'd just heard. "What?" he called out. "Has he changed the decision?"

McNaughton gestured for quiet; he wanted to hear the rest of the president's statement. But there was no mention of the 200,000 figure. There was nothing about the importance of this decision—that it was a major commitment to long-term war.

As Johnson began taking questions from the press, Ellsberg again asked if there'd been a last-second change of plans.

"You'd better find out," McNaughton said.

Ellsberg ran down the hall to the Joint Chiefs' offices. He asked the general whose job it was to schedule the deployment of troops if the president had changed his mind. He had not. Westmoreland was going to get his 200,000 troops.

In the short term, Johnson's speech was a success. Congress and the public were relieved by the relatively small size of the military commitment.

In the long term, the speech set Johnson's presidency on a muddy mountainside. If the president wasn't exactly lying, he certainly *was* going out of his way to downplay what he knew was a major commitment to war. What would happen when it became clear to the country that the Vietnam War was not going to end anytime soon?

General Earle Wheeler, chairman of the Joint Chiefs of Staff, knew the president was playing a dangerous game. "We felt that it would be desirable," he later said, "to make sure that the people of the U.S. knew that we were in a war, and not engaged at some two-penny military adventure. Because we didn't think it was going to prove to be a two-penny military adventure by any manner of means."

Ellsberg's new office had no window. He shared the small space with another analyst, whose desk was pushed up against his so that they worked facing each other—a symbol of Ellsberg's fallen status. Any chance he'd had at advancing his career in the Pentagon was gone.

But he'd learned a lot in a year. He now knew that the American public had very little idea of how decisions were really made in Washington. That didn't particularly bother him, though. "If you can't live with the fact that presidents lie," he later said, "you can't work for presidents."

What bothered him was that American policy in Vietnam was failing. He believed the war was worth fighting. Maybe he could find a way to help win it. But that wasn't going to happen from ten thousand miles away.

And then, very suddenly, things went wrong between him and Patricia Marx. She went to a conference and met a German poet. When she got back, she couldn't stop talking about how brilliant and wonderful the guy was. She didn't deny that she had a bit of a crush on him.

"I took that to mean," Ellsberg recalled, "that she had fallen out of love with me."

Marx tried to tell him he was overreacting, but she could see him locking up emotionally; he just wouldn't listen.

To Ellsberg, his relationship with Marx was the one thing that still felt right about life. Without her, there was nothing keeping him in Washington.

That's when he decided to go to Vietnam.

KILL RATIO

PHILIP CAPUTO, THE YOUNG LIEUTENANT who had led his platoon on some of the earliest combat missions in Vietnam, walked into his executive officer's tent at U.S. Marine headquarters at Da Nang, South Vietnam. Caputo had seen friends shot and blown apart by land mines. In the summer of 1965, he'd been assigned this new job, a safer job—though not one he'd ever wanted.

"I was death's bookkeeper," he later wrote.

On a typically sweltering day, Caputo stood in front of a chart on the wall. Written in grease pencil on the acetate surface of the chart were columns and rows of numbers—the numbers of American and enemy troops killed or wounded in battle. Sweat dripping from his hands and nose, Caputo began to update the chart.

"How recent are those figures?" a colonel asked.

"As of this morning, sir."

"Very good," the colonel said. An important general was coming for a briefing, he explained. The statistics needed to be up-to-date.

American strategy in Vietnam was to rely on superior firepower to kill enemy troops faster than they could be replaced. Success was measured not in territory captured, but in numbers. The "body count" was the number of enemy fighters killed. The all-important "kill ratio" was the ratio of enemy troops to Americans killed. General Westmoreland believed that if the kill ratio was high enough, for long enough, the enemy would eventually crack.

Part of Caputo's job was to verify the numbers by inspecting bodies brought into the base. With Americans, he matched the faces of the dead with photos on file. If they didn't have faces, he used dental records. Vietnamese dead were much harder to identify. How could he tell if they were Viet Cong or unlucky civilians? When in doubt he relied on the unwritten rule his superiors had taught him: "If he's dead and Vietnamese, he's VC."

That day four dead Vietnamese were brought in on a trailer. Caputo counted the mangled corpses and sent them on for burial. Then came word that the colonel wanted the visiting general to see the bodies—a tangible sign of the progress being made.

Caputo had the trailer brought back into camp. He checked to make sure there were still four bodies. It was hard to tell. Several limbs had come loose. The floor of the trailer was streaked with blood and brains.

"If that general's going to look at those bodies," a marine suggested, "we'd better hose the trailer down."

While the general listened to a briefing in a nearby tent, Caputo and his men sprayed water into the trailer. Then they tipped the trailer to let the liquid drain. The general came out to have a look. Caputo saluted. The general, followed by other high-ranking officers, walked past the trailer, glancing quickly at the contents.

"A rivulet of blood-colored water flowed from under the trailer and soaked into the dust," Caputo later recalled. "The brass stepped over it carefully, to avoid ruining the shine on their boots."

In early November, the top commanders of the U.S. military gathered outside the Oval Office in the White House. Waiting with the Joint Chiefs was a young officer, Major Charles Cooper, holding a map of Vietnam mounted on a three-quarter-inch thick slab of plywood.

The chiefs had asked Cooper to prepare the map. The thing was heavy, and he'd called ahead to request that an easel be set up in the president's office. He expected to set the map on the easel and then wait in the hall.

An aide showed the group into the Oval Office. President Johnson was there. The easel was not.

"Come on in, Major," the president said to Cooper. "You can stand right over there."

Cooper stood in the middle of the room thinking, "If I'd known I was going to have to hold the damn thing, I would have used thin plywood."

"It's really nice to have you people over here," Johnson said to his military chiefs. "What have you got?"

"Well, Mr. President," began Joint Chiefs Chairman Earle Wheeler, "we fully realize that what we're going to present to you today requires a very difficult decision."

In short, Wheeler explained, what they were doing in Vietnam was not working. American troop levels in Vietnam were nearing 200,000, but the enemy was adapting by breaking into small groups and moving unseen through the rugged mountains and forests. American soldiers were winning individual battles, and the kill ratio was favorable—about 2.5 to 1. Yet the Communists were easily replacing their losses. And no territory was being gained, because as soon as American troops left an area, the Viet Cong slipped right back in. No progress was being made. Worse, the war was being fought without a strategy that could possibly lead to victory.

Pointing to the map in Major Cooper's arms, Wheeler described a more aggressive alternative: mine North Vietnamese harbors to block Soviet and Chinese ships bringing in military supplies. Pummel Hanoi with a massive bombing campaign. These steps, he said, might force the North's leaders to rethink their position.

"So you're going to cut them off," Johnson said, "keep them from being reinforced, and then you're going to bomb them into the Stone Age."

"Well, that's not exactly it," said Air Force Chief of Staff John McConnell, "but you've got to punish them."

Johnson turned to the others. He wanted to know if they supported this plan, which risked escalating tensions with the Soviet Union and China.

They all did.

"You're trying to get me to start World War III with your idiotic bullshit!" the president shouted. "I've got the weight of the Free World on my shoulders and you want me to start World War III?"

Johnson lit into the military men, dropping the f-bomb, Cooper noted, "more freely than a marine in boot camp." The chiefs listened in stunned silence. Presidents did not talk to top commanders like this.

Finally calming a bit, Johnson asked the men to put themselves in his shoes.

"Imagine that you're me—that you're the president of the United States," he said. "What would you do?"

"I can't do it, Mr. President," said the badly offended Wheeler. "No man can honestly do it. It's got to be your decision and yours alone."

Cooper saw the anger rising in Johnson's face. He was about to explode again.

Daniel Ellsberg spent much of the fall of 1965 in the passenger seat of an International Harvester Scout, bouncing down rural roads outside of Saigon. Driving the car at high speed was John Paul Vann, a retired army colonel, now working as a civilian advisor for the government. Vann held the steering wheel in one hand, and in the other an AR-15 rifle, pointed out the open window. He had extra ammunition draped over his shoulder and grenades on his belt.

"You're safest in a single, unmarked vehicle," Vann told Ellsberg, "driving fast at irregular times during the day."

Ellsberg was still determined to help win the Vietnam War.

Now employed by the State Department, he was part of a team working to find non-military ways to defeat the Communists. The goal: to win over the "hearts and minds" of the people of South Vietnam, to help convince them they'd be better off siding with the Americans than with Ho Chi Minh. When Ellsberg first arrived in Vietnam, he'd been given an air-conditioned apartment in Saigon, with security guards at the door. It quickly became obvious that he wasn't going to learn much from that comfortable spot. He needed to get out of the city, to where the war was being fought. Vann had offered to take him.

Over six weeks, Vann and Ellsberg drove to all the provinces around Saigon. Vann explained that the biggest danger came from roadside mines set by the Viet Cong. He taught Ellsberg to constantly scan the barbed wire fences along the road, looking for a shiny edge that hadn't had time to rust, the telltale sign of a recent slice.

When they pulled into villages, children invariably crowded around the car, smiling and calling out any English they knew:

"Okay! Okay!"

"Hallo!"

"Number one!"

Ellsberg's thoughts flashed back to his own son and daughter, to the time when they'd all lived together. "I remember my children running out to climb over me at the end of the day," he wrote in a letter from Vietnam, "and my heart turns over."

As they toured villages, Vann pointed out buildings damaged in recent Viet Cong attacks. The villages had militias, Vann explained, but they tended to avoid confronting the Viet Cong. It's

Daniel Ellsberg with children in South Vietnam, 1965. On the back of the photo, Ellsberg wrote, "It's an exciting challenge and I'm very grateful to be here."

not that villagers supported the communist fighters; rather, they were outgunned and afraid. Even South Vietnam's large army, which was supposed to patrol and protect these areas, avoided the enemy.

"Only the Viet Cong were out at night," Ellsberg realized. "They owned the night."

Late one afternoon, driving along a dirt road between thatch huts, Ellsberg saw fear on the faces of the villagers. Moments later the car rolled past a group of twelve young men in loose black pants.

"There's little doubt you're looking at a VC squad," Vann said.

Ellsberg snapped a photo.

Viet Cong commanders, Vann explained, paid a large reward for dead Americans.

Ellsberg put down his camera.

"We're safe for a little while," Vann said, "because they don't expect to see us and it takes them a few minutes to react."

Vann turned around and drove slowly back through the center of town.

"Eventually," he said, "one of the people back there is going to start thinking about collecting the twenty-thousand piaster reward and the gold medal the VC gives out for a dead American."

But the people in these towns always seemed so friendly, Ellsberg pointed out.

"They're friendly people," Vann said. "They don't hate individual Americans, even in VC territory." But don't be fooled, Vann added, they won't help you either; they're all too scared of the Viet Cong.

"These people smiling at us right now," said Vann, "would smile just as warmly if they knew that in another ten yards we were going to be blown up by a mine the VC laid last night."

ESCALATION

A LITTLE OVER A YEAR AFTER his flight above the Gulf of Tonkin on the night it all began, Commander James Stockdale was shot down. He was on a bombing run over North Vietnam when his plane was ripped open by antiaircraft fire. Stockdale ejected and parachuted toward a small village, shattering his left leg as he hit the dirt street.

Within moments, shrieking villagers—men, women, and children—ran up and started kicking and punching him. Before blacking out from pain, Stockdale heard the drone of American planes above. They were looking for him.

"It's not worth the risk, guys," he thought. "I've had it."

He was loaded into a jeep and driven through the night, his broken leg jammed into the narrow backseat. Whenever he screamed in pain, the soldiers in the front grunted something he took to be Vietnamese for "Shut up!"

The next morning, soldiers carried him into a roadside building and laid him on a cement slab. A short man in a white surgical mask stepped up and looked at Stockdale's bloated, discolored limb. He pulled a large saw from his medical bag.

"No, no!" Stockdale shouted, sitting up suddenly.

The surgeon shrugged. He put down the saw. He filled a needle with a clear liquid and stuck it in Stockdale's arm and the pilot almost immediately lost consciousness. When he awoke he was relieved to see his leg still attached, covered in plaster from hip to foot. Stockdale was then driven to Hanoi and carried on a stretcher into Hao Lo prison—the "Hanoi Hilton," as American prisoners bitterly joked. Everett Alvarez was still there. So were about fifteen other American pilots.

Alone in his freezing cell, Stockdale communicated with the other Americans using an ingenious "tap code." The alphabet was divided into five rows of five letters each—*A* through *E* in the first row, *F* through *J* in the second row, and so on. There's no *K*; *C* is used for both *C* and *K*. To send a message, a prisoner would tap the number of the row, and then, after a brief pause, the number of the letter in that row.

"WHEN—DO—YOU—THINC—WE—WILL—GO—HOME" Stockdale tapped to the pilot in the next cell.

The answer came back: "THIS—SPRING"

It was what they had to believe.

Patricia Marx moved back to her New York City apartment and continued working on her radio show. She was furious with Daniel

Ellsberg for heading to Vietnam without even discussing the decision.

They started exchanging letters soon after he left, though. She wanted Ellsberg to realize he'd blown the appearance of the German poet way out of proportion, and he got the message. That became obvious one day that fall, when Marx pulled a postcard from her mailbox. She recognized Ellsberg's handwriting. There was only one sentence:

"Will you marry me?"

She decided to fly to Vietnam for a visit. "Not that I was ready to get married to Dan," she later said. "But I was very ready to explore whether I was ready to get married to Dan."

Ellsberg got leave for Christmas, and they set off on a tour through Thailand, Nepal, and India. "The most romantic trip I've ever had in my life," Marx later said. "I was totally madly in love." Early one morning they hired a boat to row them into the Ganges River, a waterway sacred to Hindus. Many people were bathing in the river, and Ellsberg decided to try it. He pulled off his shirt and pants and leaped in in his underwear. Garbage from the city and ash from a nearby crematorium floated past on the water's surface.

Marx watched for a moment—then yanked off her jeans and jumped in.

"I was impressed," Ellsberg later said. "I didn't think I knew many American girls who would have gotten into that water."

While they stood together in the shallow water, he asked her again to marry him. She said yes. The moment was too magical *not* to say yes.

And yet, as they headed back to Saigon, she felt some hesitation.

Ellsberg and Patricia Marx in the Ganges River, India, on the day Ellsberg proposed marriage to her.

"It wasn't totally clear that this was a man that would be a reliable husband," Marx said of her thinking. He was so intense, so impulsive. And there was the war. They argued a lot about Vietnam. Ellsberg tried to convince her that he—that the United States—was fighting for a noble cause.

"I disagreed with him, but I always felt he was a man of absolute integrity," Marx said of these debates. "What I sensed was that this was a man who was totally idealistic."

And to that, as a further explanation of her feelings, she added: "Love is not rational."

In late December, President Johnson and his top advisors sat around the table in the White House Cabinet Room. McNamara had just returned from Vietnam with familiar bad news. American forces were inflicting heavy casualties, but the enemy was growing stronger. South Vietnam's army couldn't hold on by itself. General Westmoreland wanted another 200,000 American troops in Vietnam, which would bring the total to over 400,000.

McNamara agreed that more soldiers were needed to prevent defeat, but pointed out that if the United States escalated, so would the enemy. If they granted Westmoreland's request, Americans killed in action would likely rise to one thousand a month. And the probable result would be the same standoff they had now, just at a much bloodier level.

"A military solution to the problem is not certain," he told the group. "Ultimately we must find a diplomatic solution."

Johnson leaned forward, resting his broad chest on the table. "Then, no matter what we do in the military field there is no sure victory?"

"That's right," McNamara confirmed.

In another meeting early in 1966, McNamara saw these fears put into a language that he understood well: statistics. Marine General Victor Krulak showed the secretary a detailed report he'd written that seemed to *prove* mathematically that Westmoreland's war of attrition was doomed.

The North Vietnamese and Viet Cong, Krulak explained, could call on at least 2.5 million men to fight. So suppose the United States wanted to reduce enemy forces by 20 percent—a significant figure, though hardly enough to break their will. To accomplish that goal, at the current kill ratio of 2.5 to 1, would cost the lives of more than 175,000 U.S. soldiers.

It was a cruel kind of scorekeeping, stacking up human lives like chips in a poker game. But the point was brutally clear: the United States could not win this kind of war. In fact, Krulak argued, the war of attrition played right into Hanoi's hands. North Vietnam's strategy was to keep fighting, to keep absorbing punishment, until the American public tired of war and demanded the withdrawal of American troops. It was exactly how they had beaten the French. It was how they planned to beat the Americans.

McNamara was horrified. He simply hadn't done the math.

"I think you ought to talk to the president about this," he told Krulak.

But McNamara never followed up. He never arranged the meeting.

Johnson, meanwhile, was still wrestling with Westmoreland's request for 200,000 more troops. He was torn. He had rejected the more aggressive steps recommended by the Joint Chiefs, for fear of expanding the war and sparking greater protests at home. Yet he was as determined as ever not to go down in history as the first American president to lose a war.

Finally, he decided to approve the request. The number of American troops in Vietnam would double in 1966. This brought the war home in a whole new way. Since the 1940s, the United States had kept a draft in place, requiring all men ages eighteen to twenty-four to register for military service. Aside from the

Korean War years, though, the number actually called to serve had been small. That changed quickly with Johnson's escalation. From 1966 through 1968, an average of 25,000 men would be drafted every month. For millions of young Americans, and their families and friends, Vietnam was no longer a distant conflict.

★ ★ ★

Daniel Ellsberg pulled his car to the side of the road in a tiny hamlet south of Saigon. He grabbed his camera and started walking through the still-smoking ruins of the village.

It was late March 1966. Since his long drives with Vann, Ellsberg had continued driving the roads of South Vietnam. "I had a personal desire to beat the Communists," he explained later. "I could not believe that the United States could fail in the end to solve the problems that the French had not solved." This was a visit that would shake his confidence.

As he walked through town, Ellsberg watched villagers stooped over in the remains of their homes, sifting the ruins for anything salvageable. He saw an old woman carefully lift a single, unbroken pink teacup.

A small group of Viet Cong had come through the night before, a villager explained. South Vietnamese soldiers, stationed just down the road, had seen them enter and had opened fire on the village with rockets. The Viet Cong had moved on, without casualties, as soon as buildings began to burn.

Ellsberg watched a young girl pull something from a pile of rubble. It was a plastic doll. He saw the girl smile as she realized her doll was only partly burned.

BREAK-UP

ON A CLEAR MORNING later that spring, a small military plane cruised low over the Plain of Reeds, a contested area near Saigon. Daniel Ellsberg sat in the front passenger seat with his camera pointed out the window. This was a very different way to see the war.

American military maps showed this region of South Vietnam in different colors: one color for land controlled by the South Vietnamese government, another for territory controlled by the Viet Cong. What struck Ellsberg was how much the landscape below looked like one of those maps. There was a river, and on one side the forest burst with shades of green. The other side looked like a vast red desert. Just bare reddish-brown earth. No trees, no plants, no crops.

Ellsberg knew the cause—American planes buzzed 150 feet above the treetops, spraying a defoliant known as Agent Orange.

Spring 1966. Daniel Ellsberg stands next to a small aircraft on the Plain of Reeds after U.S. forces used napalm to kill vegetation in the area. Ellsberg noted, "Shooting at People. Got shot at" on the back of the photo.

The goal was to deny the enemy hiding places by killing all vegetation.

"We had made a desert," Ellsberg recalled. And this was the country the Americans were there to help.

As they flew over a small village, Ellsberg heard what sounded like corn popping. Someone was firing at them from the ground. The pilot called in an air strike and within minutes American planes sped over the village, dropping bombs. Ellsberg watched a phosphorous bomb hit a house, and saw the explosion spread in the air like the petals of an enormous white flower. "It's a gorgeous sight," he later said. "When white phosphorus touches flesh, however, it burns down to the bone; you can't put it out with water." He'd seen these terrible burns on children in Vietnamese hospitals. And these were the people the Americans were there to help.

As the pilot turned back toward his base, he pointed down to the wetland below.

"There is a VC down there."

Ellsberg pulled out his pistol. The pilot grabbed his M-16 and dove to just a hundred feet above the ground. Below were two men in loose black clothing. They were running. They were unarmed.

They'd probably hidden their weapons nearby, the pilot said. As the plane zipped over their heads, the men dove and lay flat on the marshy grass. Then the men jumped up and began running again. The pilot came back around, firing his M-16.

"Does this happen often?" Ellsberg asked.

"All the time."

"Do you ever hit anyone in this way?"

"Not very often," the pilot said, turning for home. "It's hard to hit anybody from a plane with an M-16, but it scares the shit out of them. They will be pretty scared VC tonight."

Ellsberg asked how he knew they were Viet Cong.

"There's nothing but VC in the Plain of Reeds."

When he got back to Saigon, Ellsberg asked around. He was told that in addition to enemy fighters, about two thousand people lived and fished in the area they'd flown over. He thought about that. And he thought about the village he'd seen destroyed.

"We had been fired at, all right, but by whom?" he asked himself. "What connection did they have to the village? Or to the people, and the children, in the burning houses?"

And the question that *really* haunted him: "How were we serving American purposes in raining down punishment on the people in these houses?"

★ ★ ★

In early 1966, Robert McNamara reached the conclusion that the United States could not win the Vietnam War. But he was unwilling to confront President Johnson. In public, he continued to support escalation. Privately, he began airing grave doubts.

"No amount of bombing can end the war," an exhausted-looking McNamara told a few reporters in an off-the-record discussion in February. The sustained bombing of Vietnam, he confided, was showing no discernable results. The infiltration of soldiers from North to South was steadily rising. According to the CIA, the bombing campaign was costing the United States nine dollars and sixty cents for every one dollar of damage inflicted on North Vietnam.

The strain on McNamara was visible, literally.

"His face seemed to be grayer and his patent leather hair thinner," one of the journalists, Stanley Karnow, later wrote. "His voice lacked the authority it had once projected when he would point briskly to graphs and flip-charts to prove his rosy appraisals."

That summer the CIA completed a report titled "The Vietnamese Communists' Will to Persist." The main point was that the American military was not hurting the enemy nearly enough to weaken their commitment to eventual victory.

McNamara read it. Johnson read it.

"Hell, don't show this report to anyone," Johnson told Mc-Namara. "Put the clamps on it."

In the summer of 1966, Patricia Marx flew to Vietnam to visit her fiancé. They had another romantic tour planned, but at the last moment Ellsberg found out he couldn't get leave from work.

Stuck in Saigon, and as intensely curious as ever, Marx started looking around for stories. Teaming up with another journalist, she researched an article about families that had been driven from their homes by the fighting. She walked through squalid refugee camps. She spoke with people who had been forced to come to the city after their villages had been destroyed by American bombs, their crops wiped out by Agent Orange.

She had been against the Vietnam War from the start. This is when she became really furious about it. "I looked at those kids in the streets," she remembered. "The poverty, and the thought of what was happening to those human lives was just intolerable, sickening."

Marx still had her radio show in New York and took the opportunity to tape an interview with Neil Sheehan, a *New York Times* reporter who had been in Vietnam for three years. Sheehan's view was bleak. Years before, he explained, the country's best leaders had gone north to fight the French. North Vietnam simply had more talent, more discipline. The only thing holding off the Communists was American firepower.

"What's going to happen?" Marx asked, frustration in her voice. "Are we just going to keep slugging it out?"

Patricia Marx with
children in Vietnam,
summer 1966

"I don't see any quick end to the thing," Sheehan said. "What I suspect, from what most American officials say here, is that it'll be a long war."

The blow-up with Ellsberg was inevitable. It came one night in Saigon, when they went to a party thrown for Sheehan, who was heading back to the States. Everyone was drinking and talking about the war. A European diplomat described a recent trip to North Vietnam, and the destruction he'd seen from American bombs. Marx listened, fuming.

As they walked home, she turned to Ellsberg and demanded, "How *can* you be a part of this?"

"But I'm trying to *stop* these terrible things."

"It doesn't matter," she said. "You're part of something that's so awful. And you seem to be engaged in it."

This exchange really stung Ellsberg. He was against the bombing of North Vietnam, and she *knew* that. *I'm trying to do the best I can to moderate the killing, and I'm not getting any credit*, he thought as they walked in silence. *She's holding me responsible for the whole war.*

Over the next few days, Marx watched Ellsberg locking up again, closing himself off exactly as he had before he'd left for Vietnam. "His heart withdrew into a safe I didn't have the combination to," she remembered.

She soon left for the States. She had no idea where they stood, but held out hope they would eventually patch things up.

Ellsberg figured they were broken up for good. He blamed her critical words. "I thought she was unreasonable to hold me accountable for policies I was opposing," he said many years later.

"Of course," he added, "now I think she was right."

MAKING PROGRESS

ROBERT MCNAMARA TRAVELED to Vietnam in October 1966. As always, the closer he got to the war, the worse it looked.

On the long flight back to Washington, D.C., he stood in the back of his windowless military airplane, arguing about the situation with Bob Komer, one of President Johnson's aides on Vietnam. They were going back and forth about whether any progress was being made, when McNamara realized there was someone on the flight who could help settle the argument, someone who'd been on the ground in Vietnam for over a year.

McNamara walked up the aisle to where Daniel Ellsberg was sitting. Ellsberg, who was heading home for a short leave, got up and followed the secretary to the back of the plane.

"Komer here is saying that we've made a lot of progress," McNamara began. "I say that things are worse than they were a year ago. What do you say?"

"Well, Mr. Secretary, I'm most impressed with how much *the same* things are as they were a year ago," Ellsberg said. "They were pretty bad then, but I wouldn't say it was worse now, just about the same."

"That proves what I'm saying!" McNamara shouted. "We've put more than a hundred thousand more troops into the country over the last year, and there's been no improvement. Things aren't any better at all. That means the underlying situation is really *worse!*"

"You could say that," agreed Ellsberg.

"We are approaching Andrews Air Force Base," the pilot announced. "Please take your seats."

When the plane door opened a few minutes later, McNamara walked down the steps into a foggy Maryland morning. A crowd of reporters pointed microphones and cameras and television lights.

"Gentlemen, I've just come back from Vietnam," McNamara told the group, "and I'm glad to be able to tell you that we're showing great progress in every dimension of our effort."

Ellsberg walked behind the gathering, unnoticed. He was thinking, *I hope I'm never in a job where I have to lie like that.*

A month later, McNamara headed to Boston for a scheduled visit to Harvard University. He was not expecting a friendly welcome.

The students on the roofs of campus buildings were the first to spot him. Watching through binoculars, communicating over walkie-talkies, they tracked the secretary of defense's car across the campus. McNamara couldn't see them from the backseat of his car. But he could see the hand-painted signs hanging in dorm windows:

"Mac the Knife"

"How many people have you killed?"

This was becoming routine. At ceremonies at Amherst College and New York University, students had turned their backs when he stepped on stage. They'd heckled him at his daughter's college, where he'd been invited to give a commencement address. Another time, he'd been sitting at a restaurant with his wife, Margaret, when a woman walked up shouting, "Baby burner! You have blood on your hands!"

Now he'd been invited to Harvard to speak to the graduate students of Henry Kissinger, a professor of international relations. A crowd of protestors—tipped off by the rooftop observers—surrounded the car the moment it came to a stop. The students rocked the car back and forth, challenging McNamara to come out.

The panicked driver shifted into reverse and moved his foot to the gas pedal.

"Stop!" McNamara yelled. "You'll kill someone!"

The driver lifted his foot.

"I'm getting out," McNamara said.

"You can't do that," the driver insisted. "They'll mob you."

McNamara pushed the door open and stepped out. When he saw one of the protest leaders shoving his way forward with a microphone, he suggested they both climb onto the hood of the car.

"I want you to know," McNamara announced from the hood, "I spent four of the happiest years of my life on the University of

November 1966. Robert McNamara faces an angry protest during a visit to Harvard University.

California, Berkeley, campus doing some of the things you are doing today."

The crowd booed and bunched tighter.

"I was tougher than you then, and I'm tougher today," McNamara called out. "I was more courteous then, and I hope I am more courteous today."

More jeers, more sharp questions:

"Why didn't you tell the American people that the Vietnam War started in 1957 and 1958 as an internal revolution?"

"How many innocent women and children have been killed?"

McNamara tried to speak, but was drowned out by the shouting.

Beginning to feel he was in actual danger, the secretary jumped off the car, pushed through the crowd, and sprinted toward a nearby building. A student led him into a system of tunnels running beneath the campus. McNamara made it to Kissinger's classroom just in time.

At dinner that night, while chatting with faculty members, the day's unnerving events sparked a new idea in McNamara's mind. "For the first time," he later recalled, "I voiced my feeling that, because the war was not going as hoped, future scholars would surely wish to study why. I thought we should seek to facilitate such study in order to help prevent similar errors in the future."

It was a thought that would have consequences far beyond anything he could possibly have imagined.

Back in Vietnam later that year, Ellsberg sat with an elderly couple in the living room of their home. An American Army captain and an interpreter also sat in the wooden chairs arranged beneath the couple's sleeping loft. This village was supposedly "pacified"— cleared of Viet Cong activity. Ellsberg had come to see for himself.

As they sipped tea, Ellsberg asked the husband when he thought the war would end.

"I have only a few years left. The war will not end while I am alive."

"Who do you think will win?"

The man pointed to the sky. "Heaven will decide."

A thunderous boom of artillery fire shook the building. Ellsberg watched sunlight shimmer on the quivering surface of a hanging mirror. He was amazed by the couple's reaction, or lack

Daniel Ellsberg in a Vietnamese village, 1966

of it. They didn't even blink. *This is their life,* he realized. *This is normal.*

The Viet Cong controlled the village down the road, the man explained. The Americans shelled the village. The Viet Cong fired back.

Ellsberg asked the man which side he would like to see win.

"He does not care which side wins," the interpreter said. "He would like the war to be over."

There were several bursts of small-arms fire. They seemed to be getting closer. The captain said it was time to leave the pacified village.

"Now, before you go, he would like to ask you one question," the interpreter said.

"What is his question?"

"You are Americans," the man began. "In your opinion, when will the war end?"

Ellsberg was unsure what to say. There was more gunfire outside. The old man smiled with polite patience. He was waiting for an answer.

Daniel Ellsberg felt himself slipping into a deep depression. The break-up with Patricia was a big factor. So was his sense of utter powerlessness to change the course of events in this failing war. He tried to snap himself out of it by focusing on happier things. "I would make myself think about my future, my career, but nothing made any difference," he later said. "Not even when I thought about my children."

There was just one thing left to do in Vietnam. One thing left to understand. It might end up costing him his life—but that didn't trouble him.

"I'm thirty-six," he told himself. "I've lived long enough."

On December 23, Ellsberg flew by helicopter to the Mekong Delta, south of Saigon. The Viet Cong had a strong presence in the region. American forces were just beginning a major offensive to clear them out. This would be a good place to see combat up close.

SEARCH AND DESTROY

THE HELICOPTER SET DOWN IN RACH KIEN. The village's dirt streets were lined with huts. In the center of town were a few plaster buildings with corrugated tin roofs.

Ellsberg jumped out, carrying a pack with extra clothes and a sleeping bag, and was met by the colonel in charge of the American battalion at Rach Kien. They walked through town together, meeting other officers, shouting to be heard over the roar of the helicopters bringing in artillery and ammunition. The Viet Cong had been living in the village, the colonel told Ellsberg. They'd scattered when the Americans arrived. Now the Americans were setting up a makeshift headquarters in the same buildings recently used by the Viet Cong.

"You'll be mortared tonight," an officer who knew the area well told Ellsberg. "Remember, they've been living a long time right where you're standing."

"Are you kidding?" another officer asked. "This is a reinforced American battalion, with artillery and air support. There won't be a VC for ten miles around tonight."

Ellsberg was given a canvas cot next to the colonel's in one of the plaster buildings. After supper he strung up a mosquito net around his cot and fell asleep in his clothes.

A few hours later, he was jolted awake by the sound of exploding shells.

"WHOOMP!" is how he described the noise. "WHOOMP! WHOOMP!"

He sat up in the dark and saw the colonel pulling on his boots. He did the same.

They ran into the street, shoelaces dangling, as shells fell all over town and machine gunfire flew in from the darkness. As they ducked into the crowded command post, Ellsberg noticed a look of terror on the young private standing guard outside. It was his first day in Vietnam.

Just as they shut the door, a shell hit right outside. The building shook and maps fell from the walls and half-full coffee cups spun through the air. The hanging lantern that lit the room rocked and spun, projecting shadows of falling men onto the walls.

"Everyone scrambled for his helmet," Ellsberg remembered. "I was suddenly sorry I hadn't had one of my own."

The soldier outside was hit by the blast. He died in a helicopter on the way to the nearest hospital.

The shelling stopped as suddenly as it had begun. Ellsberg went back to his cot and fell asleep, and it was not until the next morning that he noticed an unexploded .60 mm shell sticking into the floor a few feet from his bed. He figured it must have landed just seconds after he'd run out. Ellsberg took out his camera to document his brush with death. He was snapping pictures as a demolition team came in to defuse the bomb.

"For Christ's sake," one of them barked at Ellsberg, "that round is live!"

A few days later, an American platoon sloshed through a paddy of waist-high rice plants, scanning in all directions for enemy fighters. With his camera and a borrowed submachine gun over his shoulder, Ellsberg walked with them.

He was pretty sure he remembered reading some rule against civilians bearing weapons in war zones. As an employee of the American embassy in Saigon, he was positive he was not supposed to fire at anyone.

A few shots whistled in from a line of trees at the edge of the field. The Americans grabbed their M-16s and started moving toward the tree line, blasting as they went. Ellsberg lifted his camera and photographed the scene.

When they reached the cover of the trees, the enemy was gone. A furious sergeant charged toward Ellsberg.

"Are you a reporter?" the sergeant demanded.

"I'm from the embassy," Ellsberg said.

"Were you taking personal photographs in a firefight?"

"No. I'm here observing for the deputy ambassador, and I'm taking pictures for him."

Disgusted, the sergeant turned and walked away. A civilian

observer was a dangerous liability for the platoon—they'd have to watch out for him when they should be focused only on the mission.

As a former marine, Ellsberg understood. "After that," he later said, "when people around me were firing, I was too."

He had plenty of opportunities. Walking patrols for a week, Ellsberg lived the life of an infantryman in Vietnam. Lugging packs weighing more than fifty pounds, the young men slogged across

Photograph taken by Daniel Ellsberg of his unit on combat patrol, 1967

muddy rice fields and cut through dense forests. Their heads baked in their helmets as temperatures soared over one hundred degrees. Clouds of mosquitoes were a constant torment, and during brief breaks they had to pull off their boots and soaking socks to pick leeches off their feet.

The long marches were grueling, miserable, boring—and, without warning, deadly. Any step could trigger a hidden mine. Gunfire could erupt from behind any clump off trees. When it did, the men got low and returned fire. They called in air strikes at what they guessed were the enemy positions. They called in helicopters to evacuate the wounded. Then they moved forward again. They never saw who was firing at them. Other than Americans, the only dead body Ellsberg saw was that of a teenage girl killed by a stray American shell.

"That didn't improve morale," he recalled.

The pattern continued, day after day. They would chase the Viet Cong from an area one day, and then take fire from the Viet Cong in the same exact area the next day. Ellsberg saw anger and frustration on the faces of the men.

"It was hard to believe we were accomplishing anything at all," he said.

In a rice paddy on the first day of 1967, Ellsberg finally saw the enemy.

The platoon was conducting another search-and-destroy mission. Ellsberg and three other soldiers were walking point, about fifty yards out in front of the other men. Their job was to locate the Viet Cong by drawing their fire. The water in the paddy was up to their knees. The plants came to their chests and swayed in the breeze. As they stepped out of the paddy, they heard shots coming from behind.

Lifting his weapon, Ellsberg spun and saw a very young soldier, maybe fifteen, wearing nothing but black shorts. He was crouched in the rice plants, blasting a Russian-made AK-47 at the American platoon. At least two more Viet Cong fighters were with him. Ellsberg saw their black hair and heard their guns. They were firing from the exact spot Ellsberg had just walked past—they must have been lying still in the water, he realized. They'd let the men walking point go past, and then, when they were between the point men and the rest of the platoon, opened fire. Ellsberg and the three soldiers with him couldn't fire at the Viet Cong without the risk of hitting their own men.

As usual, the firefight was brief. Ellsberg saw the teenage gunman crouch lower and disappear. Then, silence.

The patrol resumed. The men walking point crossed a dirt path and splashed into another paddy. The rest of the platoon followed fifty yards behind. Ellsberg could see no more than a few feet in any direction through the tall plants. He had the disturbing realization that each time he put down his boot he might literally step on an enemy soldier.

Again, they were fired at from behind. Ellsberg saw a flash of black clothing, then nothing.

Again, they resumed the march.

Later in the day the men rested on a dirt levee between rice fields. They saw a few men setting up a machine gun on a tripod among trees on the far side of the paddy.

The platoon leader picked up the radio and called headquarters.

"Who are the friendlies ahead of us?" he asked.

He listened to the answer and grunted, "Hunh."

"What do they say?" one of the men asked.

"There are no friendlies ahead of us," the platoon leader reported. He put on his helmet.

Ellsberg asked, "What are you going to do?"

"I guess we're going to find out who they are."

Moments later, Ellsberg and a few soldiers were crawling on knees and elbows through shallow water, holding their guns above their heads. From behind, men from the platoon opened fire on the enemy machine gun. The machine gun fired back.

Ellsberg in combat in Vietnam, 1967

"You didn't need to be told to keep your ass down," Ellsberg noted.

They got within about fifteen yards of the gun. "I took two grenades off my belt," Ellsberg recalled, "pulled the pin on one, and, lying on my side, tossed it with a straight arm at the machine gun. I pulled the pin on the other one and threw it too. Both went off, and the machine gun stopped firing."

Then he and the other Americans jumped out of the mud and charged toward the trees. They heard twigs snapping, footsteps on brush, and then nothing. The gun and tripod were gone. Any dead or wounded had been carried away.

"Very good soldiers," Ellsberg thought.

The Americans continued into the next rice paddy and were fired at from a different patch of trees. Several men were hit. A helicopter carried them off. The platoon continued toward the spot they'd taken fire from, and found only spent cartridges, blood on the dirt. So they moved on, and were soon fired at from a new location.

"This happened three or four times," Ellsberg later said, "taking fire and zigzagging toward it every half hour or so." There were two groups of Viet Cong fighters out there. One fired at the Americans while the other retreated to a new position and waited. "They were playing with us," Ellsberg realized, "a kind of leapfrog."

As the sky grew dark, the exhausted Americans sat on the ground gulping water from canteens and licking melted chocolate bars from the wrappers. Ellsberg remembered the stories he'd read in school of the American Revolution, of young British soldiers in heavy packs and red uniforms marching around the

New England woods, taking fire from the cover of trees and stone walls, chasing a highly motivated enemy that moved faster and knew the local geography better.

He turned to the young radio operator resting beside him. "Sergeant, do you ever feel like the Redcoats?"

The man said, "I've been thinking that all day."

LASTING IMPRESSION

AFTER TWELVE DAYS in Rach Kien, Ellsberg was due to head back to Saigon. He decided to go on one last march.

"Every patrol that's come near that spot has drawn fire," an officer told Ellsberg, pointing to a map. "There's heavy cover there and all along the riverbank, but there must be VC there all the time. I'm sending a company there tonight. We'll take them by surprise in the morning and clean it out."

The men set out at two o'clock in the morning. Walking along the dikes with empty pockets and everything on their packs tightly strapped, they moved almost silently over the soft dirt. It was a warm, cloudless night with no wind, and the reflection of the full moon glowed on the still, black water of the rice paddies.

They marched all night. Reaching their objective just before dawn, the men lay in the muddy water behind a dike, watching the grove of trees in front of them. The enemy was there. When the sky began to lighten, Ellsberg looked to his left and watched a massive red sun rising, it seemed, straight out of the water.

As soon as Ellsberg's platoon started moving forward, a burst of machine gunfire erupted from the tree line. The Americans fired back, heads low as they waded through thigh-high water toward the trees. By the time they reached the grove, the enemy was gone.

The men were ordered forward and were suddenly in thick jungle. They slashed with machetes at branches and vines to clear a path toward the river, sinking deeper and deeper into the swampy soil beneath them.

They stopped. For a moment, there was silence. Then voices. Voices speaking in hushed tones. Speaking in Vietnamese. They were across the river, no more than twenty yards away.

The platoon leader called in artillery, whispering the map coordinates over his radio. Moments later, a series of well-placed shells slammed into the trees across the river. Fragments of metal and clumps of leaves and torn branches rained into the water.

Exhausted, frustrated at again having no real chance to confront the enemy, the Americans marched into a nearby village. As they neared the first hut, Ellsberg watched some of the marines open fire. No one shot back.

They went inside. The hut was empty, but ashes in the fireplace were still warm. There was food on the table and a few handmade toys on the floor.

Ellsberg asked the platoon's lieutenant why his men had fired at the hut.

"Reconnaissance by fire," the man answered.

It was a way of determining if enemy fighters were hiding inside—a lot safer than walking into a potential ambush.

What if there's a family inside? Ellsberg asked.

"Tough shit," the lieutenant said. "They know we're operating in the area, they can hear us, and they ought to be in their bunker. I'm not taking any unnecessary chances with my men."

Most huts, Ellsberg saw, did have some kind of shelter—holes in the ground, or sandbags in the corner. But did that mean they were used by the Viet Cong? Or were the families just trying to survive the crossfire? There was no way for the Americans to know.

As they moved through the village, Ellsberg watched a young marine hold the flame of his cigarette lighter to the thatch roof of a hut. Black smoke and orange flames were already rising from two other huts.

"These are VC huts," the lieutenant told Ellsberg. "Tonight they'll have to hump it in the rain, same as us!"

Of course, the men knew this would have no impact on the war. But Ellsberg understood the angry impulse. "It was the first thing they had done in two weeks that had any visible effect at all," he later explained. "It was the only sign they were able to leave that they had ever been there."

Ellsberg headed back to Saigon later that day. The marines soon packed up and moved out of Rach Kien. The Viet Cong moved back in.

Ellsberg spent the first month of 1967 flat on his back in Bangkok.

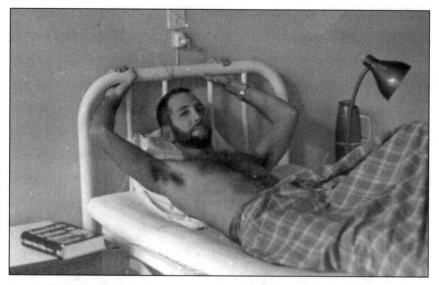

January 1967. Daniel Ellsberg recuperating from illness in a Saigon hospital.

He'd gone to Thailand on leave, looking forward to lounging on a beach he and Patricia had enjoyed when she'd first come to visit. But a debilitating case of hepatitis spoiled the vacation. He figured he must have picked up the liver disease while wading through one of those rice paddies. After a month in Bangkok, he was just strong enough to fly to Saigon—where he spent another month in bed. Too weak to move around, he balanced a type-writer on his stomach and typed reports on what he'd learned in Vietnam.

And he had a lot of time to think.

There had been one other time in his life like this, when he'd been flat on his back for months. It was the summer of 1946. Ellsberg was fifteen. The family—Dan; his younger sister, Gloria; and their parents, Adele and Harry—were driving from Michigan to Colorado to attend a party at Adele's brother's place.

113

They had gotten a late start the first day, and by the time they reached the motel where they'd been planning to stay, the rooms they'd reserved were taken. Gloria and Adele slept in the car, while Dan and his father stretched out on the ground under a shared blanket. Ellsberg later remembered his father tossing and turning all night.

The next day, July 4, they drove all morning before stopping for a roadside picnic in Iowa. Gloria had sat up front that morning, so it was Dan's turn next. But as they walked back to the car, Gloria raced ahead and jumped in the front passenger seat, calling out, "I'm going to sit here if it kills me!"

Dan had to cram himself, among the suitcases and blankets, into the seat behind his father. Adele sat behind Gloria.

They drove through endless cornfields. It was a hot day. Harry felt himself nodding off.

"I've got to stop and sleep," he said.

Adele urged him to push on, or they wouldn't make it to Denver in time for the party.

Shortly after one o'clock, Harry fell asleep. The car swerved off the road and slammed into the side of an overpass. The impact ripped off the right side of the car.

Dan opened his eyes thirty-six hours later.

He was in a bright white room. Everyone was wearing white. A doctor was bending over him.

"You were in an automobile accident," the doctor said. "You are very lucky to be alive."

"How is my mother?"

"She died instantly."

Gloria was also dead. Dan's father was not seriously hurt.

Ellsberg spent the next three months in a hospital bed, recovering from a severe concussion and a broken knee. He watched his father struggle with overwhelming guilt. He didn't blame his father for the accident, not exactly. Instead, he grappled with an intensely painful realization—one that would have unsettling relevance to his bitter experience in Vietnam.

"I think it probably left an impression on me," Ellsberg said of the accident, "that someone you loved or respected, like my father—an authority—could fall asleep at the wheel, and had to be watched. Not because they were bad, but because they were inattentive, perhaps, to the risks."

PART II

SECRETS AND LIES

CREDIBILITY GAP

"YOU WILL WRITE APOLOGY to peace-loving people of the Democratic Republic of Vietnam," the prison guard demanded. "Confess your crimes. Promise never to bomb Vietnam again."

Everett Alvarez said, "Heck, no."

This is how the torture sessions always began.

"You have bad attitude!" the guard raged. "Do not forget you are air pirate and capitalist warmonger! You are criminal aggressor who has bombed and killed peaceful Vietnamese!"

When Alvarez refused to sign a confession shoved in his face, guards cuffed his hands behind his back. They pushed his head down while yanking his arms up, holding him in this excruciating position until he cried out. The louder he shouted, the harder they punched and kicked him.

By 1967 there were more than a hundred American prisoners held in camps in and around Hanoi. Alvarez knew the same thing was happening to the other pilots. He could hear their screams through the walls of his cell.

Guards forced James Stockdale's badly healed broken leg into irons and left him until his limbs turned blue. Navy pilot John McCain, shot down in 1967, was held in solitary confinement for years, dragged out only for interrogations and beatings. The ability to communicate with other prisoners through the cement walls was the only thing that kept him sane.

The pilots became so adept with the tap code that they started inventing shortcuts, a kind of low-tech texting. The question on everyone's mind became, "WN DO U TC WE GO HM."

By the start of 1967, nearly 400,000 Americans were serving in Vietnam. More than six thousand American soldiers had been killed, and as the fighting intensified that year, the death toll rose sharply to nearly one thousand a month.

Every night on the television news, Americans watched film from the Vietnam War: falling bombs, firefights, burning villages, the wounded on stretchers, and body bags loaded onto planes for the long flight home. The president kept saying America was winning the war. But the images on the TV screen did not look like victory. For the first time, the American public's approval of Johnson's handling of the war slipped below 50 percent.

On April 15, more than 300,000 protestors gathered in New York City's Central Park for what became the largest antiwar march yet in American history. Young men stood on boulders and held cigarette lighters to their draft cards while the crowd shouted:

"Resist! Resist!"

For many of the men running the war, the growing protests hit uncomfortably close to home. Robert McNamara's teenage son Craig shocked his father by hanging a Viet Cong flag in his bedroom. Stevie Westmoreland, the general's daughter, watched in horror as college students set flame to an effigy of her father. Nearly everywhere he went, President Johnson was confronted by protestors chanting:

"Hey, hey, LBJ, how many kids did you kill today?"

Reluctant to face hostile voters, the president began to feel like a prisoner in the White House. The isolation only worsened what the press had begun calling the "credibility gap"—the gap between what Johnson was telling the public and what the public believed was really happening in Vietnam.

Asked by journalists why he didn't just cut American losses and leave Vietnam, Johnson repeated a pledge he had made many times: "I'm not going to be the first American president to lose a war."

In public, both Johnson and General Westmoreland continued to speak of steady and encouraging success in Vietnam. In private, the conversation was different. "This war could go on indefinitely," Westmoreland told Johnson at a meeting in March.

Under the existing plan, U.S. forces in Vietnam would rise from 400,000 to 470,000 by the end of 1967. It wasn't enough, Westmoreland reported. With 100,000 additional troops, or ideally 200,000, he believed he could begin to win the war of attrition.

"When we add divisions, can't the enemy add divisions?" asked Johnson. "And if so, where does it all end?"

Yes, Westmoreland agreed, the Communists were likely to match American escalation. But with the requested reinforcements, the stalemate might be snapped.

This is when Robert McNamara broke with the policy of open-ended escalation. In a secret memo, he urged the president to deny Westmoreland's request.

Johnson griped, "That military genius, McNamara, has gone dovish on me."

The president grappled with the usual indecision. He was terrified of losing the war, and scared of sparking wider protests. As he'd done several times before, he compromised. He approved another fifty-five thousand troops, raising the total to 525,000. And as usual, he assured Americans he was giving military leaders everything they asked for.

"We are very sure that we are on the right track," Johnson told the country.

By March of 1967, Daniel Ellsberg was finally well enough to travel. He decided it was time to leave Vietnam. On his way home, he called Patricia Marx from Europe and asked her to come join him.

She hadn't heard from him in months, and was ticked that he had the nerve to expect her to drop everything and come running.

She said, "Bug off."

Ellsberg continued on to Washington, D.C. He resigned his post at the State Department. Though still weak from his bout with hepatitis, he spent some time in the capital trying to share what he'd learned in Vietnam. His hope was to use his position as an insider to influence key decision makers. It did not go as planned.

"Dan, it looks very good," Walt Rostow, Johnson's national security advisor, told Ellsberg in a White House meeting. "The other side is near collapse. In my opinion, victory is very near."

Ellsberg couldn't believe what he was hearing. When he began to object, Rostow cut in—

"But Dan, you've got to see the latest charts. I've got them right here. The charts are very good."

"Walt, I don't want to see your charts," Ellsberg said. "I've just come back from Vietnam. I've been there for two years."

"No, you don't understand. Victory is near. I'll show you the charts. The charts are very good."

"Walt, I don't want to hear it. Victory is not near."

"But, Dan," insisted Rostow, "the charts are very good."

Varying versions of the same scene played out in offices at the Pentagon and State Department. Former colleagues thought Ellsberg's outlook was too negative. "He is in a very sour mood," one official commented. "He has had hepatitis so I think that contributes to his attitude."

"I was mad," Ellsberg later conceded. "Maybe it *was* my liver."

But there was more to it, of course. What really struck Ellsberg was that government leaders seemed to have learned nothing from three years of failure in Vietnam. Even more maddening was the lack of any sense of urgency to change course.

William Bundy, a top State Department official, told Ellsberg, "I don't think we can have any movement till after the election." Meaning the presidential election of 1968.

"But that's a year away!" Ellsberg cried.

Bundy sighed and shook his head.

★ ★ ★

Robert McNamara, following a very different path, came to the same conclusion as Ellsberg about Vietnam.

"We had failed," McNamara later wrote. "Why this failure? Could it have been prevented? What lessons could be drawn from our experiences that would enable others to avoid similar failures?"

In June McNamara asked his assistant, John McNaughton, to start collecting classified documents for future use by government officials and scholars. "Tell your researchers not to hold back," he told McNaughton. "Let the chips fall where they may."

This was the report that would become infamous as the Pentagon Papers, but at the time it had a less catchy name: "History of U.S. Decision-making in Vietnam."

A Pentagon official named Mort Halperin took charge of forming teams to study the various eras of American involvement in Vietnam, dating back to 1945. He offered Ellsberg a job on the project. Ellsberg jumped at the chance to expand his knowledge of the war. It was made very clear that the entire contents of the study—the very *existence* of the study—was to be kept secret, even from the president. McNamara feared Johnson would kill the project if he knew of it.

He was probably right. The study was a secret history of the Vietnam War. And the documents revealed a vast discrepancy between what government officials had been saying publicly and what they knew to be true.

"You know," McNamara said, referring to the growing pile of papers, "they could hang people for what's in there."

THE POWER OF LEAKS

"AN EMOTIONAL BASKET CASE"—that was how President Johnson described Robert McNamara's state of mind by late 1967. "The pressure got so great that Bob couldn't sleep at night. I was afraid he might have a nervous breakdown."

In meetings, McNamara would rail against the war, shouting, "The goddamned Air Force, they're dropping more on North Vietnam than we dropped on Germany in the last year of World War II, and it's not doing anything!"

Then he'd turn to the window to hide his tears.

"He does it all the time now," one of his secretaries told a visitor. "He cries into the curtain."

Johnson gently pushed McNamara out of the Pentagon, giving him the prestigious but less controversial job of president of the World Bank. "I do not know to this day whether I quit or was fired," McNamara said years later. "Maybe it was both."

Anyway, he was out. And, on Johnson's orders, the rest of the administration worked to change the mood of the country by spreading good news about Vietnam. During a brief visit to the States, General Westmoreland joined the effort. "I have never been more encouraged in the four years that I have been in Vietnam," he announced as he stepped off the plane. "We are making real progress."

"A new phase is now starting," Westmoreland told the press later in November. "We have reached an important point when the end begins to come into view."

November 1967. William Westmoreland, commander of U.S. forces in Vietnam, briefs the press during his visit to Washington, telling them, "We are making real progress."

★ ★ ★

On the night of January 31, 1968, fireworks lit the sky above Saigon. The streets were crowded with people celebrating Tet, the Vietnamese New Year.

Amid the all-night festivities, nineteen young Vietnamese men gathered at a car repair shop. For months, they had been sneaking ammunition and TNT into Saigon under loads of firewood and inside baskets of rice. The woman who owned the shop, a longtime secret agent of the Viet Cong, had helped them hide the weapons.

Now the men distributed the guns and bombs, and their squad leader went over the details of the mission. At 2:45 a.m., they crammed into a small truck and a taxi and drove, headlights off, along the dark, tree-lined avenue leading to the concrete walls surrounding the embassy of the United States.

Moments later, a massive explosion rocked the embassy compound. Two American military policemen ran toward the explosion and opened fire on the figures climbing through a three-foot hole in the wall.

"They're coming in!" one of the MPs shouted into his radio. "They're coming in!"

★ ★ ★

It was the middle of the afternoon in Washington, D.C. Walt Rostow was meeting with reporters when an aide came and handed him a slip of paper.

"Looks like some trouble in Saigon," he told Rostow.

January 1968. The U.S. Ambassador to South Vietnam, Ellsworth Bunker, looks at the body of a dead Viet Cong soldier in the grounds of the U.S. embassy at the end of the Tet Offensive.

That was an understatement. The battle at the American embassy was one small part of the massive Tet Offensive—that night seventy thousand communist soldiers launched surprise attacks on more than a hundred cities and towns all over South Vietnam.

Americans turned on their televisions and saw American diplomats firing guns out the windows of the embassy. There was rubble strewn everywhere, and the bodies of Americans and Viet Cong attackers. A little after nine in the morning, Saigon time, when the embassy was finally secured, General Westmoreland arrived to show reporters around the battlefield. Over the sounds of firefights still raging elsewhere in Saigon, Westmoreland declared victory, saying, "The enemy's well-laid plans went afoul."

"The reporters could hardly believe their ears," one *Washington Post* journalist recalled. "Westmoreland was standing in the ruins and saying everything was great."

On one level, Westmoreland was right. Tet was a military disaster for the Communists. American and South Vietnamese forces repelled the attacks everywhere, killing more than fifty thousand Viet Cong and North Vietnamese soldiers.

And yet, Tet was a disaster for the United States too—a psychological disaster. For years, the president had been telling the public how well things were going in Vietnam. But now people were watching American troops fighting brutal battles to retake territories and cities that were supposed to be secure. There were more than 500,000 Americans in Vietnam. More than twenty thousand had been killed. For what? If, nearly four years into the war, the enemy was able to launch an attack of this size, what exactly had been accomplished?

Walter Cronkite, anchor of the nation's most watched TV news program, summed up the mood of the country. After presenting an update on the fighting in Vietnam, he turned away from the camera as the show went to a commercial.

"What the hell is going on?" he said. "I thought we were winning the war."

★ ★ ★

Daniel Ellsberg watched it all from his new home in Southern California. After leaving government service, he had decided to return to the Rand Corporation, where he'd worked before joining the Pentagon. "I wanted to be free again to tell what I knew and what I believed about our Vietnam policy," he said of the decision. "After three years of largely listening and learning, I believed that I knew things about the situation in Vietnam worth passing on in my own voice."

Ellsberg let his hair grow longer and rented a tiny cottage on the beach in Malibu. The flimsy structure was still settling into the sand, causing the floor of each room to tilt at a different angle. And there was a problem with the wiring that caused electricity to spray out of the shower along with the water. "I used to take a

Ellsberg with his children, Robert and Mary, outside his Malibu beach house, 1969

131

shower leaning slightly out," he remembered, "so that if the electricity came on at that moment, you could fall outside the shower."

He loved it. He lived near his kids. He lived near Rand headquarters. He swam in the ocean every day. At night he lay in bed listening to the waves.

But Ellsberg was still a trusted Washington insider. In the wake of the Tet Offensive, Rand sent him briefly to D.C. to join a group of consultants advising Clark Clifford, the new secretary of defense.

President Johnson was pacing the halls again. Unable to sleep, he would put on his robe and slippers and walk down to the situation room in the White House basement.

"We couldn't break him of the habit," Secretary of State Dean Rusk recalled, "even for health reasons, of getting up at 4:30 or 5:00 every morning to go down to the operations room and check on the casualties from Vietnam, each one of which took a little piece out of him."

In the wake of Tet, the Joint Chiefs and General Westmoreland submitted another request for more troops. Now was the time to go on the offensive, they said. "We face a situation of great opportunity as well as heightened risk," Westmoreland told the president. He wanted another 206,000 troops.

While Johnson wrestled with another agonizing decision, a copy of the troop request came across Ellsberg's desk. It was top secret, Ellsberg knew. Not even Congress was aware that the president was considering another major escalation.

This was not a decision that should be made in secret, Ellsberg thought. The people had a right to know.

★ ★ ★

On Sunday, March 10, Ellsberg picked up his copy of the *New York Times* and read the stunning headline: "***WESTMORELAND REQUESTS 206,000 MORE MEN, STIRRING DEBATE IN ADMINISTRATION.***"

The article, by Neil Sheehan and Hedrick Smith, laid bare all the details of the military's secret request.

Ellsberg was shocked. He had no idea who had leaked the story.

The impact was immediate. Members of Congress started speaking out against further troop increases. Senator William Fulbright, who had helped steer the Tonkin Gulf Resolution through Congress, now declared that he regretted that action. Previously, Johnson had increased troop levels in Vietnam little by little, without making dramatic announcements. Thanks to the leak, that was no longer an option.

"As I observed the effect of this leak, it was as if clouds had suddenly opened," Ellsberg later said of this turning point in his life. "In the past, I had instinctively accepted the ethos of my profession, the idea that leaking was always inherently bad, treacherous . . . I had been wrong. Obviously, leaking could be a patriotic and constructive act."

LOW POINT

LYNDON JOHNSON MOST DEFINITELY did not agree.

A government employee, Johnson argued, had every right to make his case within the government. "But once a decision has been made, he has an equal obligation to carry it out with all his energy and wisdom," the president wrote in his memoir. "If he cannot do so in good conscience, he should resign. He has no right to sabotage his president and his own government from within."

Either way, the story was out, and it hurt Johnson. Polls put his approval rating at just 36 percent. Only 26 percent supported his handling of the war. The credibility gap was a major issue. One aide put it bluntly: "A majority of people believed he regularly lied to them."

"I want war like I want polio," Johnson groaned in private. "What you want and what your image is are two different things."

Then Johnson's reelection campaign got started, and the news got worse. In the first Democratic primary in New Hampshire, the president barely squeaked past Eugene McCarthy, an antiwar senator who had not been expected to pose a serious challenge. Johnson's obvious vulnerability encouraged Senator Robert Kennedy, President John Kennedy's younger brother, to jump into the race. Kennedy quickly surged into the lead.

On the night of March 31, Johnson addressed the nation from his desk in the Oval Office. He began by talking about Vietnam, announcing he had decided against further escalation of the war. He told Americans he was ordering a sharp reduction in the bombing of North Vietnam, in the hope that this would lead to peace talks with Hanoi.

Then he came to the part of the speech about his own future.

March 31, 1968. Lyndon Johnson gives a television address from the Oval Office, announcing that he will not seek reelection as president.

Even as the words he'd written rolled onto the Teleprompter, Johnson's closest aides didn't know if he was going to read them. Johnson hesitated, glancing at Lady Bird, who was watching from behind the cameras. Then he continued.

"With America's sons in the fields far away, with America's future under challenge right here at home," he said, "I do not believe that I should devote an hour or a day of my time to any personal partisan causes . . . Accordingly, I shall not seek, and will not accept, the nomination of my party for another term as your president."

A few days later, North Vietnam agreed to begin peace talks in Paris.

"We have just toppled a president, or come as close to it as our system allows," Tom Hayden, an antiwar activist, told the crowd at a conference in Princeton, New Jersey. "We have ended a war."

Sitting in the audience, surrounded by pacifists and draft resisters, was Daniel Ellsberg. He had come to the conference to listen, to hear different points of view. Like everyone there, he wanted very badly to believe the war was over.

It wasn't over. Not even close. The next few months would be among the darkest of Ellsberg's life.

A woman at the conference introduced him to Martin Luther King, Jr.'s writings on nonviolent protest. Ellsberg was particularly impressed by King's recent speeches against the Vietnam War. The next day, April 4, Martin Luther King was killed by an assassin in Memphis, Tennessee.

Horrified by what the country had lost, Ellsberg returned home to California. He lived alone in a Malibu beach house slightly sturdier than the last one. He began pitching in with Robert Kennedy's presidential campaign. He admired Kennedy's determination to end the war, and helped the candidate craft speeches in preparation for the pivotal California Democratic primary. On June 5, hours after winning the California primary, Robert Kennedy was killed by an assassin in Los Angeles.

Ellsberg was shaving when he heard the news.

"What!" he cried. "What? What is this?"

He sat on the edge of his bed and sobbed, tears carving tiny paths through the shaving cream on his cheeks. *Maybe there's no way*, he thought, *no way to change this country.*

The Paris peace talks opened in May—and went nowhere. The United States insisted that North Vietnam stop supporting the war in the South. North Vietnam demanded that the government of South Vietnam be replaced by one that included representatives of the Viet Cong.

The war went on. Nineteen sixty-eight was the deadliest year yet.

"If in November this war is not over," declared Richard Nixon, the Republican presidential nominee, "I say that the American people will be justified in electing new leadership, and I pledge to you that new leadership will end the war and win the peace."

After serving for eight years as Eisenhower's vice president, Nixon had lost a heartbreakingly close race for president to John

Kennedy in 1960. In 1962 he'd run for governor of his home state of California, and lost again. Now, *finally*, he had an advantage—the public's anger with Johnson and the Democrats for mishandling the Vietnam War. On the campaign trail, Nixon repeatedly promised to end the war "with honor." He did not specify how.

The Democratic candidate for president, Vice President Hubert Humphrey, played right into Nixon's hands. Humphrey was a harsh critic of the war—in private. He believed the president was moving too slowly to find a negotiated settlement. But he was not willing to risk Johnson's wrath by saying so publicly. The result was an absolute disaster at the Democratic convention in Chicago. Inside the convention hall, Humphrey infuriated antiwar voters by blocking the adoption of a strong antiwar platform. Outside on the streets, police clashed violently with crowds of antiwar protestors.

Philip Caputo saw the riots up close. After surviving his tour in Vietnam, he had returned to the States and found work as a newspaper reporter in Chicago. He watched protestors taunting cops and smashing windows, police tossing tear gas and bashing heads with nightsticks. Police cars and ambulances lit scenes of chaos in flashing blue and red.

"Things were spinning out of control," Caputo reflected. "American society had come to resemble a shattered mirror still in its frame."

That's when Daniel Ellsberg turned off the television. That's when he completely tuned out.

Ellsberg spent time with his kids that summer, though they never knew when he'd be around. He barely showed up for work. When he did, colleagues thought he seemed jumpy, wired, unfocused.

"Most of my energy went instead, obsessively, into a bachelor private life," he later said. "I was fighting an extreme case of powerlessness."

Troubled by feeling so depressed, so detached from life, Ellsberg started seeing Dr. Lewis Fielding, a psychiatrist, four days a week.

By summer's end, Nixon led Humphrey by fifteen points in the polls. He was cruising to victory. Then, in late September, things suddenly got interesting.

At a speech in Salt Lake City, Humphrey summoned the nerve to break with Johnson. "I'm going to seek peace in every possible way," he declared. "Come January, it's a new ball game. Then I will make peace."

With a month to go before the election, the race began to tighten.

Then came the news of unexpected progress at the Paris talks. The Americans agreed to halt the bombing of North Vietnam, and in exchange North Vietnamese negotiators agreed to sit down with representatives of the government of South Vietnam. Johnson announced the breakthrough on television on October 31. Renewed peace talks, he told the nation, would begin within days.

Humphrey drew even with Nixon in the polls.

That got Ellsberg's attention. He picked up a "Humphrey for President" poster and taped it to the front of his Spitfire.

"It wasn't a big contribution to the campaign," he admitted, "though the tape did take paint off my hood."

★ ★ ★

After running the best campaign of his life, Richard Nixon watched his hard-earned lead evaporate. "The bombing halt undercut one of my most effective campaign issues," he later explained, "the inability of the Democratic leadership to win a permanent peace."

But if peace talks undermined Nixon's chances to win the election, Nixon was prepared to undermine the peace talks.

On October 31, John Mitchell, Nixon's campaign manager, picked up the phone and called a woman named Anna Chennault.

"Anna, I'm speaking on behalf of Mr. Nixon," Mitchell told Chennault. "It's very important that our Vietnamese friends understand our Republican position and I hope you have made that very clear to them."

Born in China in 1925, Chennault was fiercely anti-communist, and chair of the Republican Women for Nixon. She had agreed, if necessary, to use her contacts to convey secret messages on Nixon's behalf to Nguyen Van Thieu, the president of South Vietnam. It now became necessary. The message was straightforward: urge President Thieu to refuse to participate in the Paris peace talks. Tell him to hold out for a Nixon victory, tell him Nixon will be a better ally to South Vietnam than Humphrey.

During the last week of the presidential campaign, Mitchell called Chennault every day. Chennault relayed the messages to Bui Diem, South Vietnam's ambassador to the United States, and he cabled the notes to Thieu in Saigon.

"I am regularly in touch with the Nixon entourage," Bui Diem wrote in one of the cables. "Many Republican friends have contacted me and encouraged us to stand firm."

A November 2 poll showed Humphrey leading Nixon by three points.

That same day, Chennault repeated her message to Bui Diem. "Tell your boss to hold on a while longer."

In Saigon, Thieu announced he would not participate in the peace talks. Without Thieu, the talks stalled again. It was a crushing letdown to American voters.

At a rally in Texas, Nixon spoke of his own disappointment. "The prospects for peace," he said, "are not as bright as they looked only a few days ago."

"This is treason!" roared Lyndon Johnson.

What Nixon didn't know was that the CIA had bugs in President Thieu's office. American agents routinely intercepted cables between the South Vietnamese embassy and Saigon, and listened in on Bui Diem's phone conversations. Johnson knew exactly what Nixon was up to.

"It would rock the world if it were known that Thieu was conniving with the Republicans," he told aides. "Can you imagine what people would say if it were known that Hanoi has met all these conditions and then Nixon's conniving with them kept us from getting it?"

Did Johnson *want* to rock the world forty-eight hours before the election? Did he want to tell Americans that one of the candidates for president was sabotaging his effort to end the Vietnam War? He wasn't sure. In need of advice, he called his old senate colleague Everett Dirksen, a Republican from Illinois.

"I want to talk to you as a friend, and very confidentially," Johnson began, "because I think we're skirting on dangerous ground." The president detailed Nixon's sneaky maneuverings. "I can identify him, because I know who's doing this," he told Dirksen. "What do you think we oughta do about it?"

Dirksen said, "I better get in touch with him."

MADMAN THEORY

LYNDON JOHNSON'S TELEPHONE RANG early on the afternoon of November 3. He picked up the receiver. The machine that recorded all of Johnson's calls was rolling.

"Mr. President, this is Dick Nixon."

"Yes, Dick."

Nixon, sounding nervous, said he'd heard from Senator Dirksen. There had clearly been some kind of misunderstanding, he told Johnson. Nixon stated his position: he backed the president and believed Thieu should go to Paris.

"I just wanted you to know that I feel very, very strongly about this," Nixon said. "Any rumblings around about somebody trying to sabotage the Saigon government's attitude certainly have no, absolutely no credibility as far as I'm concerned."

"I'm very happy to hear that," Johnson replied, "because that *is* taking place."

Nixon laughed. "My God, I would *never* do anything to encourage Saigon not to come to the table. We want them over in Paris, we've gotta get them to Paris, or you can't have a peace."

"Well, I think if you take that position you're on very, very sound ground."

Nixon assured Johnson he took that position, he wanted the war over. "The quicker the better," he said, "and the hell with the political credit, believe me."

"That's fine, Dick."

Johnson hung up. He was far from convinced by Nixon's performance.

He still didn't know what to do about it, though. The only evidence of Nixon's shady dealings came from bugs and wiretaps, which Johnson certainly did not wish to make public. Besides, he agreed with Walt Rostow's assessment: "The materials are so explosive, that they could gravely damage the country, whether Mr. Nixon is elected or not."

Johnson finally decided to say nothing. It was one more secret from the American people.

Is it fair to say Nixon prevented the Vietnam War from ending in 1968? Probably not. President Thieu knew his government would not last long against the Communists without American help. He was in no rush to cut a deal that would send American soldiers home. So when Humphrey came out in favor of a quick end to the war, it was only logical that Thieu would favor a Nixon victory.

What does it say about a man's character that he would

sabotage peace talks to win votes? To Nixon, that's just how the game was played. Politics and elections were high-stakes fights, not for the faint of heart. "And," he told aides, "I play it gloves off."

On the morning of November 5, Election Day, Nixon climbed the stairs to his campaign plane, *Tricia,* named for one of his daughters. The inside of the plane was decorated with balloons and campaign posters. He stopped in front of one of the posters and read the slogan: "Nixon's the One."

"I hope it's right," he said.

That afternoon, in New York City, Nixon joined his family in a suite of rooms on the thirty-fifth floor of a Manhattan hotel.

"I treated myself to a long hot soak in the huge bathtub," Nixon recalled. "I took my time shaving and dressing, and then I called Haldeman to find out what was happening."

Bob Haldeman, one of Nixon's closest aides, was watching the news in the next room. Pat Nixon and the Nixon daughters, Julie and Tricia, both in their early twenties, also had the TV on. Nixon was the only one who wouldn't watch—it made him too nervous.

Polls closed on the East Coast and results began pouring in. Nixon sat alone on a couch, sipping coffee, taking notes on a yellow legal pad on his lap. The vote was close, but he thought he saw a path to the 270 electoral votes needed for victory.

The counting went on all night. Nixon tried to nap, but couldn't. Finally, at eight thirty the next morning, an aide came in with an update: "ABC just declared you the winner! You got it. You've won."

November 11, 1968.
President-elect Richard
Nixon with outgoing
president Lyndon
Johnson.

Nixon ran down the hall to hug his wife and daughters.

Julie said, "Daddy, I never had any doubt you would win."

"By November 6," Daniel Ellsberg later said, "the day after the election, I was back to my regular obsession with Vietnam."

Beginning to feel engaged again, and eager to get back to work, Ellsberg was in the Rand offices when Henry Kissinger came for a visit. The Harvard professor was known for his vast knowledge of

146

National Security Advisor and future
Secretary of State Henry Kissinger, 1968

international affairs—and his habit of insulting whoever was not in the room.

"Richard Nixon is not fit to be president," Ellsberg heard Kissinger proclaim at Rand.

A few weeks later, Nixon asked Henry Kissinger to be his national security advisor. Kissinger jumped at the opportunity.

Ellsberg was encouraged. He had known Kissinger at Harvard, and had spent time with him in Vietnam. He knew Kissinger supported peace talks. He assumed Kissinger would advise Nixon that it was time to end the war.

And right away, Ellsberg got a chance to influence the new administration from the inside. When Kissinger accepted the job with Nixon, he called Ellsberg's boss at Rand, Harry Rowen.

147

Kissinger wanted Rand to prepare a paper analyzing the range of policy options open to Nixon in Vietnam. Rowen gave the job of drafting the paper to Ellsberg.

Ellsberg's report didn't argue for one option over another—that's not what Kissinger wanted. But he *did* try to subtly emphasize the benefits of his preferred option: peace talks and the withdrawal of American troops.

"Dan, you don't have a 'win' option," Kissinger said when they met to review the paper.

"I don't think there *is* a win option," Ellsberg countered. "You could double the number of troops and that would keep things quieter—until they left. You could use nuclear weapons and kill all the people. I wouldn't call that a win."

Ellsberg had no idea if he had swayed Kissinger's thinking. But he was satisfied. He had done all he could.

On January 20, 1969, Lady Bird and Lyndon Johnson ate breakfast looking out the White House windows at a gray and windy Washington morning. At ten thirty they stepped out onto the porch under the North Portico. A car drove up and stopped. Out stepped Richard Nixon, his wife Pat, and their two daughters, Tricia and Julie.

In the Red Room, in front of a warm fire, they shared coffee and awkward silence. Nixon so dreaded social events he sometimes asked aides to write ideas for conversation topics on index cards—when he got stuck, he could sneak a look at the cards.

Johnson tried to break the ice. "I'm curious," he said to Nixon, "How long will your inaugural address take?"

About twenty minutes, Nixon replied. Turning to Hubert Humphrey, he attempted a joke.

"Hubert, why don't you deliver the address for me?"

"Dick, I had planned to do that," Humphrey said, "but you sort of interfered."

They all drove to the Capitol for the traditional outdoor inauguration ceremony. Johnson watched Nixon take the oath of office, wondering what lay ahead. "I reflected on how inadequate any man is for the office of the American Presidency," he later recalled. "The magnitude of the job dwarfs every man who aspires to it."

Later that day, the Johnson family headed home to Texas.

The Nixon family attended a series of inaugural balls, finally making it back to the White House at one thirty in the morning. Scrounging in the fridge for a snack, Tricia and Julie were thrilled to find peanut-butter brittle ice cream and Dr. Pepper left behind by Johnson's daughters.

Nixon sat at the piano in the family quarters and played a few melodies, including one he'd written specially for Pat before they were married. It was a happy moment. Yes, Nixon knew he'd just taken on the toughest job in the world. He knew the Vietnam War had destroyed Johnson's presidency, and that it could do the same to him.

But Nixon was convinced he had something Johnson never had. He had a plan.

"I call it the madman theory," Nixon had explained to his aide Bob Haldeman during a walk on the beach before the election. "I want the North Vietnamese to believe I've reached the point where I might do anything to stop the war. We'll just slip the word to them that, 'for God sake, you know Nixon is obsessed about Communists. We can't restrain him when he's angry—and he has his hand on the nuclear button'—and Ho Chi Minh himself will be in Paris in two days begging for peace."

The French, Lyndon Johnson—they simply hadn't been tough enough, Nixon believed. He was confident he could frighten North Vietnam into backing down.

"I'm the one man in this country who can do it, Bob."

THE PENTAGON PAPERS

"A VERY ODD MAN, an unpleasant man," Henry Kissinger would later say of his new boss, Richard Nixon. "He didn't enjoy people. What I never understood is why he went into politics."

But if Kissinger did not exactly relish the president's company, he did come to admire Nixon's intelligence, and his willingness to make bold moves. Both were hard-core cold warriors. Both liked to work in secret. Together, over the next five years, they would remake American foreign policy.

Priority number one, of course, was Vietnam. There were 525,000 Americans in Vietnam when Nixon took over, and more than thirty thousand had already been killed. More than three hundred were dying every week. About four hundred pilots were stuck in horrific North Vietnamese prison camps. Peace talks in Paris were going nowhere. On March 16, Nixon sat down with Kissinger and General Earle Wheeler to discuss options in Vietnam.

"Gentlemen," the president began, "we have reached the point where a decision is required: to bomb or not to bomb."

Lyndon Johnson had halted the bombing of North Vietnam, and Nixon was reluctant to resume it. Doing so would be hugely controversial with war-weary American voters.

"But we have to look at what we're up against," he said. "I am convinced that the only way to move the negotiations off dead center is to do something on the military front. That is something they will understand."

It was time to test the madman theory.

On March 17, American B-52s began striking targets across the Vietnamese border in Cambodia. Nixon felt justified, because the Communists were using Cambodian territory to move supplies and stage attacks in South Vietnam. But he didn't believe the American people needed to know.

"My administration was only two months old," Nixon later explained. "I wanted to provoke as little public outcry as possible at the outset."

Nixon was well aware that voters had not elected him to escalate the war. To keep the Cambodia operation secret, the military prepared phony reports for Congress, stating that the bombs were actually falling on Vietnam.

At the Pentagon, the team working on Robert McNamara's secret Vietnam study was finally finishing up. The study ran seven thousand pages. Only fifteen complete copies were made.

During one of his frequent visits to Washington, D.C., Ellsberg asked Mort Halperin to let him borrow one. He really wanted to read it. Halperin, who was working for Kissinger, hesitated—he couldn't have word leaking out that the study existed. Ellsberg promised to be discreet.

Over several cross-country flights, Ellsberg carried portions of the Pentagon Papers from Washington to Los Angeles in his briefcase. He locked a complete copy in the safe in his office at Rand.

Back home in California, Ellsberg got a surprising phone call—from Patricia Marx. The last time they'd spoken was when he'd called from Europe on his way home from Vietnam. She was still angry about that call, she now told him, and still upset about his silence before and after it. She also told him she still loved him.

Later that spring, Marx flew to California to interview Governor Ronald Reagan for her radio show. She visited Ellsberg, and both immediately sensed that their relationship was not over. "The same old spark was there," Marx remembered.

"It was exciting to see her," Ellsberg agreed.

When Marx flew back to New York City, they had no definite plans to get together again. But Daniel and Patricia would continue thinking about each other in the months ahead.

On the morning of May 9, Henry Kissinger sat by the pool in Key Biscayne, Florida, where Nixon owned a vacation home. Scanning the papers as he ate breakfast, he turned to the *New York Times*—and suddenly leaped from the chair.

On the front page was the headline: ***"RAIDS IN CAMBODIA BY U.S. UNPROTESTED."***

The story described the supposedly secret American bombing raids in Cambodia.

"Outrageous!" Kissinger chanted as he paced beside the pool. "Outrageous!"

He ran to show Nixon the front-page story.

"We must do something!" Kissinger fumed. "We must crush these people!"

"Find out who leaked it, and fire him," snapped Nixon.

Within hours, at Kissinger's request, the Federal Bureau of Investigation began placing wiretaps on the phones of Kissinger's assistants. When that didn't turn up the leaker, the FBI tapped the phones of several journalists. But the illegal taps never led to the identity of the leaker—the *Times* reporter had actually gotten the story from a British journalist in Cambodia.

The Pentagon, meanwhile, publicly denied that the United States was bombing Cambodia. No other newspapers followed up. The bombing continued; the story went away.

One of the very few Americans to know the truth was Daniel Ellsberg.

"It's right," Mort Halperin told him, referring to the *Times* story.

Halperin explained the strategy behind the secret bombing. "Nixon's staying in," he informed Ellsberg, "he's not getting out."

Without revealing the source of his information, Ellsberg tried to persuade colleagues at Rand of the danger—Richard Nixon was secretly escalating the Vietnam War.

"I couldn't make anyone believe it," Ellsberg remembered. "In those days, a government denial was all it took to make a reality disappear."

Later that month, Ellsberg was invited to give a lecture at Ohio University. The subject was Vietnam.

It was an antiwar crowd, and Ellsberg sensed the students' mistrust of a former Pentagon insider. To get the conversation going, he asked for a show of hands—who believed that the majority of the people in South Vietnam were hoping for a victory by the Viet Cong?

Almost all the students raised their hands.

"You could be right," Ellsberg said, "but I don't think so."

Based on what he'd seen in Vietnam, Ellsberg explained, most people were neither communist nor strongly anti-communist. They didn't see the world in Cold War terms. "I suspect that for some time now," he told the class, "most of the people of South Vietnam have preferred that the war be over—with a victory by *either* side—than that it should continue at anything like the present scale."

It was only later, after the class had left, that he followed this thought further.

"What was the implication of saying that the majority of South Vietnamese wanted the war to be over no matter who won?" he wondered. "What did that say about the legitimacy of imposing our will to continue the war?"

He thought late into the night. In the morning he called Mort Halperin.

"Let me put a question to you, Mort. What would be your best guess of the proportion of Vietnamese, by now, who would rather see the war over, no matter what?"

"I suppose about 80 or 90 percent."

Ellsberg agreed. "But here's a question that's new for me. It's starting to bother me a lot. If it were true that most of the South Vietnamese wanted the war to be over," he asked, "how could we be justified in prolonging the war inside their country? Why would we have the right to keep it going even one more day?"

Halperin said, after a long silence, "That's a very good question."

With the question still burning in his brain, Ellsberg spent the summer reading the Pentagon Papers.

McNamara's study was a beast, weighing in at forty-seven volumes in thick three-ring binders. There were about a million words worth of secret government and military documents, and another 1.5 million of narrative history written by the researchers. Ellsberg knew the story, so there was no single item he found shocking.

What struck him was the pattern of deception—and how clearly it was documented.

It was all there, starting with Truman's decision to back France's war to recapture its former colony, knowing a majority of people in Vietnam supported independence and Ho Chi Minh. Other documents covered the years after France's defeat, as Eisenhower worked with the government of South Vietnam to delay and undermine elections they knew Ho Chi Minh would win.

"So we opposed elections," Ellsberg concluded as he read, "while pretending to support democracy."

The pattern continued in the 1960s. Documents showed that President Kennedy sent Special Forces troops to South Vietnam in the spring of 1961, putting Americans into combat in Vietnam for the first time. The public was not told. Most of the study focused on the Johnson years, covering Johnson's misleading public statements about the Tonkin Gulf incident, and everything that followed. Here were CIA reports stating that the bombing of North Vietnam was having "no measurable or direct effect on Hanoi's ability to mount and support military operations," and that casualties from the bombing in 1965 and 1966 alone were about thirty-six thousand, "about 80 percent civilians." Here was evidence that Johnson knew Americans were dying to prop up a South Vietnamese government that was corrupt and unpopular.

"What I had in my safe at Rand," Ellsberg would later recall, "was seven thousand pages of documentary evidence of lying, by four presidents and their administrations over twenty-three years."

WHOLE VOTE

ELLSBERG CONTINUED READING all summer, with the door of his office closed.

And as he dug deeper into the Papers, another form of deception began to emerge, one even more troubling than the lies. It was something he had begun to sense in 1967, when he'd worked briefly on the study after returning from Vietnam.

Now it hit him full force. In over twenty years of war, the United States had never actually tried to win.

Each president, of course, had *hoped* to win, and had *wanted* to win. And yet what the Pentagon Papers showed was that each president made decisions to escalate American involvement in Vietnam *knowing that what he was doing had little chance of success.* Time and time again, military leaders told presidents what it would take to win. Time and time again, presidents escalated—but stopped short of giving the generals what they said they needed.

"The same sets of alternatives began to appear to each president," Ellsberg realized, "and ultimately the choice was neither to go for broke and adopt military recommendations, nor negotiate a settlement to get out. The decisions year after year were to continue the war, although all predictions pointed to a continued stalemate with this kind of approach."

It was most obvious in the Johnson years. Johnson knew that the North Vietnamese were matching his escalations step for step. He knew the morale of the communist forces was high and that they were prepared to fight indefinitely. "Only atomic bombs could really knock them out," McGeorge Bundy cautioned Johnson in a 1967 memo. That, Bundy said, or an all-out invasion of North Vietnam, which would probably draw in the Chinese army and turn into an even bigger calamity.

So . . . why? Why continue to send Americans to Vietnam?

The missing piece of the puzzle, Ellsberg decided, was domestic politics.

Lyndon Johnson had repeatedly said, "I'm not going to be the first American president to lose a war."

That was a clue.

"No American president, Republican or Democrat, wanted to be the president who lost the war or who lost Saigon," Ellsberg realized. "They were willing to send men and women to death to avoid being called losers. They would rather keep going, no matter how many people died, to save face. In Vietnam, the crucial thing was, don't lose."

Each president had done just enough to avoid "losing" South Vietnam before the next election. This sickening deduction changed the way Ellsberg saw the Vietnam War. He had been against the war for a while, but had always seen it as an essentially noble struggle. "A worthy effort gone wrong," he had believed, "a case of good intentions that failed."

"Now I realized that it was not just the continuation of the locally devastating, hopelessly stalemated war that was unjustified—it had been wrong from the start."

He had often heard antiwar protestors shouting that Americans were fighting on the wrong side of the Vietnam War. They were missing the point.

"It wasn't that we were *on* the wrong side," Ellsberg concluded, "We *were* the wrong side."

The pattern was repeating itself. Nixon knew there was no realistic military path to victory in Vietnam—not at a cost that would be acceptable to the American people. The challenge, as he saw it, was to somehow convince North Vietnam to make concessions at the bargaining table. That would allow the president to gain the "peace with honor" he had promised Americans.

In June, Nixon made a bold move, announcing that he would begin withdrawing American troops from Vietnam, starting with twenty-five thousand men. His approval rating soared above 70 percent.

This move, Nixon hoped, would nudge Ho Chi Minh into offering a concession of his own. Kissinger traveled to Paris to make the president's position clear to North Vietnamese negotiators: Nixon had not resumed the bombing of North Vietnam and had begun pulling out American troops. He expected this would lead to a peace deal.

"But at the same time," Kissinger warned, "I have been asked to tell you in all solemnity, that if by November 1 no major progress has been made toward a solution, we will be compelled—with great reluctance—to take measures of the greatest consequences."

The North Vietnamese refused to budge. Ho Chi Minh died on September 3. Other North Vietnamese leaders vowed to continue the struggle.

That put the ball back in Nixon and Kissinger's court. They had tried concessions; they had tried threats. Remaining options were severely limited.

"I refuse to believe that a little fourth-rate power like North Vietnam does not have a breaking point," Kissinger told his staff. "You are to sit down and map out what would be a savage blow."

Nixon decided to give the North until November 1 to make a concession. If not, a "savage blow"—code-named Operation Duck Hook—would be ready.

In private talks with Republican congressional leaders, Nixon hinted at his military plans. He declined to give details, but assured them: "I will not be the first president of the United States to lose a war."

★ ★ ★

Ellsberg stood on the sidewalk outside of a Philadelphia court-house, feeling like an absolute fool. In front of him marched a group

161

of antiwar demonstrators. They were carrying signs, chanting slogans, passing out leaflets.

Cast your whole vote, Ellsberg thought, *not a strip of paper merely, but your whole influence.*

He couldn't get the words out of his head. They were from Henry David Thoreau's famous essay, "Civil Disobedience," written in 1849. Thoreau, to protest slavery and what he saw as America's unjust war in Mexico, had refused to pay taxes. He'd been arrested and jailed, but had no regrets.

Cast your whole vote . . . your whole influence . . .

It was an inspiring idea. But Ellsberg still felt like a fool.

He had flown across the country to attend the War Resisters' International Conference, held at a college near Philadelphia. He thought he'd be going to lectures and discussions. Instead, everyone had trooped to the courthouse to demonstrate—inside, a fellow activist named Bob Eaton was being sentenced to prison for resisting the draft. Ellsberg had tried to think of an excuse to duck out. Could he say he was sick? And then do what, hide in his room all weekend?

His only previous peace march had been the one with Patricia Marx in 1965, and he'd only gone to that one hoping for a date. He felt the same fear now that he had then. What if his picture showed up in the newspaper? He could hear the mocking laughter of colleagues in Washington and at Rand.

But he knew how he felt about the war. He looked around. There were no TV cameras or reporters. No police in sight. People hurried past on their way to work, hardly seeming to notice the demonstrators.

Ellsberg stepped out to join the rally.

Why are we doing this? he thought at first. *What am I doing here?* It seemed a preposterous way to confront the colossal power of the United States government. He watched the other protestors marching, waving signs. He picked up a stack of antiwar leaflets and held them out to people passing by.

And suddenly, to his surprise, he began to enjoy himself.

The threat of being cut off, of being thrust out from the club of insiders, had always terrified Ellsberg. And the club had very definite rules. "You could not have the confidence of powerful men, and be trusted with their confidences, if there was any prospect that you would challenge their policies in public," he later explained. "It was the sacred code of the insider."

He had lived by that code his entire adult life. This was the moment he crossed the line. He held out leaflets to people passing by. Most didn't take them. It didn't matter.

"I was no longer held in line by that fear. I was about to become a dangerous person to know."

The day after the courthouse demonstration, Ellsberg sat in the back row of a packed auditorium at the War Resisters' conference. A young activist named Randy Kehler stood in front of the group.

"Yesterday our friend Bob went to jail," Kehler began. "Last month David Harris went to jail. Our friends Warren and John and Terry and many others are already in jail."

Kehler stopped to clear his throat. From his seat in the back, Ellsberg could see the tears in the speaker's eyes.

"I'm not really as sad about that as it may seem," Kehler said. "There's something really beautiful about it, and I'm very excited that I'll be invited to join them very soon."

The audience knew that Kehler was facing jail time himself for refusing to cooperate with the draft. A few people began to clap. Then a few more, then everyone stood and clapped.

"I can look forward to jail without any remorse or fear," Kehler continued, "and that's because I know that everyone here, and lots of people around the world like you, will carry on."

Everyone was clapping and cheering, many were crying. Ellsberg fell back into his seat, suddenly dizzy, short of breath. He had to get out, he needed space. He pushed out of the row and ran into the hall to the men's room. He turned on the light, stumbled to the far wall, slid down to the tile floor and sobbed.

"We are eating our young," he said to himself.

Those young men and women in the auditorium were just like the friends he'd known in the marines—patriots, fighting for their country. The best young Americans were going to war or going to jail. What about his own son, Robert, now thirteen? Would the war still be raging in five years, when Robert hit draft age?

Ellsberg sat on the floor. He could not stop shaking.

Finally gaining control, he took a few deep breaths. He stood and stepped to a sink and splashed water on his face. He looked at himself in the mirror.

"Now," he asked, "what can I do to help end this war?"

NIGHT WORK

ON THE MORNING of September 30, 1969, the phone in Tony Russo's apartment began ringing. He lifted the receiver, said hello.

"I want to come over and talk to you about what we've been discussing," said the man on the other end. "I've made a decision."

Russo recognized the voice of Daniel Ellsberg. He knew exactly what Ellsberg was referring to. It was not a subject to discuss over the phone.

Thirty-two, with shaggy sideburns and frizzy hair to his shoulders, Tony Russo did not look much like an establishment insider. And he wasn't, not anymore. Until the beginning of 1969, Russo had been an analyst at Rand, with an office across the hall from Ellsberg's. The two had had long talks about Vietnam. Russo was the more outspoken war critic, and it had gotten him fired. His boss cited "budgetary problems" for the dismissal, but the reality

Anthony Russo

was that Rand often worked directly for the Pentagon, and Rand bosses were reluctant to offend their employers.

"I wasn't sorry to leave," Russo later said of his abrupt exit. Like Ellsberg, he'd set out to change government policy from within. Like Ellsberg, he was ready to try another approach. They had remained friends, talking over dinner and on walks on the beach. During one conversation, Ellsberg had mentioned the McNamara study he had in his safe.

"Dan," Russo said, "you should leak that to the press."

Ellsberg had not seemed ready to make that leap.

Now there was a knock on the door. Russo let Ellsberg in.

"You know the study I told you about a couple of weeks ago?" Ellsberg began. "I'm going to put it out."

"Great!" Russo said. "Let's do it."

166

The document was enormous, Ellsberg explained. It would take time to make photocopies, and the work obviously couldn't be done in a public copy shop.

"Can you get ahold of a Xerox machine?" he asked.

Russo smiled. "I've got the very place."

The next day, like every day, security guards checked the ID badges of everyone coming and going from Rand headquarters. Guards with binoculars kept watch from the roof. Just a block to the west, waves crashed on the wide, sandy beach beside the Santa Monica pier.

Inside, Ellsberg sat in his office, waiting for his co-workers to leave.

After dark, when the surrounding offices were empty, he opened his safe. He looked over the thick blue binders, each stamped "Top Secret." It was far too much material to take out unnoticed. He fit what he could into his leather briefcase and walked into the hall.

When he got to the downstairs lobby, he saw two guards at the security desk in front of the glass doors to the parking lot. The guards did not normally check employees' briefcases. But they did sometimes.

Ellsberg walked toward the guards. The lobby was decorated with World War II posters reminding citizens of the importance of secrecy in times of war.

"Loose Lips Sink Ships," warned one.

"What You See Here, What You Say Here, Let It Be Here, Let It Stay Here."

With his free hand, Ellsberg waved to the guards and he walked past.

"Good night, Dan," they both said.

Ellsberg parked outside Russo's apartment building. Inside, Russo introduced Ellsberg to Lynda Sinay, a woman in her twenties. Sinay, who was Russo's girlfriend, explained that she ran a small advertising agency. She had a Xerox machine they could use after business hours.

"I wanted to help," she would later say. "I never imagined the consequences would be so grave."

They drove together to Sinay's office, which was on the second floor of a small building, above a flower shop. She unlocked the office door and showed Russo and Ellsberg which key to use to disarm her burglar alarm, confessing with a laugh she could never remember if you were supposed to turn the key to the left or the right.

Sinay gave the men a quick tour, then showed them the large Xerox machine next to the reception area. Ellsberg pulled out one of the blue binders and opened the metal tabs holding the pages. He set the first sheet facedown on the glass and pressed "Copy." The machine's bright green light flashed in his eyes.

Photocopy machines were a lot slower in 1969—each sheet had to be set on the glass by hand, and it took several seconds to copy a single page. Ellsberg had wanted to make four copies of each page, but quickly realized this would take forever. He decided to settle for two. He worked the machine and Russo carried

168

the copies to Sinay's desk, where he collated the pages into neat stacks.

A loud knock on the glass door broke Ellsberg's focus.

He looked up. Two policemen stood outside the office door. One held the nightstick he'd just used to rap the glass.

Trying to make it look casual, Ellsberg dropped a blank piece of paper over the "Top Secret" stamps on the page he'd been about to copy. He went to the door.

"What's the problem, officers?" Ellsberg asked.

"Your alarm has gone off."

"Lynda, there are some people here to see you!" Ellsberg called out, hoping this would alert Russo in time.

The police walked into Sinay's office. Ellsberg followed. He shot a glance at Russo's stacks of papers. They were covered.

"Hi, Lynda," one of the officers said. "You've done it again, huh?"

"Oh, God, I'm so sorry," she said. "I'm hopeless with that damned key."

"Oh, no problem," the policeman said. "You've got to get a lesson on that thing."

"I will, I will."

The cops waved, and left. Ellsberg and Russo looked at each other. Then they got back to work.

Russo and Sinay headed home after midnight. Ellsberg worked until dawn.

At five thirty in the morning, he carefully put the originals back in the binders, and carried everything out to his car. He was eager to get the study back into his safe, but he couldn't go yet—he never showed up at Rand this early. It would look unusual to the guards. So he went to a restaurant and lingered over breakfast.

At eight o'clock, he strolled through the Rand lobby and up to his office. He locked the binders in his safe and drove home. It was a gorgeous morning, with clear blue skies. Too keyed up to sleep, Ellsberg pulled on his bathing suit, ran down the beach, and dove into the surf. He let a powerful wave lift and carry him toward shore, then swam back out.

Bodysurfing in the Pacific was one of his absolute favorite things on earth. How many more times would he get to do it?

"In a month or so I might be behind bars," he told himself, "probably for the rest of my life."

Three days later, Daniel Ellsberg and his son Robert carried plates of barbequed chicken to an outdoor picnic table. This roadside restaurant had been a favorite of theirs for years. But today they were not there for fun.

Ellsberg had spent the last three nights at the copy machine at Sinay's office, and knew he had weeks of sleepless nights ahead. He had been trying not to dwell on the likely consequences of what he was doing, but was tormented by the image of his children coming to visit him in prison. "Within a couple of weeks I would lose the chance to talk to my children face-to-face, ever again, except through glass," he worried. "They would read right away, and hear on television, that their father was a traitor."

Mary was just ten, maybe too young to understand, Ellsberg thought. But Robert was nearly fourteen, and the thought of the boy being sent to this never-ending war in Vietnam was one of Ellsberg's main motivations. He wanted his son to know what he was doing, and why. Over lunch, he told Robert about the Mc-Namara study, and what it revealed. He explained why he looked so tired.

Robert did not seem shocked. At his father's suggestion, he'd been reading Thoreau's "Civil Disobedience," and about the life of Gandhi, the leader of India's nonviolent independence movement. He agreed that there were times when a person seeking justice might need to take action that could land him in jail.

Ellsberg asked his son if he'd like to help photocopy the Pentagon Papers.

Robert said yes. "I had a sense," he later said, "of being included in something very secret and important."

They drove to Sinay's office. Lynda was there, working at her desk, but the rest of the staff was off for the weekend. Ellsberg showed Robert the system he'd worked out: after each copy was made, the "Top Secret" stamps at the top and bottom of the page had to be cut off with scissors. Then the shortened sheet was copied again, producing a full-sized page with blank white space where the "Top Secret" stamps had been. It was a tedious process, but Ellsberg wasn't sure what he was going to do with this report, or how long he'd be carrying it around. The clean copies would be safer to handle.

Robert made the copies. Ellsberg sat on the floor, cutting off the tops and bottoms of the pages.

The police knocked on the door. Three of them this time. Robert let them in.

"Your alarm's gone off again," one of the cops told Ellsberg.

"Sorry," he said from his spot on the floor, surrounded by thin strips of paper stamped "Top Secret." "I've got to figure out how to do that."

The police looked around. A woman at a desk, a man on the floor with scissors, a teenage kid at a Xerox machine. Some kind of family craft project?

"Okay," one of the cops said on his way out, "be more careful."

Ellsberg dropped his son off at home later that evening.

"I learned how to work a Xerox today," Robert announced to his mother.

"Oh, did you, dear? That's nice."

"Yes," he said. "Daddy was copying all these top secret documents."

TROUBLEMAKER

"I WENT BALLISTIC," Carol Cummings later said of her reaction to hearing about her ex-husband's night work. "I privately felt that he must have had a psychotic break."

She picked up the phone and called Ellsberg.

"I need to talk to you right away about these documents."

"Don't do it on the phone."

"Well, I need to talk to you," she said. "This is very serious."

They agreed to meet at a Chinese restaurant. They'd been getting along better since Ellsberg returned from Vietnam. "This tore it," he lamented.

At dinner he tried to explain what he and Robert were doing, and why.

"Listen, I don't know what you're copying," she interrupted. "I don't want to know. I don't want to hear about it." She was against the war too; that wasn't the point. The point, she insisted, was simple: "You do not take children along to commit felonies."

Ellsberg said he wouldn't involve Robert again. Carol felt slightly reassured. She could see that he was determined and, in her view, reckless. But clearly not out of his mind.

After dinner, Ellsberg drove to Rand and got another batch of documents from his safe.

A week later, on October 15, Richard Nixon sat in the White House watching football on television while thousands of protestors circled the building.

October 15, 1969. Demonstrators circle the White House at the end of a nationwide day of protests against the war in Vietnam.

"Don't get rattled," Nixon jotted on a notepad. "Don't waver—don't react."

After a brief lull at the start of Nixon's presidency, the war protests had been growing lately. This was the biggest one yet. In cities and towns all over the country, more than two million people gathered for marches and demonstrations. Church bells tolled for the dead, over forty thousand and counting.

The note on his pad notwithstanding, Nixon was rattled.

At that very moment, down the hall, speechwriters were working on the speech the president would read to announce Operation Duck Hook, the "savage blow" he and Kissinger hoped would shove North Vietnam into making some concessions. But Nixon was having second thoughts.

"I knew that after all the protests," he later wrote, "American public opinion would be seriously divided by any military escalation of the war."

Duck Hook was shelved—for the time being. The protestors had no idea what a major impact they'd had.

In Los Angeles, Ellsberg was invited to speak on a local television show. He took Robert and Mary along to watch. On the way home, he stopped at Lynda Sinay's office. He told Mary that he and Robert were going to run inside to pick up some papers, but that she should wait in the car. She said she didn't want to sit there alone. All three went inside.

Ellsberg had intended to just grab copies he'd made earlier, but since they were there he decided to get a little work done.

Remembering the promise to his wife, he asked Mary to sit on a couch in a room away from the copy machine. As before, he cut while Robert worked the Xerox—Robert was already involved anyway, Ellsberg figured.

Mary got bored.

"It was obvious that something secret was going on," she later said. "I knew it had to do with ending the war and that it was dangerous."

She got up from the couch and went to see what her brother and father were doing. Ellsberg gave her a pair of scissors. They sat on the floor together, cutting "Top Secret" stamps off the copies.

"I asked her that night not to tell her mother what we had done," Ellsberg recalled. Only in retrospect would he realize how unfair it was to Mary to put her in the middle of a dispute between her parents.

The copying continued through October. Russo, who helped out many nights, devised the time-saving innovation of taping two strips of cardboard to the glass of the Xerox machine. When they laid a sheet of the study on the glass, the cardboard covered the "Top Secret" stamps, but not the text on the page.

"Instant declassification," Ellsberg joked.

On November 2, Ellsberg peeked out the window of his Malibu beach house, looking toward the road. He was waiting for a cab. He was waiting for Patricia Marx.

They had continued talking by phone since her visit earlier in the year. He wanted them to give it another try, and she had agreed to fly out from New York City for a weeklong visit. She'd be at his place any minute.

The phone rang. An important antiwar organizer introduced himself and asked Ellsberg to fly to Washington, D.C., right away for a strategy meeting. Ellsberg had the phone to his ear, listening, when Patricia knocked. He opened the door and gestured for her to come in.

He watched Patricia carry her bag into his house. He told the guy on the phone he'd come, and hung up.

"It was a touchy situation," he recalled. "This was to have been the longest Patricia and I had been together in three years."

But he didn't want to miss the meeting in D.C. And the trip would give him an opportunity to take his next step—to tell Senator William Fulbright about McNamara's secret study, and offer him a copy.

He told Patricia he had to fly to Washington. It felt a little like when he'd left suddenly for Vietnam. Only this time, he asked her to come. She never even unpacked.

Something about Ellsberg had changed, Marx sensed. "He had the same dedication, but it was infused with a compassion, and a humanity," she later said. "And we were able to love each other then."

In the morning they drove to the airport. The first thousand pages of the Pentagon Papers were hidden under the clothes in Ellsberg's suitcase.

That evening, hoping to counter the massive protests of October 15, President Nixon spoke to the nation about the war in Vietnam.

"Let us all understand that the question before us is not whether some Americans are for peace and some are against peace," he said. "The great question is: How can we win America's peace?"

He reviewed the attempts he'd made to negotiate with North Vietnam, and blamed the North for the continuation of the war. His strategy from this point on, he said, would be to gradually turn over the fighting to South Vietnam—a policy he called Vietnamization. There was no timetable for American withdrawal. That, he said, would depend upon progress on the battlefield and at the negotiating table.

"And so tonight—to you, the great silent majority of my fellow Americans—I ask for your support," he concluded. "Let us be united for peace. Let us also be united against defeat. Because let us understand: North Vietnam cannot defeat or humiliate the United States. Only Americans can do that."

Nixon was thrilled by the public's positive response. His approval rating rose. "I had the public support I needed," he later explained, "to continue a policy of waging war in Vietnam and negotiating for peace in Paris until we could bring the war to an honorable and successful conclusion."

The Vietnam War would go on.

A briefcase in each hand, Ellsberg walked into Senator Fulbright's office and sat on the sofa. The curtains were drawn, the large space lit dimly by lamps.

The senator and a top aide, Norvil Jones, listened to Ellsberg describe what he had in the briefcases and why he thought the papers should be made public. He spoke quickly, gesturing with his hands. "He was articulate," recalled Jones, "but nervous."

Fulbright was immediately intrigued. By this time he knew he'd been lied to about the Tonkin Gulf incident, and probably a lot of other things. He told Ellsberg to give the material to Jones. They'd read it right away, the senator said, and set up a public hearing of the Senate Foreign Relations Committee—a dramatic setting in which to unveil the Pentagon Papers to the American people.

Jones led the way to his office, and Ellsberg opened his briefcases and stacked the papers on the desk. Jones locked them in his office safe.

Before heading home, Ellsberg told Patricia Marx about the Pentagon Papers. She was worried about the risk he was taking, but supported his decision to expose the study.

"Now we were agreeing totally," she later said of their views on Vietnam.

Back in California, on the beach in Malibu, he proposed to her for a third time. She told him she needed some time to think about it. "She still wasn't sure I was so reliable," Ellsberg recalled. In early 1970, she said yes.

When Marx told her father, he warned her about the man she'd chosen. "He's a troublemaker," Louis Marx told his daughter.

But she already knew that.

BEHIND THE MASK

ONE WINTER DAY in early 1970, Everett Alvarez and a few other American prisoners were loaded onto a jeep and driven to downtown Hanoi. They had no idea where they were being taken.

The jeep stopped outside the Museum of the Revolution. The prisoners were led inside and shown exhibits celebrating Vietnam's bloody victory over the French and the ongoing fight against America. There were large photos of downed planes and captured pilots. Alvarez was stunned to see his own flight helmet and uniform on display, clearly labeled with his name.

But the real shock came when he was given permission to use the bathroom. The urinal was an almost unimaginable luxury after five and a half years of crusted buckets. Then, while washing up, he looked at himself in the mirror for the first since becoming a prisoner.

"My God!" he gasped. "Could that be me?"

The torture had let up in the past year, but Alvarez could see the damage on his face. He ran fingertips over his bony cheeks, over lines around his eyes that looked like those of a man of middle age. His hair was streaked with gray. He was thirty-two.

On February 21, Henry Kissinger sat in the small living room of a house on the outskirts of Paris. This was the first of many secret meetings between Kissinger and Le Duc Tho, a high-ranking member of the North Vietnamese government. Nixon and Kissinger were still looking for a way to pressure North Vietnam into concessions. These talks were their latest effort.

Kissinger and Le Duc Tho sat in red easy chairs, a few feet apart. Tho, fifty-nine, had gray hair and manners Kissinger later described as "impeccable." Yet Kissinger could see right away he'd met his match. Tho had joined the anti-French rebels at age sixteen, and had spent ten years in French-run prisons in Vietnam. His entire life had been dedicated to revolution.

In his opening remarks, Tho referred to the Saigon government as an American "puppet," one that could never stand without a foreign power holding its strings.

"Although we have suffered great sacrifices and losses," Tho said, "and undergone a great deal of hardship, we have won."

"You have won the war?"

"Before, there were over a million U.S. and Saigon troops, and you failed," Tho explained. "How can you succeed when you let the puppet troops do the fighting?"

This was precisely the question that had been tormenting

Kissinger. It was the weak point of Nixon's Vietnamization strategy. Still, Kissinger cautioned Tho not to underestimate President Nixon, not to test his will too boldly. The men agreed to meet again the next month.

Nixon stuck with Vietnamization, announcing his decision to withdraw another 150,000 soldiers from Vietnam over the next twelve months. This would drop American troop strength to half of what it had been when he took office.

At the same time, he did not abandon hope of finding some way to budge the North Vietnamese. "We had to think," he later wrote, "about initiatives that we could undertake to show the enemy that we were still serious about our commitments in Vietnam."

There was no news from Senator Fulbright. In the months after his meeting with Fulbright, Ellsberg called Norvil Jones over and over. Jones kept putting Ellsberg off, saying the senator was still weighing options. In fact, Fulbright was having serious doubts about being the one to release top secret documents to the public.

On April 7, Ellsberg's thirty-ninth birthday, Carol Cummings called to tell him FBI agents had just come to her door. They had asked if she knew anything about a classified report her ex-husband may have been copying. She had told them she did not.

Ellsberg could not imagine how the FBI had found out. He drove to Carol's house.

"Have you been talking to people about it?" he demanded.

"No," Cummings said.

Mary was there, listening to the argument.

"Mary, you must have told somebody," Ellsberg said.

"We didn't tell anybody, Daddy," Mary said, badly hurt by the unfair accusation.

That's when Cummings found out that Mary, too, had been involved in the copying.

It was only years later that Ellsberg found out what had actually happened. The previous Christmas, at a visit to her father's house, Carol Cummings had told her stepmother what Ellsberg was up to. Cummings was just trying to release some stress by confiding in someone; she assumed it would go no further. But as soon as she headed home, her stepmother called the FBI.

Ellsberg didn't know how seriously the FBI was taking this investigation, but he figured time was short. He hid the copies he'd been making at friends' houses, and made the decision to leave his job. "The sheriff would soon be at my door," he later explained, "and I didn't want the door to be Rand's."

Ellsberg called a friend at the Massachusetts Institute of Technology and was offered a position, at half his current salary, at MIT's Center for International Studies.

"It's too bad it has to end like this," said Harry Rowen, Ellsberg's friend and longtime boss at Rand.

Ellsberg agreed, though he knew it was far from over. He thought about a quote from the novelist E. M. Forster: "If I had to choose between betraying my country and betraying my friend, I hope I should have the guts to betray my country."

It was the exact dilemma Ellsberg faced. Releasing a secret

document he had essentially stolen from Rand was a betrayal of Rowen's trust and would hurt him, both personally and professionally. But *not* releasing the document was, in Ellsberg's view, another form of betrayal: a betrayal of the country he loved, and the people who were still dying in Vietnam.

In this case, he decided, Forster was wrong.

Nixon tossed and turned, unable to sleep. Finally he gave up and walked down to the Lincoln Sitting Room. He sat alone until dawn. It was April 30, 1970.

He had a major announcement to make that day, and was expecting trouble. Four of Kissinger's top staffers, including Mort Halperin, had already resigned in protest over the president's decision. Nixon was particularly anxious about his daughter Julie, a student at Smith College. "It's possible that the campuses are really going to blow up after this speech," Nixon told his secretary.

That night, sitting beside a large map of Southeast Asia, Nixon addressed the nation. "To protect our men who are in Vietnam," he said, "and to guarantee the continued success of our withdrawal and Vietnamization programs, I have concluded that the time has come for action."

Pointing to Cambodia on the map, he explained that communist forces were using this territory to store supplies and stage attacks in South Vietnam. For this reason, he had decided to send American soldiers across the border into Cambodia.

"We will not be humiliated," Nixon told Americans. "We will not be defeated."

★ ★ ★

Nixon's Cambodia invasion sparked the biggest protests to date. And he was right—college campuses absolutely erupted.

Philip Caputo, the marine-turned-journalist, was home when his editor at the *Chicago Tribune* called. There was a major disturbance on the campus of Kent State University in Ohio, his editor told him. Protestors had smashed windows and set fire to a building used by the military. The National Guard had been called out to occupy the campus.

Caputo flew to Cleveland and rented a car. While driving to Kent, the news came on the radio—the guardsmen had opened fire at Kent State. He sped the last few miles.

May 4, 1970. A woman reacts with horror on seeing the body of a student shot dead by National Guardsmen during protests at Kent State University.

The campus looked like a war zone. There were no students in sight. Caputo saw the ruins of the burned building. Guardsmen crouched behind trees, holding rifles with bayonets fixed. In a parking lot, patches of asphalt were soaked with blood.

He got the story from another reporter: protestors had assembled for a demonstration that morning. Guardsmen in gas masks shot tear gas at the crowd. Some students threw rocks at the guardsmen. Most were just shouting. A platoon of guardsmen fired their rifles. Four students had been killed, two women and two men.

Caputo couldn't believe it. "To answer stones and bad language with a random volley of .30-caliber bullets was not imaginable in America," he later reflected. "Or maybe it was, because America had changed."

"Those few days after Kent State were among the darkest of my presidency," Nixon later said. "I could not help thinking about the families, suddenly receiving the news that their children were dead."

The protests grew even more intense. Furious students completely shut down 450 college campuses, and protestors poured into Washington, D.C. When a rowdy crowd circled Henry Kissinger's apartment, he moved into the White House basement to get some sleep. But the president's home was under siege. A young White House aide, Egil Krogh, came up with the idea of parking sixty buses around the building, bumper to bumper, to form a makeshift barricade. "The purpose," he later explained, "was to keep over 100,000 angry protestors from storming the White House."

Demonstrators sat in the streets, blocking access to the White House. Canisters of tear gas came arcing out from behind the bus barricade, landing among the protestors. Everyone inside was exhausted and on edge, Nixon in particular.

"He's very disturbed," Haldeman noted in his diary. "I am concerned about his condition."

At four fifteen in the morning on May 9, Egil Krogh was at his desk in the Secret Service command post across the street from the White House. He was preparing for another day of mayhem.

A voice on the loudspeaker announced: "Searchlight is on the lawn!"

Krogh looked up from his work. *Searchlight* was the Secret Service's code name for President Nixon.

"Searchlight has asked for a car."

Krogh was seriously alarmed. It was the middle of the night. Wasn't Nixon asleep in bed?

He ran out of the building, across the street to the White House, through the first floor and out the back door to the Rose Garden lawn. He got there just in time to see the taillights of Nixon's limo disappear through the gate.

Nixon's limo pulled to the curb about five minutes later. The president got out and looked up at what he considered the most beautiful sight in Washington—the Lincoln Memorial at night. He climbed the monument's white marble steps and stood in front of the imposing, seated figure of Abraham Lincoln.

Protestors were camped all around. Eight or ten sleepy students walked up to see who the visitor was. Nixon shook hands and introduced himself. At first the students thought he was a celebrity impersonator.

"I know that probably most of you think I'm an SOB," Nixon said, "but I want you to know that I understand just how you feel."

Intensely frustrated with his inability to connect with young people, Nixon tried to get a conversation started. He talked of the pacifist views he'd held before World War II. He talked of his love of world travel and the environment and college football.

May 9, 1970. President Nixon made an unannounced late-night visit to the Lincoln Memorial in Washington, where he spoke with antiwar protestors.

The group of students grew to about thirty. The top of the Washington Monument picked up the day's first rays of faint pink light.

"I hope you realize that we are willing to die for what we believe in," one student said.

"I certainly realize that," Nixon replied.

More students were walking up. Nixon's valet, Manolo Sanchez, pleaded with him to come back to the car.

Nixon shook hands with a few of the students. "Remember," he said, "this is a great country, with all its faults."

He got in the limo, but the bizarre journey was not over. Nixon told the driver to take him to the Capitol building, where he got out and led Sanchez to the House chamber. A custodian unlocked the door. Nixon walked in and sat in the seat that had been his when he'd served in the House as a young man. He told Sanchez to go up to the Speaker's chair and make a speech.

"No, no, Mr. President. I shouldn't do that."

"Yes," insisted Nixon, "go on up, Manolo, and give a speech!"

Egil Krogh arrived in time to see Sanchez walking sluggishly to the Speaker's podium. Sanchez spoke very briefly about how glad he was to be an American.

Nixon's applause echoed in the cavernous chamber.

"I was too dumbfounded to react," Krogh later said of the president's behavior. "I saw him in an exposed, emotionally raw state." It only strengthened his loyalty to Nixon.

"I felt more devoted to him than ever before," Krogh said. "I had seen behind the mask."

BRIDGES BURNED

ON AUGUST 8, 1970, at the home of her brother in the New York City suburbs, Patricia Marx married Daniel Ellsberg. After the ceremony, the newlyweds climbed into a helicopter and flew to the city for the night. The next day they headed to Hawaii for their honeymoon.

Whatever would happen from this point on, they were in it together.

Back home in California a few weeks later, Ellsberg arranged a meeting with Henry Kissinger at Nixon's beachfront home in San Clemente. As Ellsberg pulled up to the tall gate surrounding the estate, a voice from a speaker atop the guardhouse directed him to a parking spot. He was then led to a small waiting area that reminded him of a dentist's reception room. The president smiled down at him from large color photos on the walls. He sat for a long time.

August 8, 1970: Daniel and Patricia after their wedding ceremony, about to leave by helicopter for their honeymoon.

When the meeting finally began, Kissinger immediately started lecturing about tensions in the Middle East. "I'm afraid that that situation may blow up," he said.

Ellsberg cut in. He'd come to talk about Vietnam. "I think *that* may blow up."

Kissinger drummed his fingers on the table. "I do not want to discuss our policy," he told Ellsberg. "Let us turn to another subject."

For Ellsberg, there *was* no other subject. Hoping there was still some way to influence the White House's Vietnam policy, Ellsberg asked Kissinger if he'd heard about the secret McNamara study.

Yes, Kissinger said, he knew of it.

"Have you read it?" asked Ellsberg.

"No, should I?"

"I very strongly think that you should."

"But do we really have anything to learn from this study?" Kissinger asked.

Ellsberg felt his heart sink. Were Nixon and Kissinger really unwilling to learn from the failure of four presidents before them?

"Well, I certainly do think so," Ellsberg continued. "It is twenty years of history and there's a great deal to be learned from it."

"But after all," Kissinger said, "we make decisions very differently now."

"Cambodia didn't seem all that different."

Kissinger shifted in his chair. "You must understand," he said, "Cambodia was undertaken for very complicated reasons."

Too gloomy to guard his words, Ellsberg shot back, "Henry, there hasn't been a rotten decision in this area for twenty years which wasn't undertaken for very complicated reasons."

As he drove home, Ellsberg knew he had just burned his bridges to the president's inner circle. "That wasn't the way you talked to a high official," he later said, "if you wanted to get another visit to his office."

Dan and Patricia moved into a one-bedroom apartment on the third floor of a house in Cambridge, Massachusetts, near Ellsberg's new job at MIT. They still wondered when the FBI was going to come calling. In fact, the investigation had cooled. Agents suspected

Carol Cummings's stepmother's accusations were true, but could find no solid evidence.

The Ellsbergs furnished their new living room with a white couch and wicker chairs with colorful cushions. They stacked boxes of records by the stereo, and hung photos from their travels on the walls. Ellsberg set up his typewriter on a table and, much to the irritation of downstairs neighbors, pounded away late into the night.

He was supposed to be working on a book about Vietnam, but was far more focused on figuring out what to do with the Pentagon Papers. Senator Fulbright was still refusing to give him a straight answer. It was not a good sign, Ellsberg figured, that Norvil Jones was urging Ellsberg to find some other way to make the papers public.

Back in Washington in January 1971, Ellsberg had better luck with Senator George McGovern of South Dakota. McGovern, an outspoken war opponent, told Ellsberg he'd be willing to go public with the study.

"I want to do it," McGovern said. "I will do it." He just needed a little time to think. "I'll call you in a week," he told Ellsberg.

Ellsberg left the papers with McGovern's staff and flew home to tell Patricia the good news. McGovern called a week later.

"I'm sorry," the senator said. "I can't do it."

"I understand."

And Ellsberg did understand. McGovern wanted to run for president in 1972. Releasing classified documents would not exactly help him convince Americans he'd make a good commander in chief.

"At this point," recalled Ellsberg, "it was looking as though Congress was closed off."

Tony Russo, only half jokingly, suggested they hire a helicopter and shower the papers on Capitol Hill.

Patricia was a bit more practical. "These senators don't seem to think it's worth the risk," she said. "Why are you so sure that they're wrong?"

"I can't be sure about that," Ellsberg said. "The problem is, I'm the only one who's read these documents. They haven't. So I can't go by their judgment. I have to rely on my own."

They agreed—it was time for her to read the papers. He went through the files, picking out key memos and cables. She carried them into the bedroom and shut the door. Aside from Pentagon typists, she realized, she was the first woman to read these documents.

She came out of the bedroom an hour later. Her eyes were wet.

"These have to be exposed," she told him. "You've got to do it."

★ ★ ★

Later in January, Henry Kissinger came to MIT to give a talk. As he walked into the conference room he saw Daniel Ellsberg. They shook hands.

Kissinger then gave his usual lecture about how the Vietnam War was a "tragedy," but not one for which the Nixon Administration could be blamed.

If that was the case, a student asked, why was the war still going on?

"You're questioning me as if our policy was to stay in Vietnam,"

Kissinger replied. "But our policy is to get *out* of Vietnam." American troops were leaving Vietnam, he explained. American casualties were down.

Ellsberg could not let that go. He stood.

"You failed to mention Indochinese casualties, or refugees, or bombing tonnages, which in fact are trending up," he said. "By your omission, you are telling the American people that they need not and ought not care about impact on the Indochinese people."

The room was absolutely silent.

"So I have one question for you," Ellsberg continued. "What is your best estimate of the number of Indochinese that we will kill, pursuing your policy in the next twelve months?"

For a moment Kissinger was too stunned to respond.

"You are accusing us of a racist policy," he finally said.

"Race is not the issue here," Ellsberg pressed on. "How many human beings will we kill under your policy in the next twelve months?"

"What are your alternatives?"

"Do you have an estimate or not?" Ellsberg demanded.

There was a long, tense silence. The student who had introduced Kissinger stood.

"Well, it's been a long evening, and I think we've had enough questions now," he said. "Perhaps we should let Dr. Kissinger go back to Washington."

Richard Nixon was hardly the first president to do it.

In 1940, Franklin Roosevelt hid a microphone in a lamp on his desk in the Oval Office, and another in a telephone. Every president since had secretly recorded some of his White House conversations.

"You know, boys, it's a good thing when you're talking to someone you don't trust to get a record made of it," President Eisenhower once advised a group of aides, including Vice President Richard Nixon.

Kennedy kept Eisenhower's system, flicking a switch under his desk to activate mics concealed around the room. Johnson taped thousands of phone calls. Nixon liked the idea of having a precise record of everything that was said in his office. He asked Bob Haldeman about setting up the kind of system Kennedy had used.

"Mr. President, you'll never remember to turn it on," Haldeman said, "and when you do want it you're always going to be shouting—afterwards, when it's too late—that no one turned it on."

So they decided to hide voice-activated devices around the Oval Office, and under the table in the Cabinet Room. Everything was wired to recording machines in the basement. Over the next two and a half years, the tape machines picked up nearly four thousand hours of meetings and phone conversations—including an excellent record of the president's imminent showdown with Daniel Ellsberg.

But at the time, even the existence of the recording system was secret. When it first went into operation in February, Haldeman asked Nixon if he wanted an aide to type up transcripts of the recordings.

New York Times reporter Neil Sheehan.

"Absolutely not," Nixon said. "No one is ever going to hear those tapes but you and me."

In early March, Ellsberg traveled again to Washington, D.C. After another frustrating day on Capitol Hill, he called his friend Neil Sheehan, a Washington-based *New York Times* reporter he'd known in Vietnam. Ellsberg asked if he could come over and stay the night. Sure, Sheehan said.

Thirty-five, with round glasses and thick black hair, Sheehan was a veteran reporter with what one colleague called "bulldog tenacity" and "an almost perfect nose for news." He had come away from Vietnam sick to death of being lied to by American officials. He was about to be offered the chance to expose those lies on the front page of a newspaper read all over the world.

When Ellsberg arrived, Sheehan could see he was upset. They went into the den. Sheehan got out some sheets for the sofa.

Ellsberg didn't use the bed. He and Sheehan talked all night.

WAR ROOM

THE NEXT DAY, in the newsroom of the *New York Times* Washington bureau, Sheehan asked his boss, Robert Phelps, to step out to the lobby for a private conversation. Standing in front of the elevators, Sheehan explained that a source had offered to give him a copy of a secret government study about Vietnam.

"You better go to Scotty Reston," Phelps said, referring to James "Scotty" Reston, a top editor in the New York offices. "We can't get into something like this without knowing what it involves."

He told Reston about the Pentagon Papers.

Reston said, "You have my permission to proceed, young man."

"You've been talking about making more copies of those papers for months," Patricia Ellsberg told her husband when he returned from Washington. "You'd better get off your ass and do it."

She was right. After giving a complete set to Fulbright, Ellsberg had just one copy of some sections, two of others. He'd put off making more copies because the process was so stressful. But now, for what they were planning to do, they would need extra copies.

He pulled out the boxes and spent several nights going through the papers, looking for "Top Secret" stamps he'd missed the first time through. Patricia carried stacks of papers to all-night copy shops near Harvard, different shops on different nights, always glancing nervously over her shoulder before entering. They spent several sleepless nights making the copies, sorting the papers into boxes, and stashing them with friends all over Boston.

Ellsberg was glad to have help, though working with his wife only raised the stakes higher. "As soon as I got together with Patricia, got engaged and married, what I had to lose grew very much worse," he later said. "The feeling of losing Patricia—that was really like death."

On March 12, a Friday, Patricia Ellsberg unlocked the door of her brother Spencer's Boston apartment. She walked in, followed by her husband and Neil Sheehan. Spencer was away for the weekend.

Sheehan had flown to Boston to get a look at the secret study Ellsberg had offered him. He could see that both Daniel and Patricia were exhausted, and thought Dan seemed particularly fretful. Probably worried about being arrested, Sheehan figured, and feeling guilty about betraying his friends at both Rand and the Pentagon.

Sheehan was nervous too. He had, almost within grasp, the story of a lifetime.

Ellsberg retrieved a file from a hiding place in the apartment and brought it to Sheehan. Sheehan's eyes widened as he started to flip through the pages. He asked to make a copy of his own.

No, Ellsberg said. First he wanted to be assured the *Times* was really going to run with the story.

Sheehan said he'd need some time with the study before knowing. Ellsberg handed Sheehan a key to Spencer's apartment, saying he could stay and read, but must not remove any documents.

After two days with the Pentagon Papers, Sheehan returned to D.C. and showed his notes to Max Frankel, the *Times*'s Washington bureau chief.

"If this is the quality of most of the thing," Frankel said, "it's a gold mine."

Henry Kissinger continued to meet with Le Duc Tho in the Paris apartment. The sessions consisted mainly of the North Vietnamese negotiator lecturing Kissinger about the need to replace the American "puppets" in South Vietnam.

To the American public, the president insisted Vietnamization was working. The slow pace of withdrawal was necessary, he explained, because American forces needed to stay long enough to ensure an "honorable" end to the war.

A March 19 conversation in the Oval Office revealed a different reason for prolonging the Vietnam War.

"Well, we've got to get enough time to get out," Kissinger told

Nixon. "We have to make sure that they don't knock the whole place over," he said, referring to the Communists. "We can't have it knocked over, to put it brutally, before the election."

Nixon said, "That's right."

The presidential election of 1972 was more than a year and a half away.

That same day, March 19, a man representing himself as "Mr. Johnson, of the Control Data Corporation" checked into the Treadway Motor Inn in Cambridge, Massachusetts. After dropping off his bags, the guest stepped out to a pay phone on the street and called his wife. He told her to come to the motel, and to check in as Mrs. Johnson.

Neil Sheehan hung up the phone. He went to his room to wait for his wife, Susan Sheehan, a writer for *The New Yorker* magazine. When she arrived, they went together to Spencer Marx's apartment, carrying empty shopping bags. When they left the apartment, their shopping bags were full.

Sheehan knew the Ellsbergs were away for the weekend. He figured this was his chance to make his own set of copies of the Pentagon Papers.

Neil and Susan carried the bags to a local copy shop and handed the papers to a man behind the counter. The guy looked through the pages. He asked about the Top Secret markings on a few of the pages—Ellsberg never did catch all of them. Sheehan flashed his White House press pass. He explained that the documents had been declassified.

The job took all weekend. First the copy machine broke down and Sheehan had to haul everything to another shop. Then, late Saturday night, he ran out of money. In desperation, he called the *Times* Boston bureau chief, asking him to hurry to the copy shop with six hundred dollars in cash. Sheehan wouldn't say what the money was for.

The Boston editor called Gene Roberts, his boss in New York, for guidance. Roberts called Max Frankel in Washington.

"What the hell is going on in New England?" Roberts demanded.

"Please relax," Frankel said. "I can't tell you about it on the phone, but in any case it's a Foreign Desk matter."

"Foreign Desk! Hell, it's up in New England!"

"I'm sorry, Gene, I can't talk about what Neil is doing," Frankel said. "Just let him have the money."

Sheehan got the cash. He finished the job, replaced the originals before Ellsberg knew they were missing, and flew with his wife to New York, lugging five bulging bags. Did he feel any guilt about this deception? No, he later explained, because the Pentagon Papers did not really belong to Daniel Ellsberg. "They belonged to the people of America and of Indochina, who had paid for them with their blood."

On April 7, 1971, Daniel and Patricia Ellsberg celebrated Dan's fortieth birthday with friends at their Cambridge apartment.

He had no idea what was going on at the *New York Times*.

Ellsberg called Sheehan many times that month. Sheehan said his editors still couldn't make up their minds whether to run with the Pentagon Papers. Meanwhile, Sheehan said, he'd been assigned to cover other stories.

None of that was true. The fact was, Sheehan didn't trust Ellsberg to keep his mouth shut. Any leak at that point would ruin Sheehan's chances of breaking what James Reston was now calling "the greatest story of the century."

"Have you heard about the papers we have?" *Times* managing editor Abe Rosenthal asked James Goodale, the paper's thirty-seven-year-old general counsel.

Goodale said he had.

"Would you like to come to a meeting we are having tomorrow to discuss them?"

"Yes, of course," said Goodale. As the paper's in-house lawyer, it would be his job to advise the editors about the possible legal fallout from publishing classified documents.

The next day, he joined about ten editors and executives in James Reston's office. Most sat on chairs and couches; a few found spots on the carpet. The space was cluttered with piles of papers and stacks of magazines. While Reston sat at his desk, puffing on a pipe, Sheehan told the group of the origin of the Pentagon Papers, and of how the study clearly documented government lies about the war. He referred to the person from whom he'd gotten the secret study only as "my source."

No one asked Sheehan to name his confidential source, but Reston did want assurance the source could be trusted.

He's the real deal, Sheehan promised. "Now that we have the

documents," he said, "you can read them and see for your-selves."

Max Frankel asked the group to consider the risks of publishing classified documents in a time of war. Was the story important enough to justify defying the government? Was it worth facing legal action?

All agreed that it was. They turned to the lawyer.

James Goodale cautioned that if they published the Pentagon Papers, Nixon would likely come after them using the Espionage Act. Passed in 1917, this law states that anyone who "willfully communicates or transmits" documents related to national defense to others who are not authorized to see them can be fined and/or sent to prison.

The law was designed to prevent information that could harm the United States from reaching an enemy. That wasn't the *Times*'s intention, argued Goodale. The intention was to inform the public of a story it had every right to know. Besides, he added, the most important relevant law was the First Amendment: "Congress shall make no law . . . abridging the freedom of speech, or of the press."

But that was just his view. Once the case went to court, any-thing could happen.

"Everyone has to remember, be quiet!" Goodale advised as they stood to leave. "Because everyone in this room may have participated in a felony."

A MATTER OF PATRIOTISM

WITH TALL, WHITE WALLS and arches at the entryway, La Tuna Federal Correctional Institution looked like an old Spanish mission. It sat on the desert of west Texas, barren mountains rising behind.

Behind the imposing facade, the building looked like what it was—a prison. In a concrete courtyard patrolled by armed guards, Daniel Ellsberg sat talking with Randy Kehler, the antiwar activist whose words had so inspired him. Kehler was now serving two years at La Tuna for resisting the draft.

After exchanging personal news and talking about the war, Ellsberg asked about prison life. How was the food? Do they let you exercise? Is there anything decent to read? Kehler knew nothing of the unfolding Pentagon Papers drama, but got the sense there was something more than concern for a friend behind the questions. He wondered if Ellsberg might be expecting to spend some time in jail.

Daniel Ellsberg with Randy Kehler, before the publication of the first excerpts from the Pentagon Papers by the *New York Times*.

When visiting time ended, Ellsberg asked one last question, the significance of which would hit Kehler a few weeks later.

"Do you have a subscription to the *New York Times*?"

"No."

"Would you like one?"

"Sure," Kehler said, "that would be great."

A poll taken in the spring of 1971 revealed that 71 percent of Americans believed that U.S. intervention in Vietnam had been a mistake. Over 70 percent wanted all American troops home by the end of the year.

Even some veterans began publicly criticizing the president. On April 22, twenty-seven-year-old John Kerry became the first

Vietnam war veteran and future Secretary of State John Kerry with Daniel Ellsberg, 1971

Vietnam combat vet to testify before Congress against the war. Some saw this as a kind of betrayal of other men in uniform. In Kerry's view, it was the government that was guilty of betraying the troops. More than six thousand Americans had been killed in Vietnam in 1970; another twenty-four hundred would die in 1971. And for what? Why was the pace of Nixon's Vietnamization so agonizingly slow?

"Each day," Kerry charged, "someone has to die so that President Nixon won't be, and these are his words, 'the first president to lose a war.' We are asking Americans to think about that, because how do you ask a man to be the last man to die in Vietnam? How do you ask a man to be the last man to die for a mistake?"

That same day, at the Hilton Hotel in Manhattan, there was a knock on the door of room 1106. Neil Sheehan opened the door. Fellow *Times* reporter Hedrick Smith stood in the hall.

"Man, am I glad to see you," Sheehan said.

Smith stepped into what looked like some kind of makeshift war room. The three-room suite was crammed with desks, chairs, typewriters, file cabinets, and three large safes. The bosses had decided the Pentagon Papers were too hot to handle in the *Times* building, so Sheehan had moved his operation to the Hilton.

Through the end of April and into May, a team of sixteen editors, reporters, and secretaries worked twelve-plus-hour days going through the thousands of pages Sheehan had brought back from Boston. Sheehan and Smith worked in adjoining rooms, each reading documents and typing stories as fast as he could. When one found something particularly interesting, he'd run into the other's room shouting, "Look at this, look at this!"

Rough drafts of articles and scrap paper with notes were carried back to the *Times* building and put through the basement shredder.

Meanwhile, in the fourteenth floor boardroom of the *New York Times*, publisher Arthur Sulzberger listened to arguments against publication from Lord, Day & Lord, the prestigious law firm that had represented the *Times* since the late 1800s. The paper would be prosecuted under the Espionage Act, warned Louis Loeb, one of the firm's partners. The editors would wind up in jail. What's more, he insisted, making the Pentagon Papers public was just plain wrong. The government had deemed the information secret, and it was not up to any individual or newspaper to blow the whistle.

"It's a matter of patriotism," Loeb insisted.

Though Daniel Ellsberg did not know what was happening in New York, he suspected he may soon need legal representation. He and Patricia went to see a Harvard Law professor she knew. In the lawyer's living room, Ellsberg described what was in the Mc-Namara study and what he'd done with the documents thus far.

"I have to stop you right now," the professor cut in, holding his hand in the air. "I'm afraid I can't take part in this discussion any further."

"Pardon me?"

"You seem to be describing plans to commit a crime. I don't want to hear any more about it. As a lawyer I can't be a party to it."

Ellsberg jumped out of his easy chair. "I've been talking to you about seven thousand pages of documentation of crimes," he growled. "Twenty years of crime under four presidents."

The lawyer was unmoved.

Ellsberg was going to need a different lawyer.

On the morning of Saturday, June 12, Daniel Ellsberg got a call from Tony Austin, a *New York Times* editor he knew casually. Ellsberg had once mentioned the McNamara study to Austin, and even shown him a few pages.

"That study you showed me part of, the *Times* has the whole study," Austin now told Ellsberg. "They're starting to bring it out today. The building is shut down tight. They're checking everybody who wants to come in or out. They're afraid the FBI will come after them before they can print."

Ellsberg was shocked. He had heard nothing from Neil Sheehan. "Are you sure?" he finally asked.

Austin was sure. The presses would start rolling in a few hours.

"Well, I'm glad you told me," Ellsberg said.

Heart hammering, he dialed Sheehan's desk at the *Times*. The phone rang once, twice, three times. "He hasn't given me any warning over the last week or the last month, or, for Christ's sake, this morning!" Ellsberg thought as the rings echoed in his ear. "When was he going to tell me?"

Someone in the newsroom picked up and took a message.

Ellsberg dialed Tony Russo's L.A. apartment. No answer.

Patricia came home, and he told her what was going on. They had a complete copy of the Pentagon Papers in the apartment and agreed they'd better find a hiding place. Ellsberg called his friend Howard Zinn, a Boston University professor and antiwar activist. Zinn told Ellsberg to bring the box right over.

Abe Rosenthal, the *New York Times* managing editor, sat at his desk in the newsroom with his head in his hands.

"Let it be four thirty," he chanted. "Just let it be four thirty."

Four thirty was the so-called "magic hour"—after that point, no more changes could be made to the next day's paper. At four thirty, all the copy would go to the composing room, where the text was set into lead type for the printing presses in the basement. At six, the massive presses would roar into action, rolling out 200,000 copies of the *Times* every hour.

Sulzberger, after all the back and forth, had approved publication of Sheehan's stories.

But until four thirty, anything could happen.

Rosenthal got up and paced in the vast newsroom. Typewriters clacked as reporters worked on stories, but two-thirds of the desks were empty. Saturday afternoon was usually slow.

Richard Nixon peeked out the White House window, checking the weather again. It was still overcast, still drizzling.

Nixon's older daughter, Tricia, was getting married that afternoon, and she had her heart set on an outdoor ceremony in the Rose Garden. The skies above Washington were not cooperating. The forecast called for clouds and intermittent rain all day. Pat Nixon, their younger daughter Julie, and the entire White House staff were trying to convince Tricia to move the event inside.

"I would prefer to have it in the Rose Garden as we planned," Tricia told her father.

"Then that's the way we'll do it," he said.

Nixon got on the phone to an Air Force meteorologist and was told there'd likely be a clearing between four thirty and four forty-five. He announced that the wedding would start promptly at four thirty. The rain stopped, exactly as predicted, and ushers ran outside and pulled plastic covers off four hundred chairs on the lawn. The guests moved quickly to their seats. Moments later, as a band played, Nixon and his daughter, both beaming, walked arm-in-arm down the White House steps and into the Rose Garden. Guests thought the president looked happier and more relaxed than they had seen him in years.

Later, during the indoor reception, White House press secretary Ron Ziegler got a message from a reporter at the *New York Daily News*. The reporter didn't know details, but he'd gotten wind that something big was about to break in tomorrow's *New York Times*, something about Vietnam. Ziegler didn't think it sounded like a big deal.

Most of the staff from room 1106 in the New York Hilton went to the *Times* building to watch the first copies roll off the press. Sheehan stayed at his typewriter in the hotel suite, banging out stories for later in the week.

A little after six thirty that evening, a copyboy walked in with a stack of papers. He dropped a few copies on Sheehan's desk. Sheehan jumped up and yelped with joy.

When word came that 100,000 copies had been printed—too late to turn back—Sheehan picked up the phone to call Ellsberg. "I owe him this!" he shouted as he dialed.

There was no answer.

The Ellsbergs were at a restaurant with Howard Zinn and his wife, Roz. Ellsberg was annoyed he hadn't heard from Sheehan, but his mood lifted as the evening went on. The important thing was that the Pentagon Papers were about to hit the street.

After dinner they went to see *Butch Cassidy and the Sundance Kid*, a movie Ellsberg had seen several times and loved. Then they got ice cream, and were strolling in Harvard Square, licking cones, when several stout men in suits blocked their path. One raised his hand in an aggressive "stop" signal.

The Ellsbergs and Zinns stood on the sidewalk, holding their ice cream.

The man with the raised hand demanded, in an accent that sounded Latin American, "How do we get to the Combat Zone?"

It took a moment to process the question. The Combat Zone was a nearby strip club.

In New York City, Neil Sheehan and a few *Times* colleagues crowded around a table in a small Italian restaurant.

"Well, what have we learned from all this?" asked Robert Phelps.

"I've learned," said Hedrick Smith, "that never again will I trust any source in the government."

They all lifted their glasses of Chianti in a toast to Smith's statement.

Late that night, after the guests had left, Richard Nixon sat upstairs with Pat and Julie. The television networks were broadcasting highlights from the wedding. The president watched himself walking down the aisle with Tricia.

"Well, at least I'm standing pretty straight," he joked.

Always worried how he'd look on television, Nixon did not like watching himself. This was an exception. "It had been a wonderful day," he later wrote. "It was a day that all of us will always remember, because all of us were beautifully, and simply, happy."

Just after midnight, Dan and Patricia Ellsberg walked to a subway station near their apartment. They ran down the stairs to a kiosk that sold the early edition of Sunday's *New York Times*. They came up holding several copies, staring at the front page.

In the top left corner was a photo of the president arm-in-arm with his daughter, under the headline: ***"TRICIA NIXON TAKES VOWS IN GARDEN AT WHITE HOUSE."***

In the middle, spreading across three columns, was the headline: ***"VIETNAM ARCHIVE: PENTAGON STUDY TRACES 3 DECADES OF GROWING U.S. INVOLVEMENT."***

Hardly an eye-catching headline. But the story, under Neil Sheehan's byline, was absolute dynamite.

A friend saw the Ellsbergs emerging from the station with a stack of papers.

"What's going on?" he asked.

Ellsberg smiled. "I may be going out of town for a while."

PART III

OUTSIDER

SLOW BUILD

RICHARD NIXON SAT IN BED with breakfast on a tray, scanning the *Washington Post* and *New York Times*. It was early Sunday morning. He liked the photo from Tricia's wedding in the *Times*. He was still in a very good mood.

In the afternoon, the president met with aides to prepare for the week ahead. The *Times*'s Vietnam story was not at the top of the agenda, though it was briefly discussed.

"We must be exceedingly careful not to overreact," warned Charles Colson, Nixon's top legal advisor.

Nixon agreed. Though infuriated by leaks, he thought this particular leak might not be too damaging. After all, the McNamara study only covered the years up to 1968, before Nixon even took office.

"The key for us is to stay out of it," Nixon said, "and let the people who are affected cut each other up."

Later, he would very much wish he had stuck to that position.

★ ★ ★

James Goodale, the *New York Times* lawyer, carried a portable radio down to the lake near his family's Connecticut home. He tuned to the news, expecting to hear about the earthshaking story on the front page of the *Times*.

All the talk was about Tricia Nixon's wedding.

Harrison Salisbury, a *Times* reporter, had friends over that morning. They were all *Times* readers, he knew. No one said a word about the Pentagon Papers.

"The story is a bust!" he thought.

But as the day went on, the media's attention started shifting from Tricia to the McNamara study. That afternoon in California, Tony Russo came home from a day in the park. He turned on the radio and heard the news.

"Oh, my God," he said. "It has hit."

Robert Ellsberg cheered aloud when he heard the Pentagon study had been published. "Instantly I knew what it was," he recalled. "Of course, I couldn't tell anybody about it."

His mother's reaction was less enthusiastic. "Oh, God," she thought. "Oh, no."

In La Tuna prison in Texas, Randy Kehler read that day's *Times* with a smile. Now he knew why Ellsberg had been so eager to send him a subscription.

In offices around Washington, D.C., several people opened safes to see if their copies of the Pentagon Papers were missing. All over the country, speculation about the source of this historic leak began. Washington insiders knew it had to be someone among the select few who had access to McNamara's study—and someone who had turned against the war.

"This has got to have been Dan Ellsberg," thought former State Department official William Bundy.

The reaction at Rand was the same. "We all knew in our gut that it was Dan," a former colleague remembered.

Harry Rowen sat at his desk, fielding call after call about Rand's possible connection to the leak. "I don't need this," he said, slamming down the phone. "I just don't need this."

A little after three o'clock that afternoon, Kissinger phoned Nixon from California.

"It is unconscionable," Kissinger said of the Pentagon Papers story.

"It's unconscionable on the part of the people that leaked it," Nixon agreed. "Fortunately, it didn't come out on our administration."

That was a key point, Kissinger agreed. "This is a gold mine of showing how the previous administration got us in there."

"Huh," said Nixon, laughing, "Yeah!"

But the more they talked about it, the angrier Nixon became.

"This is treasonable action on the part of the bastards that put it out," he told Kissinger.

"Exactly, Mr. President."

"Doesn't it involve secure information?" Nixon asked of the Pentagon Papers.

"It has the highest classification, Mr. President."

"Yeah. Yeah."

"It's treasonable," said Kissinger.

The next step, they agreed, was to consult with Attorney General John Mitchell about possible legal action.

On Monday, June 14, the *New York Times* continued its series on the Pentagon Papers under the headline: ***"A CONSENSUS TO BOMB DEVELOPED BEFORE '64 ELECTION."*** The story described how Johnson had decided to expand American involvement in Vietnam while telling the public he sought "no wider war." Top secret documents were printed along with the story, providing irrefutable evidence.

Their work done at the Hilton, Sheehan and his staff scrambled to evacuate room 1106.

"If the police come we'll be arrested!" shouted a secretary.

"Don't worry," Sheehan said. "I'm the only one who will go to jail."

They managed to shove all the potentially incriminating papers into an enormous suitcase. A young reporter, Bob Rosenthal, lugged the two-hundred-pound case toward the door. Sheehan handed Rosenthal twenty dollars and told him to catch a cab to the back entrance of the *Times* building. If the FBI was there, Rosenthal was to drive right past.

He made it into the building without incident. Inside, the editors were preparing a third day of Pentagon Paper stories—and wondering when they'd hear from President Nixon.

It wouldn't be long. Not if Kissinger had anything to say about it.

"I tell you Bob, the president must act—today!" Kissinger started pounding the table with his fists, yelling directly at Chief of Staff Bob Haldeman. "There is wholesale subversion of this government under way."

Years later, after the Nixon presidency had come crashing down, Kissinger would claim he had never had strong feelings one way or the other about the Pentagon Papers.

"Unfortunately for Henry," Haldeman noted, "it was recorded."

When Nixon came in, Kissinger launched into a lecture about how the president didn't seem to grasp the danger of allowing top secret documents to be leaked to the press.

"It shows you're a weakling, Mr. President," charged Kissinger.

Nixon ordered his staff to cut off all contact with the *New York Times*. "Don't give 'em anything!" he ordered. "I just want to cool it with those damn people, because of their disloyalty to the country."

Later, with his top domestic advisor John Ehrlichman, Nixon talked about taking stronger action. Ehrlichman explained that Attorney General Mitchell kept calling, asking permission to tell the *Times* to immediately halt publication of the Pentagon Papers—and threaten prosecution if they refused.

"You mean to prosecute the *Times*?" asked Nixon.

"Right."

"Hell, I wouldn't prosecute the *Times*. My view is to prosecute the goddamn pricks that gave it to them."

"Yeah," said Ehrlichman, "if you can find out who that is."

Nixon called Mitchell at his apartment.

"What is your advice on that *Times* thing, John?" Nixon asked. "You would—you would like to do it?"

"I would believe so, Mr. President."

The *Times* stories were getting more and more attention as the day went on. Secretary of Defense Melvin Laird appeared on television condemning the newspaper for printing secret military documents.

The phone at the Ellsbergs' apartment rang almost constantly. Reporters, Ellsberg figured, following up rumors that he was somehow linked to the leak. He didn't pick up.

Dan and Patricia were laying low for now, enjoying the nation's growing fascination with the Pentagon Papers. And while the content of the secret study was certainly interesting, what was really sparking the nation's interest was the mystery—where did the *Times* get this explosive document?

That night, they dropped by a friend's place for a dinner party. Everyone was having fun trying to guess the identity of the leaker.

"Patricia and I listened," Ellsberg recalled, "without contributing much."

★ ★ ★

James Goodale had been expecting to hear from the attorney general all day. At seven o'clock, he finally decided to go home.

But he couldn't relax, couldn't sit still. "Something must be going on," he said to himself. He picked up the phone and called the office.

222

"We have received a phone call from the Justice Department to stop publishing," an editor told him.

Goodale raced back to the *Times* building and rode the elevator up to the fourteenth floor. He could hear the yelling even before he got to the office where the top editors were gathered. It was a hot night. The air conditioners were off, since the executive offices were normally empty at this hour. Everyone had jackets off, ties loosened. They were arguing about the telegram that had just arrived from the attorney general.

"The material published in the *New York Times* on June 13, 14, 1971," Mitchell's message began, "contains information relating to the national defense of the United States and bears a top secret classification.

"As such, publication of this information is directly prohibited by the provisions of the Espionage Law," Mitchell charged. "Moreover further publication of information of this character will cause irreparable injury to the defense interests of the United States.

"Accordingly, I respectfully request that you publish no further information of this character and advise me that you have made arrangements for the return of these documents to the Department of Defense."

The type for the next day's *Times*—including more Pentagon Papers material on page one—was already set. The printers were waiting for word to start the presses. Most of the *Times* staff wanted to go ahead; some argued the other side. There was a lot of shouting.

"You can't stop publishing if someone sends you a telegram," Goodale contended. "If there is a court order, that's something else. But this is not a court order. There is no penalty for disobeying a telegram."

In any case, the editors knew a decision of this magnitude had to be made by the publisher, Arthur Sulzberger, who had recently left on a trip to England. It was two o'clock in the morning, London time, when they got Sulzberger out of bed and on the speakerphone.

"What does Louis say?" Sulzberger asked, referring to Louis Loeb of the *Times*'s law firm, Lord, Day & Lord.

"He's opposed to further publication," one of the editors explained.

Abe Rosenthal jabbed Goodale in the ribs, urging, "For God's sake say something!"

"It would be a very great mistake to stop publishing," Goodale said.

"Do we increase our risk by refusing to follow the government's request?" asked Sulzberger.

Yes, Goodale conceded.

Sulzberger mulled this over a moment.

"Okay," he said, "let's continue to publish."

MR. BOSTON

ROSENTHAL RAN TO THE ELEVATOR and jumped off on the third floor, where about 150 staff members were gathered.

"Go ahead!" Rosenthal shouted.

The group gave a huge cheer, then dispersed to their jobs. The presses began rolling a few minutes later.

Goodale called Louis Loeb to update him, and to suggest the law firm begin preparing to be in court in the morning. That was not going to happen, Loeb informed Goodale. The firm of Lord, Day & Lord would no longer be representing the *New York Times*.

Goodale briefly wondered if he could handle the case himself. The answer was no. "My court experience," he later said, "consisted of two uncontested divorce cases."

It was nearly midnight. He started making phone calls.

★ ★ ★

Tuesday's *Times* featured another front-page story by Neil Sheehan, this time highlighting Johnson's secret plans to send Americans into ground combat in Vietnam. But the even bigger headline reported on the attorney general's late night telegram: *"MITCHELL SEEKS TO HALT SERIES ON VIETNAM BUT TIMES REFUSES."*

The Pentagon Papers showdown was now the lead story on the radio and television news. Ellsberg was thrilled with the attention the story was getting—but not quite ready to reveal his own role. A reporter from *Newsweek* cornered Ellsberg, telling him he was going to be on the cover of the upcoming issue.

"We're convinced you're the source," the reporter said.

"I'm glad it's out," Ellsberg answered, smiling. "I'm flattered to be suspected of having leaked it."

And he did plan to take public responsibility for the leak. Just not yet. First he had to get the *whole* report out to the public. "It wasn't any one page or volume or individual revelation that was so dramatic," he later explained. "It was the tenacity and nature of the patterns of deceit."

If Nixon was able to shut down the *Times*, Ellsberg was going to need a backup plan.

"This is a very bad situation," Nixon told his staff in the Oval Office on Tuesday morning. "This guy is a radical that did it. A radical, we think."

"Ellsberg?" Haldeman asked.

"No, we don't know who the hell he is. But maybe it's him." Nixon pounded his desk. "Now goddamn it, somebody's got to go to jail."

June 16, 1971. Editors of the *New York Times* discuss an order from a federal judge halting publication of material contained in the Pentagon Papers.

Haldeman assured Nixon that taking the *Times* to court was a good next step.

"Neil Sheehan is a vicious antiwar type," Nixon moaned. "And if they're going to go to this length, we're going to fight with everything we've got. And I—I'm just—I just—we'll just take some chances."

At Nixon's order, the Justice Department went to the federal court in New York City to demand an injunction against the *Times*—a legal order to stop publication of the Pentagon Papers.

★ ★ ★

Goodale was in his office later that morning when the call came in. The *Times* was to show up in court by noon. He alerted Alexander Bickel and Floyd Abrams, respected constitutional lawyers who had agreed to take the case. Bickel and Abrams had spent the entire night preparing. When they showed up at Goodale's office, their eyes were swollen and red. The three lawyers took a cab to the courthouse downtown.

The courtroom was crowded, largely with antiwar protestors who hissed as the government lawyers argued that the *Times* was violating the Espionage Act. Alexander Bickel countered that the paper was protected by the First Amendment, and that this was the first time in American history the government had tried to silence a newspaper.

"But there has never been a publication like this in the history of the country," Judge Murray Gurfein, a recent Nixon appointee, pointed out.

Gurfein then asked if the *Times* would voluntarily stop printing for a few days, to give him time to study the case. Goodale said he'd have to ask. He ran to a phone booth in the hall and called Harding Bancroft, the paper's executive vice president.

"The judge wants us to stop publication voluntarily," Goodale told Bancroft. "Please tell me what to do."

"I'll check and call you back."

Goodale hung up and waited in the stifling booth. People lined up to use the phone. Some started shouting and banging on the glass door. Goodale wouldn't budge. Sweat soaked through his shirt. He picked up the phone and called Bancroft back.

"Harding," Goodale said, "we can't stop publication, it would be terrible."

"I agree."

He told Gurfein of the decision. The judge issued a temporary restraining order, barring the *Times* from printing more of the Pentagon Papers until the trial was concluded.

Round one to President Nixon.

The next morning, in the newsroom of the *Washington Post*, assistant managing editor Ben Bagdikian stepped out of a meeting and was handed a slip of paper. He read the short note:

"Call Mr. Boston from a secure phone."

The name sounded fake. There was a phone number with a 617 area code. Boston. Bagdikian thought he knew what this might be about. He ran out of the building and across the street to a row of pay phones. He dropped in a coin and dialed the number on the note. Someone picked up.

"An old friend has an important message for you," a man's voice said. "Give the number of a pay phone where the friend can call in a few minutes."

Bagdikian leaned to the phone beside him and read off the number on the dial. The man on the other end hung up. The phone next to him rang. Bagdikian picked up.

"If I can get you what you want, will you print them?"

Bagdikian recognized Daniel Ellsberg's voice; they'd met many times over the years to talk politics and Vietnam.

Bagdikian couldn't commit the *Post*, not without checking. "I'll have to call you back."

Ellsberg instructed Bagdikian to get confirmation from his bosses, and then to travel immediately to Boston and check into a particular motel under the name Mr. Medford. He was to bring a large suitcase.

★ ★ ★

The front page of that day's *New York Times* updated Americans on the unfolding drama: ***"JUDGE, AT REQUEST OF U.S., HALTS TIMES VIETNAM SERIES."*** If Bagdikian could get his hands on the Pentagon Papers, would the *Washington Post* risk printing this same material?

Bagdikian didn't know. He called Ben Bradlee, the paper's executive editor, and laid out the situation.

"If we don't publish," Bradlee said, "there's going to be a new executive editor of the *Washington Post.*"

Bagdikian caught the next flight to Boston and checked into the motel. As soon as he walked into his room on the third floor the phone started ringing. The familiar voice named an address in Cambridge at which he was to pick up "the material."

"Do you have back trouble?" Ellsberg asked. "This stuff is very heavy."

"I'm not worried," Bagdikian lied. Actually, his back had been killing him lately. Small price to pay, he figured.

That night, he got in a taxi and gave the driver the Cambridge address. The unlighted, tree-lined street was so dark they couldn't make out house numbers. The driver got out and struck a match and went door to door, holding up the flame to read the numbers. He finally found the right one.

Bagdikian knocked. A woman opened the door.

"Dan Ellsberg said I could pick up some things here," Bagdikian said.

The woman pointed to two large boxes. He carried them to the cab and drove back to the motel. He lugged the boxes out of the elevator and down the corridor toward his room.

Someone stepped out of the vending machine nook holding a bucket of ice. It was Daniel Ellsberg.

"He was haggard," Bagdikian recalled, "and complained of a terrible headache."

They went into Bagdikian's room and shut the door. The air conditioner was broken and the room was boiling. Patricia Ellsberg was there. They opened one of the boxes and spread documents out on both of the twin beds.

It took most of the night to get the papers somewhat organized. Bagdikian then tried to cram them into the suitcase he'd brought. They didn't fit; he'd have to take the boxes on the plane. Ellsberg suggested they find some string to tie up the boxes. The motel clerk didn't have any string, but told them to check out by the fence around the pool, where guests sometimes tied up their dogs. They found a few pieces of rope, just enough for the job.

Bagdikian headed to the airport for an early flight to Washington. He bought two tickets, one for him and one for the boxes, and flew home with the Pentagon Papers on the seat beside him.

Patricia Ellsberg, who had gone home for the night, drove back to the motel to pick up her husband. She came into the room and they turned on the TV to watch the morning news.

The first thing they saw on-screen was the front porch of their house. Press photographers were there, snapping photos. Two FBI agents stood at the door, knocking. The FBI was looking for a man named Daniel Ellsberg, the announcer explained, hoping he could help with their investigation of the Pentagon Papers leak.

Patricia stated the obvious. "We can't go back."

June 18, 1971. Antiwar demonstrators outside Daniel and Patricia Ellsberg's apartment house in Cambridge, Massachusetts.

UNDERGROUND

MARINA BRADLEE HAD NEVER SEEN so many people come to her parents' house. On the morning of June 17, the ten-year-old girl sat at a lemonade stand in front of the family's Georgetown home, watching men and women jump out of cabs and run past her to the front door. Many carried typewriters. One carried a heavy-looking box.

Ben Bradlee led Bagdikian—the one with the box—into the living room. It was already crowded with *Washington Post* staff members. As reporters went through the documents, racing to write stories for the next day's paper, the staff had the same argument that had taken place at the *Times*. The lawyers advised against publication. The *Post* was facing certain legal action by Nixon, and possibly fines that could cripple the company. The final decision lay with the publisher, Katherine Graham.

"Okay," she said after hearing both sides, "go ahead."

With the deadline for the next day's paper looming, Bagdikian grabbed the articles the reporters had typed up and jumped on the back of a copy editor's motorcycle. He clung tight to the copy editor as they wove through Washington traffic to the *Post* building.

Early that evening, Nixon, Kissinger, Haldeman, and Ehrlichman sat in armchairs in the Oval Office, yellow legal pads on their knees. They were now convinced the leak had come from Daniel Ellsberg.

"Curse that son of a bitch," Kissinger began. "I know him well."

Nixon sounded surprised. "You know him?"

"Well. First of all he's—"

Haldeman cut in: "He's nuts, isn't he?"

"He's nuts," Kissinger agreed.

Nixon asked, "Why did they have him in the Defense Department?"

"Well, Mr. President, he's a funny guy."

"Right," Nixon said, decidedly unamused.

"He's a funny kid," Kissinger tried to explain. "He's a genius. He's the brightest student I've ever had." Clearly worried his past association with Ellsberg would make him suspect in Nixon's eyes, Kissinger launched into a bizarre attack. "He was a hard-liner. He went—he volunteered for service in Vietnam. He was so nuts that he'd drive around all over Vietnam with a carbine when it was guerrilla-infested, and he'd shoot at—he'd shoot at peasants in the fields."

"He's a born killer," Ehrlichman added.

Nixon said, "Go ahead."

"Then—well, he's always been a little unbalanced—and just totally wild," Kissinger continued. He described their last meeting, at the lecture at MIT. "He then started up and heckled me and accused me of being a murderer."

Nixon wanted to know how such an unstable character had gotten hold of McNamara's study in the first place. Kissinger guessed there must have been a copy at the Rand offices in California.

"By the end of the meeting," Haldeman remembered, "Nixon was as angry as his foreign affairs chief. The thought that an alleged weirdo was blatantly challenging the president infuriated him."

Later, in the hall, Nixon spoke with Charles Colson.

"I want him exposed, Chuck," Nixon said of Ellsberg, wagging his finger. "I don't care how you do it. But get it done. We're going to let the country know what kind of a hero Mr. Ellsberg is."

The next shot was fired by the *Washington Post*.

"DOCUMENTS REVEAL U.S. EFFORT IN '54 TO DELAY VIET ELECTION" declared the paper's headline on Friday, June 18. Beneath was an article detailing how the United States, under President Eisenhower, had secretly worked to undermine elections that were supposed to unite North and South Vietnam. The proof, as the headline charged, was in the documents.

At three o'clock that afternoon, Ben Bradlee got a call from Assistant Attorney General William Rehnquist. Rehnquist warned Bradlee to cease publishing the Pentagon Papers.

"I'm sure you will understand that I must respectfully decline," Bradlee said.

After dark, as the *Post* presses pumped out a second day of Pentagon Papers stories, Ben Bagdikian carried one of the boxes he'd brought back from Boston to his car. The first box he'd left at Bradlee's place. This second one, which also contained a nearly complete copy of the Pentagon Papers, he put in the trunk. Ellsberg had given him specific instructions as to what to do with it.

Bagdikian drove to the Mayflower Hotel and parked on the street. He didn't have to wait long before a car pulled up behind him. A man stepped out. Bagdikian recognized Senator Mike Gravel of Alaska, an outspoken Vietnam War opponent. Bagdikian opened his trunk and silently handed Gravel the box.

In New York, Judge Gurfein got to his office early the next morning. The previous day's hearing had lasted late into the night. Now he was ready to write his decision—in favor of the *New York Times*.

"The security of the nation is not at the ramparts alone," the judge wrote in a passage that has been quoted ever since. "Security also lies in the value of our free institutions. A cantankerous press, an obstinate press, an ubiquitous press must be suffered by those in authority in order to preserve the even greater values of freedom of expression and the right of the people to know."

Gurfein announced the ruling early that afternoon. But in spite of the victory, the *Times* could not resume printing the Pentagon

Papers because the Justice Department immediately appealed, and the injunction remained in place while the case moved to the higher court.

In Washington later that day, a judge barred the *Washington Post* from printing any more Pentagon Papers stories until the court could rule on the government's case against the paper.

Once again, Daniel Ellsberg was going to need a new plan.

After leaving Bagdikian's motel room, Daniel and Patricia Ellsberg had checked into a different motel under false names. From there, a team of friends, many of them students, helped arrange a series of hiding spots at apartments around town. While the FBI conducted a massive nationwide hunt, the Ellsbergs moved by night from place to place. Friends brought them clean clothes and toiletries. They never left Boston.

"I tried to stay one step ahead of the Justice Department's injunctions," Ellsberg recalled. That meant relying on friends to somehow get the Pentagon Papers to another newspaper. But it was dangerous to contact anyone Ellsberg knew, because the FBI was tapping many of their phones. One day while they were in hiding, Daniel and Patricia watched from the window while "Mr. Boston" went out to a pay phone to call one of Ellsberg's friends in Los Angeles. Only minutes after Mr. Boston hung up, four police cars sped up and screeched to a stop outside the phone booth.

Dan and Patricia ducked below the window as the cops looked around. Mr. Boston—whose true identity Ellsberg has never revealed—was long gone.

237

Most of the time underground was a lot less exciting. The Ellsbergs spent long days alone, reading newspapers and watching television. The search for the fugitive leaker now dominated the news—reporters even showed up at Ellsberg's father's house in Detroit. Harry Ellsberg, an eighty-two-year-old Nixon supporter, backed his son 100 percent.

"Daniel gave up everything to devote himself to ending that foolish slaughter," Harry said of the Vietnam War. "He might be saving some boys they'd have sent there otherwise."

"The whereabouts of Daniel Ellsberg and his wife, Patricia, remained a mystery yesterday," reported the *Boston Globe* on June 20.

Globe writer Tom Oliphant hated to leave town in the midst of such a major story. Especially since he knew Ellsberg, and was hoping to be the next reporter to get his hands on the Pentagon Papers. But Oliphant had long since scheduled a visit to his parents in San Diego; he had to go.

Almost as soon as he got to his parents' place, the phone rang. The caller identified himself as a friend of Ellsberg's.

In a series of calls from a phone booth at the beach, Oliphant arranged a stealthy meeting between a *Globe* reporter and one of Ellsberg's people on the streets of Boston. The reporter returned to the *Globe* offices with seventeen hundred pages in a plastic bag. After writing up a series of stories, the staff locked the documents in the trunk of a car in an unlit parking lot.

On Tuesday, June 22, the *Boston Globe* stunned the nation by becoming the third newspaper to print the now-notorious Pentagon Papers.

The headline read: ***"SECRET PENTAGON DOCUMENTS BARE JFK ROLE IN VIETNAM WAR."*** Another article, by Tom Oliphant, contained a message from the country's most famous fugitive. "Ellsberg said he wanted his two children, who live in this state with his first wife, to know that he is well and thinking of them," reported Oliphant. "He also said he wanted his father, Harry Ellsberg, who lives in a Detroit suburb, to know that he is deeply grateful for the expressions of support."

Only hours after the *Globe* hit the streets that morning, editor Thomas Winship got a call from John Mitchell.

June 22, 1971. Editor Tom Winship holds the day's edition of the *Boston Globe*. The *Globe* was the third newspaper to publish material from the Pentagon Papers.

"Well, Tom," said the attorney general, "I see you're in the act too."

"If you want to call it that. We did print this morning."

Mitchell asked if the *Globe* would voluntarily stop publishing.

"No," Winship said, "I don't think we can."

The court quickly blocked the *Globe* from further publication of the classified documents. But Ellsberg and his friends had been busy. Sections of the Pentagon Papers were in the hands of newspapers all over the country.

Unable to find the Ellsbergs, the FBI turned up the heat on known associates. Later that Tuesday morning, Tony Russo pulled into the driveway of his apartment building. As he opened his car door, another car skidded to a stop behind him, blocking the exit. Two agents jumped out and ran to Russo. One handed him a subpoena, ordering him to show up in court the next morning.

"I showed up at the courthouse," Russo later reported, "with my toothbrush in my pocket, ready to go to jail, because I was sure of one thing: I was not going to cooperate with the inquisitors."

Russo was going to need that toothbrush. Brought before a grand jury that was considering criminal charges against Daniel Ellsberg, Russo absolutely refused to give evidence, even when offered immunity in exchange. The judge declared Russo in contempt of court and sent him to jail.

The FBI also delivered a subpoena to Lynda Sinay's door.

"For what?" she asked the agents.

"We think you know."

She knew. Threatened with prison, she told the grand jury of her role in copying the Pentagon Papers.

When the FBI visited Carol Cummings, she told them she had no idea where her ex-husband was. She reluctantly agreed to testify, telling the grand jury what she knew of Ellsberg's activities.

"Where is Dan?" reporters called out when Cummings got back to her house.

"I haven't heard from him in some time," she said.

Cummings ran inside, but press vans remained camped out at the end of her driveway. Reporters called nonstop, asking for comments. After dark, she led Robert and Mary out the back door. They climbed over a fence and hid in a friend's house.

On Wednesday, June 23, CBS News vice president Gordon Manning got a call from "Mr. Boston." Manning, who was in charge of Walter Cronkite's nightly broadcast, was offered access to Daniel Ellsberg. If interested, Manning was to come to the Harvard campus that night and stand in front of the library.

Manning was confused by the cloak-and-dagger directions, but couldn't pass up a chance to get Ellsberg on Cronkite's show. That morning, the Pentagon Papers had popped up in the Midwest, on the front page of the *Chicago Sun-Times*. The story was just getting bigger and bigger.

Manning was outside the library that night. He heard a rustle in the nearby bushes. A young, bearded man jumped out and said, "Follow me at a quick pace."

They walked to the street. The young man opened the door of a parked car.

"Jump in."

They got in the car. The driver steered what seemed like a circular route through dark streets.

"What's going on?" Manning asked. "I thought we were going to see Ellsberg."

"Well, people are always following us."

The driver pulled to the curb very near where they'd begun.

The young man said, "Jump out and go up to the third floor."

Manning climbed the stairs and knocked. The door opened. There were a few young people inside. A few boxes. And Daniel and Patricia Ellsberg. Manning was struck by the intensity of Dan's expression.

"I always remember those eyes burning a hole in you," he later said.

At one o'clock in the morning, Manning left the apartment with six stacks of paper, tied together with string. A light rain was falling as he started back toward his hotel.

A police car rolled up and came to a stop.

"Having a walk in the rain?" the officer asked through his open window. "You've got heavy bundles there."

"Yeah, but I'm young."

"Hey, get in. It's going to rain hard."

Manning sat in the front seat with the Pentagon Papers on his lap. The policeman dropped him off at his hotel.

ARREST

WALTER CRONKITE WALKED into the lobby of the Commander Hotel in Boston. The most watched news broadcaster in America was trying not to attract attention. He succeeded for about two seconds.

"Mr. Cronkite!" the hotel manager called, striding up. "What can I do for you?"

Cronkite explained that he just needed to make a quick call from the basement pay phone. Absurd, the manager protested, Cronkite should use the private phone in his office. Cronkite politely declined.

Gordon Manning had passed on instructions from Ellsberg's crew—Cronkite was to go to the hotel basement and wait by the phone booth near the men's room. He did as he was told. "It was just incredibly awkward," he later said. "People were coming up for my autograph."

"I don't know why you won't wait in my office, Mr. Cronkite," the manager said. "I'll get you out of this crowd."

Cronkite again declined. He paced in front of the bathroom, growing increasingly annoyed. He was about to leave when a young man walked up and nodded to the broadcaster. Cronkite followed the man to a beat-up car idling outside the hotel.

After driving a circuitous route, they parked outside a small, gray house in Cambridge. Cronkite went in and was relieved to see Manning inside. Daniel Ellsberg was there, in the only tailor-made suit he owned. They began setting up to film.

That night, NBC and ABC news reported that there were still no clues as to the whereabouts of Daniel Ellsberg. At the exact same time, on CBS, Walter Cronkite opened his show with a bang.

"During the controversy, a single name has been mentioned most prominently as the possible source of the *Times*'s documents," Cronkite told the nation. "Daniel Ellsberg, a former State Department and Pentagon planner, and of late something of a phantom figure, agreed today to be interviewed at a secret location."

The show cut to the living room of the gray house. Ellsberg sat with Cronkite, speaking with calm conviction.

"It must be painful for the American people now to read these Papers," Ellsberg said. "What these studies tell me is we must remember this is a self-governing country. We are the government."

Cronkite asked what Ellsberg thought was the most important lesson Americans should take from the Pentagon Papers.

June 23, 1971. Daniel Ellsberg appears on *CBS News* with Walter Cronkite, his first public statement since publication of the Pentagon Papers.

"I think the lesson," Ellsberg answered, "is that the people of this country can't afford to let the president run the country by himself."

On Thursday, June 24, the dam burst. The *Los Angeles Times, Philadelphia Inquirer, Miami Herald, Detroit Free Press*, and eight other papers around the country published parts of the Pentagon Papers.

Nixon and Mitchell decided not to haul everyone into court. Mitchell claimed it was because these papers had not printed classified material—obviously untrue, since the entire McNamara report was classified. In reality, thanks to Ellsberg's network, the Pentagon Papers were too widely dispersed to get back.

It was a busy day in court. The New York Court of Appeals ruled against the *New York Times.* Hours later, the Washington, D.C., Court of Appeals ruled in favor of the *Washington Post.* The *Post* could now publish the Pentagon Papers; the *Times* could not. It was a legal mess that could only be settled in the Supreme Court. The justices voted to hear the case right away.

In Los Angeles, a grand jury indicted Daniel Ellsberg on three felony counts, including theft and unauthorized possession of classified documents, and violation of the Espionage Act. An arrest warrant was issued. Ellsberg had just become the first person in American history to face criminal charges for leaking government secrets to the press.

From a new hiding place, he spoke by phone to Charlie Nesson, a lawyer he'd hired before going underground. Nesson advised his client to surrender to authorities.

"I can't do that," Ellsberg said. "I still have some more copies of the papers to distribute."

"How long will it take you to get rid of the rest of the papers?" asked Nesson.

"A couple of days."

They agreed that Ellsberg would turn himself in on Monday morning. He spent the next few days arranging the delivery of his remaining batches of documents. The *St. Louis Post-Dispatch* was next to publish the Papers. Then the *Christian Science Monitor,* then *Newsday.*

Ellsberg loved every minute of it. "After the last two glorious

A pressman holds a copy of the *St. Louis Post-Dispatch*, containing excerpts from the Pentagon Papers.

weeks of open and successful defiance," he later said, "I wasn't in a mood to jump when the authorities told me to."

In Washington, on the morning of June 26, James Goodale, Alexander Bickel, and the rest of the *Times*'s legal team tried to ignore the television cameras and shouted questions of reporters as they walked from their hotel to the Supreme Court building. About fifteen hundred people were lined up at the foot of the building's white marble steps, hoping to get one of fewer than two hundred seats available to the public.

The lawyers walked past the crowd, up the steps, between the majestic white columns—and into the sudden silence of the courthouse. "It was like going from Yankee Stadium into a mausoleum," recalled Goodale.

In the courtroom the nine Supreme Court Justices, wearing long black robes, sat behind a raised table. Lawyers for both sides made their presentations, and were grilled by the justices. The session lasted about two hours. The justices gave little indication of which way they were leaning, though Justice Thurgood Marshall offered a clue in an exchange with Solicitor General Erwin Griswold, who was handling the government's case. Marshall expressed worry that if the Court ruled in favor of the government, it would become easier for the government to silence the media in the future.

"Wouldn't we then—the federal courts—be a censorship board?" Marshall asked.

"Mr. Justice," Griswold replied, "I don't know what the alternative is."

"The First Amendment might be," retorted Marshall.

Goodale and Bickel left court feeling pretty good.

On Monday morning, Daniel Ellsberg put on his good suit. Charlie Nesson met the Ellsbergs at their final hideout. All three got in a taxi and drove toward downtown Boston.

News of their imminent arrival leaked out, and the streets in front of the courthouse were jammed with reporters and cheering crowds. Daniel and Patricia got out of the cab and worked their way through the mob. They were quickly surrounded by cameras and microphones.

"I think I've done a good job as a citizen," Ellsberg told the press. "I could no longer cooperate in concealing this information

June 28, 1971. Daniel Ellsberg with his wife, Patricia, outside the federal courthouse in Boston, where he was arraigned on charges relating to the leak of the Pentagon Papers.

from the American people. I took this action on my initiative, and I am prepared for the consequences." His only regret, he said, was that he hadn't acted sooner.

"This has been for me an act of hope and trust," he continued. "Hope that the truth will free us of this war. Trust that informed Americans will direct their public servants to stop lying and to stop the killing and dying."

As Ellsberg turned toward the policemen waiting for him at the top of the courthouse steps, a reporter shouted: "Do you have any concern about the possibility of going to prison for this?"

Ellsberg said, "Wouldn't you go to prison to help end this war?"

FAME

ON JUNE 29, IN WASHINGTON, D.C., Senator Mike Gravel got an enema. He put on a back brace and attached a pouch to his leg to catch his own urine. Once he started talking, Gravel figured, he would not be able to stop for at least thirty hours.

That night the senator called a special session of his Subcommittee on Buildings and Grounds—just about the least prestigious subcommittee in the Senate. He opened the session with a crack of his gavel at nine forty-five.

He was the only senator in the room.

"I have in my possession the Pentagon Papers," Gravel declared. "To not make them public would be a dereliction of duty and morality."

Gravel began reading the pile of documents he'd gotten from Ellsberg via the midnight exchange with Ben Bagdikian. A stenographer sat taking it all down. Now, no matter how the Supreme

Court ruled, the entire Pentagon Papers would be in the Congressional Record, available to anyone.

A few tourists wandered in. Gravel continued reading. Reporters got word of the weird hearing and showed up with cameras. Gravel continued reading. Antiwar activists came and cheered him on.

Early in the morning, reading a graphic description of combat wounds suffered by American soldiers, Gravel began to cry. He plowed on for several minutes, tears streaming down his face. Finally, exhausted and emotionally drained, he had to stop.

"Arms are being severed, metal is crashing through human bodies," he said, "because of a public policy this government and all of its branches continue to support." He wiped his eyes with a handkerchief. "I am overpowered with the fact that at this very moment, we are killing people in Vietnam with our tax dollars."

Senator Gravel asked for the unanimous consent of all subcommittee members to insert the rest of the Pentagon Papers into the public record. There were no objections.

Later that day, on the other side of First Street, the Supreme Court announced a 6–3 ruling in favor of the *New York Times* and the *Washington Post*. "In revealing the workings of government that led to the Vietnam War, the newspapers nobly did precisely that which the Founders hoped and trusted they would do," wrote Justice Hugo Black.

The newsrooms of the *Times* and the *Post* burst into cheers.

"Daniel Ellsberg is the most dangerous man in America," Henry

June 30, 1971. *Washington Post* editor Ben Bradlee and publisher Katherine Graham reading the Supreme Court decision upholding the right of the *Post* and other papers to publish material from the Pentagon Papers. The *Post* was the second newspaper to publish material leaked from the Pentagon Papers.

Kissinger told the president and other top aides in the Oval Office. "He must be stopped at all costs."

Less than an hour after losing in the Supreme Court, Nixon's team moved on to the next battle.

"We've got to get him," insisted Kissinger.

"We've *got* to get him," Nixon repeated. And they couldn't wait for some jury to do the job; who knew how that would turn out? "Don't worry about his trial," the president instructed. "Just get everything out. Try him in the press."

To John Mitchell, he said, "We want to destroy him in the press. Is that clear?"

"Yes," said the attorney general.

"These fellows have all put themselves above the law," Nixon said, "and by God we're going to go after them."

The discussion of next steps continued the following morning.

"I really need a son of a bitch," Nixon told his inner circle, "who will work his butt off and do it dishonorably. Do you see what I mean? And I'll direct him myself."

The way to play it, Nixon instructed, was to hire someone to dig up dirt on Ellsberg, and leak it to the press. Destroying Ellsberg in public would silence him—and other potential whistle-blowers. Nixon made it perfectly clear that staying within the confines of the law was not a priority.

"I want somebody just as tough as I am for a change," he explained. "Do you think, for Chrissakes, that the *New York Times* is worried about all the legal niceties? Those sons of bitches are killing me . . . We're up against an enemy, a conspiracy. They're using any means. We are going to use any means. Is that clear?"

"It's got to be a guy you can really trust," Haldeman cautioned, "because it's got to be—" Nixon finished the sentence: "Run from the White House without being caught."

Daniel Ellsberg was booked, fingerprinted, photographed, and released on $50,000 bail. For the first time in two weeks, he and Patricia went home.

"Thanks to the drama of Nixon's injunctions and their defiance by a large part of the press in America," Ellsberg later said, "there had been more attention to the contents of the Papers than I could ever have dreamed." More attention to him too. In the weeks after Ellsberg's arrest, reporters waited outside his apartment. They photographed him and Patricia coming and going. On July 13, he appeared on the nationally broadcast *Dick Cavett Show*.

"Mr. Ellsberg has been hailed as a hero by a lot of people," Cavett told the audience, "condemned as a traitor by others."

Ellsberg was recognized in restaurants and stopped on the street for his autograph. At a Broadway theater, after the lights had dimmed, a voice came over the loudspeaker: "We've just been informed that Daniel Ellsberg is in the audience."

The entire audience stood and clapped.

"It was a tremendous boost to my antiwar activity," Ellsberg said of his sudden fame. "It gave me a platform."

At his desk at home, he stacked the thousands of letters he'd received since his arrest. Some of his favorites were tacked to a bulletin board.

"You have done a great duty to our country," said one.

Another declared: "As far as I am concerned you are the hero of the Vietnam War, and that if more people would do the things that had to be done such as you did, the world would be a better place."

There was plenty of hate mail too, even death threats. The backlash that really bothered Ellsberg came from his former co-workers. "I was typhoid Mary," he later said. "I was a leper, with a bell around my neck."

One former Rand colleague summed up the sentiment there: "Hang him from the highest tree in town."

"I hope they hang the son of a bitch," another told Rand boss

Harry Rowen. Rowen's career at Rand was ruined. He was forced to leave.

Lyndon Johnson, from his ranch in Texas, called the leak of the Pentagon Papers "close to treason." Senator Barry Goldwater called Ellsberg a second Benedict Arnold.

Patricia Ellsberg felt the wrath of her father. "Absolutely apoplectic," was how she described Louis Marx's reaction. "And just ranting and raving. He admired Nixon, he was very anti-communist. So he just thought it was a betrayal of the country."

"Dad, I love you," she told him, "and I don't want this to come between us. But if you insist on talking about my husband in this way, I don't want to see you."

Four days after Ellsberg's appearance on *Dick Cavett*, White House aide Egil Krogh sat on the patio of President Nixon's San Clemente home. The sun was warm and the view of the Pacific was beautiful. Just beyond the whitecaps cruised a Navy destroyer, keeping watch on the president's compound.

Krogh was hoping to have some downtime that afternoon, but John Ehrlichman's secretary found him and told him Ehrlichman wanted to see him as soon as was convenient. In other words, immediately.

Krogh walked into his boss's office. Ehrlichman closed the door. Krogh sat. Ehrlichman handed him a file labeled "Pentagon Papers." It was stuffed with newspaper clippings about the secret documents and the man who had leaked them.

"As I read," Krogh recalled, "Ehrlichman told me that the

THE WHITE HOUSE
WASHINGTON
July 22, 1971

EYES ONLY

MEMORANDUM FOR: JOHN EHRLICHMAN

FROM: CHARLES COLSON

SUBJECT: Further on Pentagon Papers

As we discussed earlier this week I met today with Bud Krogh and reviewed with him what he has done to date and what his immediate plans are.

We both agreed that the major task at hand is to pull together all of the information that is available in Justice, Defense, CIA, State and outside. We must determine whether we have a case that can be made public with respect to Ellsberg and any conspiracy with his colleagues.

At the moment I think Bud has a good investigative mechanism (although he thinks he will need the full time services of Jack Caulfield, a matter I would like to discuss with you). Leddy is an excellent man. Hunt can be very useful.

July 1971 memo to top domestic advisor John Ehrlichman from Counsel Charles Colson describing the White House's investigation of Daniel Ellsberg and the involvement of Gordon Liddy (misspelled here) and Howard Hunt.

assignment he was about to give me had been deemed of the highest national security importance by the president. He emphasized that the president was as angry about the leak of the Pentagon Papers as he had ever seen him on any issue."

Nixon, Ehrlichman explained, was dissatisfied with the FBI's investigation of Daniel Ellsberg. He wanted his own team on the job. Krogh was to head the so-called Special Investigations Unit, working in partnership with David Young of Henry Kissinger's staff. Progress reports were to go to Ehrlichman, who would keep Nixon informed.

That night, in his hotel room, Krogh began to plan. Though overwhelmed by the responsibility being placed on his shoulders, he felt absolutely committed to the president. As he later said, "I certainly wasn't in the habit of questioning the orders or wisdom of my superiors."

THE PLUMBERS

IN WASHINGTON, A FEW DAYS LATER, the first recruit to the Special Investigations Unit entered Egil Krogh's office. G. Gordon Liddy, attorney and former FBI agent, stepped forward and crushed Krogh's hand in a vicelike shake. Forty years old, with a thick mustache and the posture of a flagpole, Liddy was known around Washington as intelligent, fiercely loyal, and something of a loose cannon.

"I could kill a man with a pencil in a matter of seconds," he was known to brag.

Krogh, Liddy, and David Young moved into room 16 on the ground floor of the Old Executive Office Building, across the street from the White House. The suite had several offices and a reception area. A window, behind steel bars, looked out at Seventeenth Street.

Kathy Chenow, a White House secretary, sat at the front desk. Chenow arranged for a secure phone to be installed and, to prevent whatever was going to happen in room 16 from being traced to the White House, had the phone bill sent to her home address.

The fifth and final member of the team showed up later that week.

"A short, dapper man," Krogh later said of Howard Hunt. "He could blend easily into any group without drawing undue attention to himself, a valuable characteristic for a spy." Hunt, formerly of the CIA, had been assigned to the group by Charles Colson.

The Secret Service put a new lock on the outer door and gave each team member a key. One of the team taped up a sign with a single handwritten word: *Plumbers*—a joking reference to their mission of finding and fixing leaks. The name stuck. The Special Investigations Unit would become known to history as "the Plumbers."

★ ★ ★

"A mood of manic resolve to carry out our duties drove us forward," Krogh recalled. "The unit had been given a critical responsibility by the president."

In an office with a conference table and a blackboard, the Plumbers dissected Daniel Ellsberg. They sifted through all available records on him, from recent FBI files to security checks that had been done over the years. They read about the many women he'd dated, going back to his college years, wondering if any of them might actually have been Soviet agents. Of particular interest were details that could be used to humiliate and discredit Ellsberg—tales of recreational drug use, and rumors that Daniel and Patricia enjoyed visiting nudist camps.

Liddy summarized his view of Ellsberg: "Unstable, self-righteous, egotistical."

"The picture that emerged," concurred Hunt, "was that of a brilliant, unstable man."

The most enticing tidbit was that, sometime in 1968, soon after returning from Vietnam, Ellsberg had begun seeing a psychiatrist. He must have told his doctor, Lewis Fielding, all sorts of intimate and potentially embarrassing details.

"The more Liddy and I discussed both the problem of, and the opportunity presented by, Dr. Fielding's file," Hunt recalled, "the more apparent it became that the file should be photographed by surreptitious means."

Liddy proposed a late-night visit to Fielding's office—a "black bag job," he called it. He assured Egil Krogh he'd learned such skills in the FBI.

Krogh had no experience with this sort of thing. On August 11, he drafted a memo to John Ehrlichman recommending: "A covert operation be undertaken to examine all the medical files still held by Ellsberg's psychoanalyst." Below the proposal, Krogh typed two words:

Approve ____ Disapprove ____

Ehrlichman dashed the initial "E" in the Approve slot. Underneath, he handwrote: "If done under your assurance that it is not traceable."

★ ★ ★

A few days later, Howard Hunt led Gordon Liddy into a Washington, D.C., apartment building. A man they knew only as "Steve" let them into a small studio, nearly empty of furniture.

Hunt and Liddy had promised a very nervous Egil Krogh to use "good tradecraft"—expert spying techniques, in other words. This is what had brought them to the CIA safe house. Steve, a specialist with the agency's Technical Services Division, had agreed to prepare a false identity and disguise for Liddy. Hunt was set; he had these things from previous operations.

Steve handed Liddy a Kansas driver's license in the name of George F. Leonard. Liddy got a Social Security card with this name, club membership cards, and other "pocket litter"—ordinary things like torn train tickets and scribbled notes that make a wallet look real. Steve also gave Liddy a sheet of paper with basic facts about Kansas. Liddy promised to memorize the information.

Next, Steve fit a wig of long, dark brown hair over Liddy's head and snipped the edges to make it look natural. He gave Liddy a pair of glasses with lenses as thick as bottle bottoms.

Then Steve demonstrated a miniature 35mm camera that could be hidden in the bottom of a tobacco pouch, with a tiny hole in the pouch for the lens. He also gave Liddy something he called a "gait-altering device," a lead insert placed in the shoe that caused the wearer to limp. The limp, in theory, would distract witnesses from noticing other details.

"It was a rather unsophisticated item," Hunt conceded. "A pebble would have done as well."

★ ★ ★

"I am not guilty."

Standing in a Los Angeles courtroom on August 16, speaking in a firm voice, Daniel Ellsberg repeated his plea after each charge against him was read. Outside the courthouse, reporters gathered around Daniel and Patricia. Ellsberg, now facing up to thirty-five years in prison, insisted that the contents of the Pentagon Papers justified his actions.

"The public agrees with me that they have a right to know," he told reporters.

He said he was looking forward to his trial, because it would raise issues the country needed to confront. "They are issues of life and death, war and peace. They're incomparably more important than what happens to me."

Several observers commented on Ellsberg's intensity, the fire in his eyes. "It was almost like he glowed with this fervor," noted one reporter.

With the trial set to begin early the next year, Daniel and Patricia flew to New York and stayed at the apartment she still owned in Manhattan. Any time her husband started to discuss the case in the apartment, Patricia would say, "*Shhhhh.*" She was convinced the government had her place bugged. If it was important, she and

Daniel would step onto the balcony, where the noise of the traffic fourteen floors below drowned out their whispered words.

Patricia was not being paranoid. She knew for a fact that FBI agents were questioning her friends and family. She found out that agents had interviewed her financial advisor and doctor, and had even gone to her dentist and asked to see her X-rays. The agents were searching for evidence of disloyalty, or anything else to use against the Ellsbergs—though what they hoped to discover on Patricia's teeth is difficult to say. Anyway, the dentist had refused to cooperate.

In California, agents interrogated Carol Cummings and many of Ellsberg's friends. "They asked me a whole lot of weird questions," one friend recalled, " 'What kinds of emotional troubles is he having? What kinds of wild things is he doing?' They were really looking for dirt."

From far left to right: "Plumbers" G. Gordon Liddy, Howard Hunt, and White House aide Egil "Bud" Krogh, who coordinated Liddy and Hunt's investigation of Daniel Ellsberg.

The manager of the Sandstone Ranch, a nudist retreat, remembered two men showing up and asking questions about Ellsberg. Even though the men were, as the manager recalled, "in a naked state," there was something about them that screamed government agent.

"Psychologically, it's not so bothersome, because we believe in what we're doing," Patricia Ellsberg said about the feeling of being watched by one's own government. "But I think it's troublesome for the country that there is surveillance of citizens, and that the right of privacy is being threatened."

In late August, traveling as George Leonard and Edward Warren, Liddy and Hunt flew to California to conduct a feasibility study for the Ellsberg job. Wearing their disguises, they photographed the entry and exit points of Dr. Fielding's office building. Liddy tried out the gait-altering device once, then threw it away. He was not much happier with the CIA's tobacco-pouch camera. "First your guys give me this heel lift that crippled me for life," he grumbled to Hunt, fiddling with the gadget's tiny buttons, "and now a camera I can't even see."

At night, posing as friends of the doctor, they returned to the building and convinced a cleaning woman, Maria Martinez, to unlock the door to Fielding's office. Liddy snapped pictures while Hunt stood in the hall, chatting with Martinez in Spanish.

"Steve" met Hunt and Liddy at Dulles Airport in Northern Virginia to pick up the film. The operatives then went home and grabbed a few hours of sleep. When they got to the White House that afternoon, the photos were ready. They presented the images, along with their report, to Egil Krogh.

"Very few of the pictures turned out," Krogh remembered. The only really clear photo showed Liddy beaming in front of Fielding's building.

Krogh gave the go-ahead, with one change—Hunt and Liddy were not to perform the job themselves. People working directly for the White House, Krogh explained, could not risk getting caught in a break-in.

That killed it, as far as Liddy was concerned. But Hunt suggested they contact Bernard Barker, a Cuban American living in Miami who had done clandestine work for the CIA in the past. Barker agreed to put together a team.

Hunt and Liddy set the operation for Labor Day weekend, when

Fielding's building should be quiet and empty. Krogh asked Charles Colson, the White House lawyer, for money to cover expenses.

On September 1, the Wednesday before Labor Day weekend, there was a knock on the rarely used back door of Egil Krogh's office. Krogh opened the door partway. A man's hand held out an envelope. Krogh took it and shut the door. He looked in the envelope. Fifty crisp hundred-dollar bills, as requested.

Krogh hurried from his office to room 16. Hunt and Liddy were there, bags packed. Krogh handed over the cash, enough to cover airfare, hotel, two rental cars, special equipment, and payment for Barker's crew. He reminded the men to exchange the hundred-dollar bills at a bank, to ensure that any purchases they made could not be traced back to a White House account.

"Now for God's sake," Krogh said, "don't get caught."

"We won't," Liddy assured him.

Krogh nodded nervously. "I'm going to give you my home phone number. As soon as the operation's over—whatever happens—call and let me know. I'll be waiting."

Liddy tucked the slip of paper with the number in his pocket. He promised to make the call.

"I'll be George," he said, grinning, "honest George Leonard."

BAG JOB

FRIDAY NIGHT, IN LOS ANGELES, Howard Hunt stood in a phone booth with the receiver to his ear, listening to the rings. There was no answer in Dr. Fielding's office. He dialed Fielding's home number. A man answered. Hunt hung up. So far so good.

He drove one of the rental cars to Fielding's apartment house, a walkie-talkie on the seat beside him. He parked on the dark street. He got out and walked past the driveway to make sure Fielding's Volvo was there. It was. The lights in Fielding's apartment were on.

"All was as it should be," Hunt later said.

Liddy drove the other car to Fielding's office. With him were Bernard Barker and the two men Barker had brought, Felipe De-Diego and Eugenio Martinez. Like Barker, they were Cuban-born anti-communists, trained in covert operations by the CIA.

Liddy parked in the lot behind Fielding's building. Barker and

DeDiego, wearing black delivery uniforms purchased the day before, and the wigs and glasses issued to Hunt and Liddy, got out and entered the building through the unlocked back door. Barker carried a suitcase with stickers labeled "Rush" and "Air Express" stuck to the side. They met the cleaning woman, Maria Martinez, in the corridor. In Spanish, they told her they had a delivery for Dr. Fielding. It was late for deliveries, she said.

"Well, we'd like to get this thing done," Barker said, trying to sound casual.

Martinez unlocked Fielding's door and watched the deliverymen set their cargo down. She may have noticed one of them unlocking the knob from the inside. In any case, after they left, she relocked the door.

Hunt paced the dark sidewalk in front of Dr. Fielding's apartment building. He was tempted to contact Liddy to see how things were going, but the walkie-talkies were to be used only in case of emergency.

At the doctor's building, Liddy and the entry team waited in the car. Maria Martinez finally left a little after midnight. Barker and his men got out and walked to the back door. To their surprise, it was locked.

The men returned to the car for a consult. Liddy didn't want them to break the glass door—that might attract attention. But there was a first-floor window behind a clump of shrubbery. Near the window, a central air-conditioning unit put out a steady rumble. Good sound cover. This was the way in, they agreed.

Liddy knew he couldn't go inside, but refused to leave the men exposed. He got out and positioned himself in the bushes beside the building. He pulled a Browning knife from the holster on his belt and unfolded the big blade.

Barker's team put on gloves and scurried to the low window. Martinez lifted the glass cutter given to him by Liddy and pressed the edge to the window. Nothing happened; it was too dull to cut glass. They went to plan B, laying strips of masking tape across the window and then cracking it with a crowbar. The tape muffled the sound of breaking glass.

Liddy, from the bushes, barely heard it over the hum of the air conditioner.

Martinez reached in, unlocked the window, and slid it up. All three men climbed into a dark office.

The Beverly Hills building containing the offices of Dr. Lewis Fielding, which Hunt and Liddy burglarized in an attempt to obtain Daniel Ellsberg's psychiatric records.

They hurried through the office to the hall, and up the stairs to Dr. Fielding's door. It was locked. They pried it open with a crowbar, cracking the door's wooden frame. Inside, they opened the suitcase they'd delivered earlier and took out tools: camera and film, spotlights, rope, and a roll of black plastic. They taped the plastic to the windows. The rope was set aside, to be used only if an emergency exit from the second-floor window became necessary.

Following standard procedure for covert operations, Barker had held back key information until the last moment. Now he explained what they were looking for.

"We are here because we are doing a great job for the country," he said. "We have to find some papers of a great traitor to the United States."

"Who's the guy?" asked DeDiego.

"Daniel Ellsberg."

They started the search.

Outside, Liddy returned to his car to wait. He slouched down in the driver's seat, angling the rearview mirror to give him a view down the alley to the street in front of the building. All was quiet.

Hunt relaxed when he saw the lights go out in Fielding's apartment. He walked back to his car and sat for a few minutes. Then he started the engine and cruised past for a final look.

Fielding's car was not in the driveway.

Fear flashed through Hunt's mind: *Was the doctor on his way to his office? Had Barker's men tripped an unseen alarm? Were the police already there?*

He pulled to the curb and stuck the antenna of his walkie-talkie out the car window.

"George, this is Edward," Hunt said. "Report. Repeat: George, this is Edward. Report."

No response. He tried again. Nothing but static.

Hunt sped toward the office, hoping it wasn't too late. There were no police cars in sight. He rolled through the alley and saw Liddy's parked car. The windows of Fielding's office were dark, thanks to the black plastic. The team had been inside for about half an hour.

He jogged to Liddy's car and slipped into the passenger seat. Liddy could see that Hunt was in a panic.

"What's happened?" he asked, sitting up.

"I put Fielding to bed, but fifteen minutes ago his car disappeared."

"*What?*"

"Where are the boys?" Hunt asked.

"Hell, they're inside."

"I thought they'd be out by now."

"Well, the goddamn cleaning woman," Liddy explained. "She locked both doors, so the boys had to break into a ground-floor window so they could get upstairs. That's what took so long."

"Any word from them?"

"No."

Liddy picked up his walkie-talkie. "George to Leader, George to Leader. Come in. Come in."

270

No answer.

He looked at Hunt. "What the hell's going on?"

"We'd better get them out of there."

"This goddamn Mickey Mouse gear!" Liddy shouted, collapsing the antenna of his walkie-talkie. "Let's go get them."

They got out of the car and had just reached the alley when they heard footsteps approaching. It was Barker and the team. They had the suitcase.

"Okay, back to the plan," Hunt whispered. "I'll head for the hotel room, and we'll all meet there."

★ ★ ★

In his room at the Beverly Hilton, Hunt slid a bottle of champagne into a bucket of ice. He got out five glasses.

Liddy came in smiling, and threw his jacket on the bed.

"I bet Krogh's pissing his pants!"

A few minutes later Barker's team arrived, dripping with sweat.

"Eduardo," Barker said, using the Spanish version of Hunt's cover name, "there was nothing there."

"*Nothing*?"

"We went through every goddamn file in that office," Barker said. "There was nothing there. Nothing with the name Ellsberg on it."

Hunt and Liddy looked at each other.

"You're absolutely sure?" Liddy asked.

Barker nodded. "I'm sorry, George, but that's how it was."

While the men pulled off their wigs and wiped their heads with towels, they explained that they'd pried open the filing cabinets and gone through everything. They'd ransacked the place, purposely leaving it a mess to make it look as if some junkie had broken in looking for drugs. As an added touch, Martinez swiped Fielding's prescription pads. They'd used a Polaroid camera to document everything.

"Well," Hunt said, "I guess it's time for champagne."

He popped open the bottle and poured five glasses.

"This isn't the kind of victory celebration I figured we'd have," Liddy said. "But at least nothing went wrong."

It was three o'clock in the morning; six on the East Coast. Liddy went out to a pay phone to update Krogh. The Cubans walked to their rooms. Hunt started packing.

Liddy came back a few minutes later and sat on his bed. Krogh was so relieved, Liddy reported, he'd nearly wept.

They turned out the lights. They had a few hours before their flight home.

"Do you think there is an Ellsberg psychiatric file?" Hunt asked from his bed.

"There has to be one," Liddy said, "unless Fielding destroyed it."

He was wrong—Dr. Fielding simply didn't take the types of detailed notes on his patients they were looking for. Not knowing this, they figured Fielding must have taken the Ellsberg file home. When they got back to Washington, Liddy said, he'd suggest a bag job at Fielding's apartment.

Laughing, he added, "Krogh'll go bananas."

Back in the White House after the long weekend, Liddy reported in person to Egil Krogh, showing him photos of the damage done to Dr. Fielding's office. He took pleasure in showing Krogh the Browning knife he'd carried on the operation.

"Would you really have used it," Krogh asked. "I mean, to kill somebody?"

"I would, if necessary, to protect my men."

Over the next few days, Liddy and Hunt prepared a proposal for a visit to Fielding's apartment. They submitted the plan to Krogh, who asked John Ehrlichman for guidance.

"Get them away from there, and never send them back," Ehrlichman ordered.

Good call, Krogh thought. "The White House Plumbers," he recalled, "were not the most rational group of people."

He watched the Los Angeles newspapers for anything about the Fielding break-in. There was nothing. The Beverly Hills police thought it looked like the work of a drug addict, and accused a well-known local crook named Elmer Davis. Under questioning, Davis confessed to the crime, but was not prosecuted; he was already facing several other burglary charges.

It later emerged that Davis had been in jail the night of the break-in.

The Fielding operation was over. But the impact of Nixon's determination to destroy Daniel Ellsberg was still to be felt.

"A botched break-in, evidenced in a few Polaroids, didn't seem to represent much," Krogh would say in retrospect. "In practice, however, it was the first irreversible step by which a presidency ran out of control."

CONSEQUENCES

"I WASN'T DISCOURAGED by the failure of the Fielding job to produce results," Gordon Liddy would later explain. "In that line of work there are as many dry holes as there are in the oil business."

Liddy and Hunt soon learned that Daniel Ellsberg was scheduled to come to Washington in September to accept an award from a peace organization. There would be a big ceremony in a hotel ballroom, with lots of media. This sparked a new idea in room 16.

First, they'd bring up some of their Cuban agents from Miami. "We'll make waiters out of them," Hunt proposed.

Posing as waitstaff at the award dinner, the agents would slip LSD into Ellsberg's soup. "Enough to befuddle him," Liddy added, "make him appear a near burnt-out drug case." By the time the guest of honor stood to make his acceptance speech, he'd be completely zonked.

White House Counsel Charles Colson approved the plan. Hunt went to a CIA doctor for the drugs.

On September 23, the night of the ceremony, more than a thousand people sat at tables in the hotel ballroom. The waiters carried in food, and Ellsberg ate. When he was called to the podium, everyone stood and clapped.

Ellsberg's voice seemed to shake.

"Brothers and sisters," he began, "I prepared notes appropriate to a very depressed crowd. But I had a feeling from the moment I stepped into this room tonight that this is a celebration."

The crowd cheered and stomped their feet.

And Ellsberg launched into his speech. He was emotional, but otherwise fine. By the time Hunt had procured the LSD, it had been too late to get his Cuban contacts hired as waiters at the hotel.

The Plumbers went back to the drawing board.

A week later, Ellsberg landed at night in Los Angeles and rented a green Mustang convertible. He tossed his jacket in the backseat, and drove with the top down and the radio blaring. His first stop was a friend's house, a woman who was training to be a hairdresser. Ellsberg sat at a kitchen chair while she snipped his curly, graying hair.

In the morning he drove to the Los Angeles Federal Building, where Tony Russo was scheduled to appear in court. After six weeks behind bars, Russo was finally released by the judge. Russo and Ellsberg embraced in the courtroom, then talked to the press outside.

"I realized how many men had died because those pages had been stamped top secret and because generations of bureaucrats like me kept them secret," Ellsberg said. "I realized that I had to reveal this information even if I had to go to prison for the rest of my life."

That was looking increasingly possible. In late December, the grand jury added new charges to the Ellsberg indictment. He now faced a total of 115 years behind bars. Tony Russo was also charged with theft and espionage, and was looking at a sentence of up to thirty-five years.

Russo, like Ellsberg, was unrepentant.

"Dan and I are charged with 'conspiracy to defraud the United States.'" he told reporters. "But the whole point of the Pentagon Papers is the incredible extent to which the government has defrauded the people of America."

In February 1972, Richard Nixon stunned the world with a week-long trip to China. Cameras followed him as he met with Chinese leaders and walked on the Great Wall. This visit, the first by an American president, led to a thaw in the years of icy hostility between two of the world's most powerful nations. It was the greatest triumph of Nixon's presidency. And yet there was little time to savor the moment. Almost as soon as Nixon got back home, North Vietnam launched a massive offensive in the South. There were just seventy thousand Americans left in Vietnam. South Vietnam had an enormous military, but the forces were spread out and ineffective.

America's longtime ally was nearing collapse. Nixon saw this as a grave threat to American prestige—and to his own.

"Both Haldeman and Henry seem to have an idea—which I think is mistaken—that even if we fail in Vietnam we can still survive politically," the president wrote in his diary. "I have no illusions whatever on that score." The important thing, Nixon decided, was to avoid disaster in Vietnam until after the presidential election in November.

"That's why we've got to blast the living bejeezus out of North Vietnam," Kissinger advised.

The president agreed. Lyndon Johnson had halted the bombing of North Vietnam four years before. It was time to start it up again. The only question, in Nixon's mind, was the scale of the attack.

"I still think we ought to take the dikes out now," Nixon said on April 25, referring to a long-discussed plan of leveling the walls holding back the Red River in North Vietnam. "Will that drown people?"

"That will drown about two hundred thousand people," Kissinger replied.

"Well, no, no, no. I'd rather use the nuclear bomb. Have you got that, Henry?"

"That, I think, would just be too much."

"The nuclear bomb, does that bother you?" Nixon asked. "I just want you to think big, Henry, for Chrissakes."

The president was just talking tough, just pumping himself up. That's the generous view, anyway. But he was serious about taking the violence to a new level.

"The only place where you and I disagree," he told Kissinger in early May, "is with regard to the bombing. You're so goddamned concerned about the civilians, and I don't give a damn. I don't care."

Kissinger's response was revealing. "I'm concerned about the civilians," he said, "because I don't want the world to be mobilized against you as a butcher."

"This period was one of the most intense, frightening, and meaningful times of my life," Patricia Ellsberg later said of the months leading up to the trial. "I was terrified that my husband would be physically harmed or sent to prison for the rest of his life."

Both possibilities were very real.

The Plumbers were set to strike again on May 3, when Ellsberg was scheduled to appear at a Vietnam War protest at the Capitol Building. "If heads are knocked, that's all right," Charles Colson told the team. "That's Ellsberg's problem."

Hunt and Liddy contacted Bernard Barker in Miami. Barker flew north with a crew of eight, including Felipe DeDiego from the Fielding operation. In a Washington hotel, Hunt told Barker the idea was to disrupt Ellsberg's talk, and to physically attack him.

"Our mission is to hit him," Bernard Barker briefed his fellow operatives, "to call him a traitor and punch him in the nose."

On the drizzly afternoon of May 3, about five hundred protesters gathered outside the Capitol. As a speaker railed against the never-ending war, Barker's team mingled, not exactly blending in—they were the only ones in suits. Ellsberg made his way to the mic and started talking.

"Traitor!"

"Communist!"

Ellsberg heard the shouts. He saw some pushing and shoving. He went on with his talk.

Barker's men, unable to get close to Ellsberg, tore down antiwar signs and swung fists at anyone with long hair. The police broke up the ruckus and no arrests were made. That night, in his hotel room with Hunt and Liddy, Barker bragged he'd punched a hippie hard enough to hurt his hand.

For the Plumbers it was another failure. They were quick to move on. All three got into a car and drove around Washington, Hunt and Liddy pointing out locations of potential "entry operations," as Liddy called them. The Plumbers were moving beyond Ellsberg. Their focus now included helping President Nixon's reelection campaign. One priority was installing listening devices in the campaign office of Democratic presidential candidate George McGovern.

But the next entry operation, Liddy explained, would be at the headquarters of the Democratic National Committee (DNC), located in an upscale office and apartment complex called Watergate.

On the afternoon of May 8, Richard Nixon announced that American planes had begun striking industrial targets in and around Hanoi. The Navy was placing mines in North Vietnam's Haiphong harbor. If North Vietnam agreed to a cease-fire and returned the American prisoners of war, Nixon said, he would end the bombing and withdraw the remaining American troops.

May 1972. Warehouse and shipping areas in Haiphong, North Vietnam, after being bombed by U.S. warplanes.

As usual in times of military crisis, the public rallied around the president. Nixon's approval rating rose to nearly 60 percent.

Daniel and Patricia Ellsberg were in Los Angeles, preparing for trial, when they heard the news. "I remember feeling," Ellsberg recalled, "and telling Patricia, that it was the darkest day of my life."

His depression deepened as he sat in the courtroom, watching the jury selection process. Listening to lawyers from both sides question potential jurors, it became obvious to Ellsberg that none of these people knew much about the documents he'd risked everything to expose. They'd heard of the Pentagon Papers, but hadn't taken the time to read them. The war in Vietnam went on. The bombing was escalating again.

Ellsberg leaned to a member of his defense team and moaned, "For this I'm going to do ninety-nine years?"

280

PREPOSTEROUS

Rɪᴄʜᴀʀᴅ Nɪxᴏɴ ᴡᴏᴜʟᴅ ʟᴀᴛᴇʀ ᴄᴀʟʟ the Watergate operation "a comedy of errors." It was an understatement.

Howard Hunt had his wife call the Watergate Hotel to rent a banquet room for the night of May 26. Bernard Barker and his recruits returned to Washington. The plan was for Hunt, Liddy, and the men from Miami to enjoy dinner in the rented room, lingering until late at night. When the halls were empty, Barker's team would sneak through an underground corridor connecting the hotel with the Watergate office building next door. They'd climb the stairs to the sixth floor and break into the offices of the Democratic National Committee—the objective was to place listening devices and photograph key documents.

A complication arose at ten thirty when a hotel guard told the guests he was locking up; everyone had to leave. Hunt and one of

Barker's men stayed behind, hidden in a liquor storage closet. They hoped to wait until the coast was clear, then tiptoe out and let the others back into the building. But the guard locked the banquet room door. They were unable to pick the lock, and the guard kept making his rounds, shining a flashlight into the room every hour. So Hunt and his associate spent the night in the liquor cabinet. When he could no longer resist the call of nature, Hunt reached for a half-empty bottle of Johnnie Walker Red.

Early the next morning, after the guard had unlocked the banquet hall, the exhausted operative returned to the hotel room he was sharing with Liddy.

"Gordon," he said, "I know you like scotch, but don't ever drink it at the Watergate Hotel."

The Plumbers tried again the next night. Barker and his men got inside, made it up to the door of the DNC offices, but couldn't pick the lock.

They returned the next night with better tools. They got in, took photos of files and papers, and placed bugs in the office.

But the bugs didn't work well. James McCord, a former CIA technician now working with the Plumbers, set up a listening post in a room of the Howard Johnson's motel across the street from the Watergate. McCord could barely make out what was being said in the DNC offices.

So they went in again on the night of June 16. Before the building was locked for the night, McCord put electrical tape over the bolt of a door in the parking garage that opened to an inside stairwell. The tape prevented the door from locking. At 1:30 a.m., McCord, Barker, Eugenio Martinez, and two more Miami men went into the Watergate office building through the garage door.

McCord forgot to remove the tape.

On the balcony of a hotel room at Watergate, Liddy set up a walkie-talkie antenna. He went inside and clicked on the television, with the sound turned low. Hunt flipped through a newspaper. They waited.

From the window of the listening post in the Howard Johnson's, McCord's assistant watched the Watergate building through a pair of binoculars. At 2:00 a.m., he saw something.

"There's flashlights on the eighth floor," he reported to Liddy by walkie-talkie.

Just a routine door check by guards, Liddy assumed.

"Now they're on the seventh floor."

Liddy still wasn't alarmed—not until the next communication from Howard Johnson's a few second later:

"Hey, any of our guys wearin' hippie clothes?"

Hippie clothes? That's when Hunt and Liddy knew something was terribly wrong. As they would later learn, a guard had spotted the tape on the garage door. Suspicious, he'd called the police. The first officers to respond had been working undercover, thus the "hippie" clothes.

"Negative," said Liddy. "All our people are in business suits. Why?"

"They're on the sixth floor now. Four or five guys. One's got on a cowboy hat. One's got on a sweatshirt. It looks like . . . guns! They've got guns. It's trouble!"

Liddy cursed. "Are you reading this?" he called to the entry team. "Come in!"

Nothing. Liddy tightened his grip on the walkie-talkie.

"Come in. That's an order!"

Finally, there was a response from the entry team. Three whispered words. "They got us."

Hunt and Liddy ran down to the street, jumped in their cars, and sped off. Liddy made it home, walked into his bedroom, and undressed quietly, hoping not to wake his wife.

"Is that you?" she asked.

"Yes."

"Anything wrong?"

"There was trouble," Liddy told her. "I'll probably be going to jail."

He got into bed.

★ ★ ★

Richard Nixon walked into the kitchen of his home in Key Biscayne, Florida. He poured a cup of coffee and looked over the front page of the *Miami Herald*. The main headline was a routine update from Vietnam: ***"GROUND COMBAT ROLE NEARS END FOR U.S."***

Beneath that, and to the left, a smaller headline caught Nixon's eye: ***"MIAMIANS HELD IN D.C. TRY TO BUG DEMO HEADQUARTERS."***

He started reading. Five men had been arrested in the Democratic National Committee offices in the Watergate complex. One of the men had identified himself to police as a former CIA agent.

June 17, 1972. Police check the offices of the Democratic National Committee in Washington's Watergate building after a break-in.

Several others were Cubans from Miami. They were carrying locksmith tools, electronic surveillance equipment, and, between them, fifty-three crisp, sequentially numbered hundred-dollar bills.

"It sounded preposterous," Nixon later wrote. "Cubans in surgical gloves bugging the DNC! I dismissed it as some sort of prank."

By the time he got back to Washington on June 20, the Watergate story no longer seemed funny. The ex-CIA agent had been identified as James McCord, currently employed by the Committee to Reelect the President—which was headed by Nixon's former attorney general, John Mitchell. Two of the Cuban burglars had been carrying notebooks in which the name Howard Hunt was written. Hunt, known to be a consultant to White House Counsel Charles Colson, had since disappeared.

For the rest of his life, Richard Nixon would insist he had played no role in the planning or approval of the Watergate break-in. The evidence suggests this is true. He quickly realized, though, that close advisors within the White House and his reelection campaign had been involved.

"The White House has had no involvement whatever in this particular incident," Nixon told the nation at a press conference on June 22.

In private Oval Office meetings, Nixon, Bob Haldeman, and John Ehrlichman discussed options for damage control. The president wanted to know who had ordered the job.

"Is it Liddy?" he asked. "He must be a little nuts."

"He is," Haldeman said.

"I mean, he just isn't well screwed on, is he?"

Perhaps not, Haldeman granted, but he was working for people higher up, including John Mitchell. Complicating matters, the FBI had just discovered that the hundred-dollar bills found in the burglars' pockets had all been withdrawn from a bank account belonging to the Committee to Reelect the President. It was only a matter of time before the FBI picked up Hunt and Liddy for questioning. And the problem was, they knew too much. Not just about Watergate, but about other jobs that could be traced back to the White House—most dangerously, the Ellsberg break-in.

With these facts in mind, Nixon and his team devised their strategy. They would get top officials at the CIA to tell the FBI that

Watergate had been an intelligence operation, a matter of national security.

"They should call the FBI in," Nixon ordered, "and say that we wish for the country, don't go any further into this case, period!"

All approved the cover-up plan. Everything was recorded.

In the early morning light, a lone figure churned through the water of the swimming pool outside a Los Angeles apartment complex. This was Daniel Ellsberg's daily routine now—thirty laps, starting at six o'clock.

With the trial set to begin soon, the Ellsbergs had moved into this complex near the courthouse. Patricia Ellsberg worked out her stress on the apartments' tennis courts. During one game, after she missed a shot, a friend suggested she pretend the ball was the chief prosecutor, David Nissen.

She wound up and smashed a winner.

"That's Nissen," she snapped.

Patricia sold property she owned to raise funds for the Ellsberg-Russo legal team. Her father was wealthy, but his riches were definitely not available.

"Louis Marx presently refuses to see Dr. Ellsberg," reported the *New York Times*.

For the lawyers, meanwhile, this was a difficult case to prepare for. Lawyers like to study precedents, similar cases that have come before. There were none. The government had never prosecuted anyone for leaking secret documents. One of the team,

Leonard Boudin, explained to Ellsberg that to prove espionage, the government would have to show that Ellsberg had damaged national security—something Ellsberg obviously didn't feel he'd done.

"That's great," he said. "So I'm home free!"

"I'm afraid it's not as simple as that," Boudin explained. "When the U.S. government goes into a courtroom and says to a jury, 'The government of the United States versus Daniel Ellsberg,' and presents twelve felony counts . . . you can't be sure you will walk out of that courtroom a free man."

"Well, what are my odds?"

"Fifty-fifty."

Ellsberg did not feel reassured.

"Well, let's face it, Dan," said the lawyer. "Copying seven thousand pages of top secret documents and giving them to the *New York Times* has a bad ring to it."

PEACE WITH HONOR?

NIXON WAS FEELING CONFIDENT in the summer of 1972. He repeatedly told the public he was demanding a full and vigorous investigation of the Watergate break-in. Most people believed him. After the Republican Convention that August, Nixon led Democratic nominee George McGovern by a lopsided 64–30.

When Kissinger prepared to return to Paris for talks with the North Vietnamese, Nixon emphasized that he was in no hurry to end the war. "Henry, you tell those sons of bitches that the president is a madman and you don't know how to deal with him. Once re-elected I'll be a mad bomber."

The message got through. Leaders in Hanoi knew Nixon was almost certain to win another term. And when Nixon said he'd be the mad bomber, they believed him. It was time to cut a deal. All along, the North Vietnamese had been demanding the removal from power of President Thieu's government in South Vietnam.

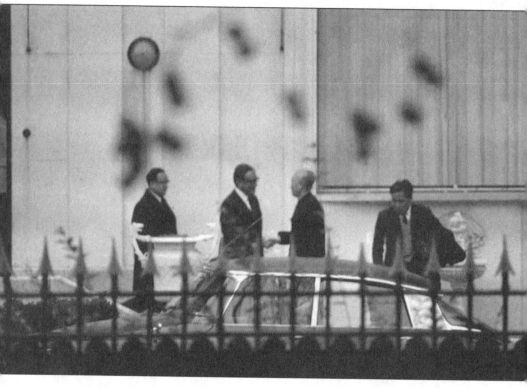

December 1972. Henry Kissinger meets with North Vietnamese negotiator Le Duc Tho in Paris during negotiations to bring an end to the Vietnam War.

Now they decided to drop that demand. This quickly led to a breakthrough. Kissinger agreed to the complete withdrawal of American forces from Vietnam. In exchange, Le Duc Tho agreed to a cease-fire and the return of American prisoners of war.

It was a cynical bargain on both sides. "The most important thing was the American withdrawal," Tho's top aide later said. With American forces gone, Hanoi would have time to remove Thieu in its own way. Kissinger realized this, of course. And he knew that when the fighting flared up again, Nixon would likely resume the American bombing missions.

But in the meantime, Nixon could declare he had finally achieved "peace with honor."

Kissinger flew back to Washington with the good news. He and the president celebrated with a bottle of French wine and steaks from the White House kitchen.

There was only one problem—no one had bothered to consult with President Thieu.

When Kissinger flew to Saigon to brief the South Vietnamese president, it did not go well. Thieu blasted the deal, and was especially enraged that North Vietnam would be allowed to keep its troops in the South.

"The South Vietnamese people will assume that we have been sold out by the United States," he complained to Kissinger, "and that North Vietnam has won the war."

Kissinger reminded Thieu that Nixon had stuck it out in Vietnam for four bloody years. "Had we wanted to sell you out," he said, "there have been many easier ways by which we could have accomplished this."

Unmoved, Thieu demanded a total of sixty-nine modifications to the deal.

Kissinger called the list "preposterous." He assured Thieu that the United States was not abandoning South Vietnam, that Nixon would continue the bombing as long as necessary. The tense visit ended without agreement.

When it was over, Thieu turned to his press secretary and said, "I wanted to punch Kissinger in the mouth."

★ ★ ★

On election night, Nixon ate dinner with his family at the White House. An hour later, he felt something in his mouth crack—a cap had snapped off one of his front teeth. He had to go on television in a few hours. A dentist hurried over to fix the tooth.

Nixon then sat in the Lincoln Sitting Room, his tooth throbbing, as election returns began coming in. It was a landslide of historic proportions. Nixon carried forty-nine states, winning more than 60 percent of the vote to McGovern's 37 percent.

It was a moment to savor. Instead, Nixon grappled with a sense of foreboding.

"I am at a loss to explain the melancholy that settled over me on that victorious night," he later wrote. "Perhaps it was caused by the painful tooth. To some extent the marring effects of Watergate may have played a part."

Nixon's cover-up was holding, but possibly not for long. Hunt, Liddy, McCord, and the four men from Miami were all facing felony charges for the break-in. Their trial was set to begin in January—just like Ellsberg's. Meanwhile, reporters at the *Washington Post* were digging closer and closer to the real story, and the FBI, in spite of Nixon's efforts, was still investigating. The shadow of secrets still to be revealed darkened Nixon's night.

So did the ongoing crisis in Vietnam. Soon after the election, Nixon wrote to President Thieu. "I repeat my personal assurances to you that the United States will react very strongly and rapidly to any violation of the agreement."

Nixon was promising to continue the bombing. It wasn't good enough. Thieu insisted on his modifications to the deal. Kissinger brought the proposals to Paris, knowing there was zero chance they would be accepted by the North Vietnamese. In a meeting with Le Duc Tho, Kissinger quipped that he had accomplished the impossible: he had unified Vietnam.

"Both North and South Vietnam hate me now."

Tho was not laughing. North Vietnam had no intention of re-negotiating points that had already been settled. "If these are your last, unchangeable proposals," he told Kissinger, "settlement is impossible."

Kissinger hinted that Nixon was likely to respond militarily.

"Threats have no effect on us!" Tho shouted. "We have been fighting against you for ten years. Our people will never give up."

The peace deal was on the brink of collapse. Nixon and Kissinger were livid with Thieu, but he was an ally. So they turned their fury on the North.

"We have no choice," Kissinger advised, "but to step up our bombing as a means of making them agree."

On the night of December 18, the lights in Hao Lo prison suddenly went out. There were now nearly four hundred American prisoners crammed into the Hanoi Hilton, many held in groups in large, concrete cells.

Lying in their bunks, the men heard the sharp shriek of air-raid sirens. And then, distant at first but growing louder, the thunder of the engines of American bombers.

"Atta boy!" shouted a prisoner.

"Sock it to 'em guys!"

Seconds later the walls started shaking. Plaster fell from the ceiling. The prisoners jumped out of bed and cheered. The guards, brushing rubble from their hair, shouted for quiet.

"They are trying to kill you!" a guard cried.

"No," said one of the pilots, "they're not trying to kill *us*."

Outside the prison walls, massive bombs fell on the city. The air raid lasted all night. "The bombers kept coming," James Stockdale later wrote, "and we kept cheering."

"Let's hear it for President Nixon!" the men shouted.

From a small window high in the wall of his cell, Everett Alvarez watched the dancing light of fires burning in downtown Hanoi.

Perspective is everything.

"Despair. Horror." That was Daniel Ellsberg's response to the renewed bombing—the "Christmas Bombing" as the press dubbed it. Over the next twelve days, American bombers struck Hanoi and Haiphong with twenty thousand tons of explosives.

The *Washington Post* called the campaign "savage and senseless."

"War by tantrum," said the journalist James Reston.

As the angry reaction intensified worldwide, Richard and Pat Nixon spent a lonely Christmas in their Key Biscayne home. Kissinger defended the attacks, pointing out that American planes were targeting military and industrial targets. Some bombs accidently hit homes and a hospital, but Kissinger dismissed the civilian deaths as hardly worth notice.

"Perhaps no more than four hundred to five hundred civilians were killed," he said.

Fifteen more American planes were shot down, the crews killed or dragged to prison camps.

But in any case, Kissinger told the press, the bombing was North Vietnam's fault.

While bombs fell in the North, Nixon sent a blunt note to President Thieu in the South: the United States was going to make a deal with or without his consent. Thieu quietly indicated more flexibility. The bombing ended on December 30.

"If both sides now return to the attitude of good will shown in October," Kissinger cabled to the North Vietnamese, "the remaining problems can be rapidly solved."

Hanoi was willing to talk. Kissinger returned to Paris.

"It was not my responsibility," he said, reaching to shake hands with Le Duc Tho. "It was not my fault about the bombing."

"You have tarnished the honor of the United States," replied Tho.

On January 8, 1973, Daniel Ellsberg was given a standing ovation when he spoke at an antiwar rally in Los Angeles. It was one of the last demonstrations against the Vietnam War.

In Paris, Kissinger and Tho worked out a peace deal—essentially the same deal they had agreed to in October. On January 9, Nixon's sixtieth birthday, Kissinger cabled the news to Washington. Nixon called it the best birthday present he'd ever gotten.

He knew, of course, that his South Vietnamese allies were unhappy. Privately, he promised President Thieu that American involvement in Vietnam would not end. "You have my assurance," he wrote, "that we will respond with full force should the settlement be violated by North Vietnam."

A week later Judge Matthew Byrne sat in a green leather chair behind a raised bench in a large, windowless Los Angeles courtroom. Sandy-haired with long sideburns, the forty-two-year-old judge had a reputation for intelligence and fairness. He knew the whole country was watching the trial that was finally under way. He knew it could make his career.

In the jury box sat ten women and two men. The rows of spectators' benches were packed with reporters and war protestors and a few curious celebrities. Patricia Ellsberg sat in the first row. At a long table, sitting with their lawyers, were Tony Russo and Daniel Ellsberg.

In a two-hour opening statement, prosecutor David Nissen told the jury that Russo and Ellsberg were unquestionably guilty of damaging America's national security. Projecting slides on the courtroom's wood-paneled wall, he discussed each charge, illustrating step-by-step how the defendants had committed theft and espionage.

For Ellsberg, the seriousness of the stakes really hit home. "The odds," he told a reporter, "are in favor of my spending a long time in prison."

A little after three thirty in the afternoon of January 22, Lyndon Johnson woke from a nap in the bedroom of his Texas ranch.

Feeling intense pain in his chest, he grabbed the phone and called the Secret Service agents assigned to the ranch.

"Send over whatever agent is on duty."

Alarmed by the agony in Johnson's voice, two agents rushed to the bedroom. They found him on the floor. He was not breathing. Johnson was flown to an army hospital in San Antonio, where he was pronounced dead of a heart attack.

★ ★ ★

The next day, in Paris, Kissinger and Le Duc Tho initialed the deal to end the Vietnam War.

That night President Nixon announced the historic news. "I have asked for this radio and television time," he began, "for the purpose of announcing that we have today concluded an agreement to end the war and bring peace with honor in Vietnam."

Nixon outlined the deal, and thanked the American people for their support. He ended with a tribute to the fallen president.

"In his life, President Johnson endured the vilification of those who sought to portray him as a man of war," Nixon said. "But there was nothing he cared about more deeply than achieving a lasting peace in the world."

There was no mention, in his tribute, of Nixon's efforts to undermine Johnson's peace talks four years before. No mention that since then more than twenty thousand Americans had died in Vietnam—all to achieve a lousy deal that allowed North Vietnam's army to stay in the South, making a lasting peace impossible. No mention that neither Nixon nor Kissinger expected their "peace with honor" to actually end the killing.

"I came away from the January negotiations," Kissinger later noted, "with the feeling that we would have to bomb the North Vietnamese again in early April or May."

In a Washington courtroom a week later, G. Gordon Liddy stood with his arms folded, his face impassive, as the clerk read the jury's verdict: guilty on eight counts related to the Watergate break-in. Moments later James McCord was also found guilty. Howard Hunt and the four men from Miami had already pled guilty.

All seven faced long prison sentences—but only for the Watergate break-in. So far, no one had talked about earlier jobs.

BIZARRE EVENTS

IN FEBRUARY 1973, after eight and a half years as a prisoner of war, Everett Alvarez was finally set free. Alvarez was with the first group of American pilots driven by bus to the Hanoi airport. Through the window, he watched an enormous U.S. Air Force jet descending toward the runway.

"There it is!" someone in the bus shouted. "There it is, guys!"

"Man, what a beautiful sight!"

Alvarez was fighting back tears as he boarded the plane. The jet engines roared and the cabin bounced as they picked up speed, and the moment they felt themselves lifted into the air, the men cheered and slapped each other on the back. Many cried. The plane flew southeast over the Gulf of Tonkin, landing four hours later at Clark Air Force Base in the Philippines.

A crowd of thousands greeted the men at the American base. Flags waved and film cameras rolled, and a military band played

as the pilots stepped out of the plane and began walking down a stairway onto a red carpet. They came off in the order they'd been shot down.

An American admiral stood on the carpet, waiting to greet the men. Alvarez walked up to him, saluted, and said, "Lieutenant J. G. Everett Alvarez, Jr., reporting back, sir!"

The Ellsberg trial continued in Los Angeles. The typical day in the courtroom lasted from nine thirty in the morning until five o'clock in the afternoon. Patricia Ellsberg never left her front row seat.

"When things are going well," noted a *New York Times* reporter, "she and her husband constantly smile at each other." At other times, Daniel Ellsberg hunched over a legal pad, making notes for his lawyers.

The days were long and the atmosphere tense. Tony Russo lightened the mood with an occasional wisecrack—he interrupted one long stretch of testimony by calling out:

"That's the only thing of substance that's been said all day."

Judge Byrne informed Russo's lawyer that such observations were not helpful.

The prosecution wrapped its case on day thirty-six of the trial. Russo took the stand and testified that it had been "an honor" to help Ellsberg copy the Pentagon Papers. "Any American who knew what we did," he said, "would consider it his official duty to get the Papers to Congress and the American people."

February 12, 1973. U.S. prisoners of war are released in Hanoi and turned over to the U.S. military.

The jury was to disregard that remark also, Judge Byrne declared.

The spectator's benches were packed tighter than ever on day sixty-eight, when Daniel Ellsberg finally took the stand. Ellsberg's father had flown in from Detroit and was in the courtroom. Robert and Mary were there to support their father.

Ellsberg had been losing weight steadily throughout the trial. Reporters thought he looked drawn and anxious. Courtroom artists complained that his restless gestures in the witness box made it impossible to get a good sketch.

Speaking almost in a whisper at first, Ellsberg told the jury he had been a hawk when the Vietnam War began. He detailed his role in helping to plan the early bombing campaigns, and told how two years in Vietnam had changed his views. He described scenes of devastation—forests turned to deserts by American chemicals, villages burning, children wounded by American bombs. He described the time he had watched a young girl poking through the wreckage of her home, lifting the charred remains of her doll.

When the court recessed for lunch, Ellsberg walked to the defense table, fell into a chair, and sobbed. Patricia came up and sat beside him.

On April 5, during a break in the trial, Judge Matthew Byrne strolled along a bluff overlooking the Pacific Ocean at Richard Nixon's San Clemente home. Beside him walked John Ehrlichman.

"If at any time what I'm saying makes it awkward or

embarrassing for you, just turn around and leave," said Ehrlichman. "I'll understand and we can talk later instead."

Byrne told him to go ahead.

Ehrlichman said that Nixon was beginning the search for a new man to head the FBI. He wanted to know, on behalf of the president, if Byrne might be interested.

Yes, the judge said, it sounded intriguing. Ehrlichman promised to pass this on to the president.

Byrne may or may not have recognized this for what it was—a brazen attempt to win influence with him. Nixon's Watergate cover-up was wobbling. With Hunt and Liddy convicted, reporters and prosecutors were looking higher, wondering who had issued their marching orders. Eventually, Nixon knew, someone would crack. Someone would talk about the Ellsberg break-in. If that happened, the Watergate prosecutors would be obliged to inform Judge Byrne, and it would be up to Byrne to decide whether to admit this evidence into Ellsberg's trial.

Byrne, of course, should have walked away. Instead, the day after his visit to San Clemente, he called Ehrlichman to ask for another meeting. They talked that afternoon in a Santa Monica park. Byrne explained that he just wanted to reiterate his strong interest in the FBI job.

They agreed to stay in touch as the Ellsberg trial neared its conclusion.

Nixon's fears played out as expected. Hoping to avoid jail, White House lawyer John Dean broke the Watergate investigation wide open by agreeing to tell prosecutors about the massive campaign of political spying and sabotage run from the White House and Nixon's reelection campaign. Dean, who had helped organize the cover-up, described the Plumbers and the Ellsberg break-in. He admitted to destroying evidence and arranging "hush money" to be funneled from the White House to Hunt and Liddy—cash in exchange for their silence.

Nixon got on the phone to Assistant Attorney General Henry Petersen, who was heading the Watergate investigation.

"I know about that," Nixon said of the Ellsberg job, "and it is so involved with national security that I don't want it opened up. Keep the hell out of it!"

He hung up.

"That should keep them out of it," Nixon told Ehrlichman. "There is no reason for them to get into that. What those fellows did was no crime. They ought to get a medal for going after Ellsberg."

It didn't work.

On April 27, day eighty of the trial, Judge Byrne called Daniel Ellsberg and Tony Russo to the bench. Attorneys from both sides huddled behind them, out of earshot of the press.

In a lowered voice, Byrne explained that he had just been sent a copy of a memo written by one of the Watergate prosecutors to Assistant Attorney General Petersen. "This is to inform you," Byrne read from the paper, "that on Sunday, April 15, 1973, I received information that at a date unspecified, Gordon Liddy and Howard Hunt burglarized the offices of a psychiatrist of Daniel Ellsberg to obtain the psychiatrist's files relating to Ellsberg."

Russo, facing the judge, put his hand behind his back and flashed a stealthy thumbs-up to the courtroom.

Byrne handed the memo to the defense team.

"Mr. Ellsberg," he said, "I don't need to reveal this information publicly."

Ellsberg realized he'd face personal questions about why he'd been seeing a psychiatrist. It was worth it. "Are you kidding? Put it out!"

Everyone returned to their seats. Judge Byrne announced the news. The reporters jumped up and sprinted for the pay phones in the hall.

"I wish I could say as a citizen that I'm surprised," Ellsberg said outside the courthouse. "How can I be surprised just because the administration breaks the law?"

Nixon addressed the nation on television on April 30.

"Today, in one of the most difficult decisions of my presidency, I accepted the resignations of two of my closest associates in the White House—Bob Haldeman and John Ehrlichman—two of the finest public servants it has been my privilege to know."

"Accepted" is not precisely correct. Privately, in another desperate attempt to cauterize the Watergate wound before it spread all the way to the president, Nixon had pressured his two closest aides to step down.

That same day, the *Washington Star-News* printed the news that Judge Mathew Byrne of the Daniel Ellsberg trial had recently met with John Ehrlichman to discuss a high-level government appointment.

Who had leaked the story? That was never determined, but not many people knew of the meeting. Suffice it to say, it hadn't come from the judge.

Judge Byrne, looking nervous and pale, announced that he had a statement to make. The crowded courtroom was absolutely silent.

Byrne described his meeting with Ehrlichman. He assured all parties that there had been no discussion of the details of the Ellsberg trial. He did not mention the second meeting he had requested.

The defense team attacked immediately. "The White House, by initiating this meeting, has irretrievably compromised the court," declared Ellsberg's lawyer in a motion to dismiss the charges.

Visibly shaken, Judge Byrne ruled that the trial would continue.

But the stunning revelations kept coming. Just days after stepping down, John Ehrlichman told federal investigators that the Ellsberg break-in was not merely the work of Hunt and Liddy, but part of a White House investigation ordered by President Nixon.

"The conduct of the President," argued the defense team, "has compromised the judiciary to the point where a fair trial is impossible, now or in the future."

Ellsberg's and Russo's lawyers again pressed Byrne to throw out the charges. The prosecutor rejected this argument, assuring the court no tainted evidence was needed to prove the defendants' guilt.

Again, Byrne ruled that the trial would continue.

On May 8, Ellsberg stepped out of the courtroom during a recess to pick up a newspaper. There were none available. To keep jurors from being influenced by the sensational Watergate headlines, Judge Byrne had ordered all newspaper boxes removed from the streets around the courthouse.

Ellsberg went into a saloon, where someone recognized him and shouted his name. A man at the bar told Ellsberg that when his trial began, local bookmakers had set the odds at four-to-one in favor of the prosecution. Then, when the story of the Fielding break-in came out, the odds swung to three-to-one in Ellsberg's favor. And now no one was betting against Ellsberg at any odds.

His chances seemed to improve again on May 10, when the FBI revealed the bugging that been done, at Kissinger's orders, on the phones of his assistants. Judge Byrne was told that a listening device on Mort Halperin's phone had picked up several conversations with Daniel Ellsberg. The records of those calls, the FBI explained, had been given to the White House and had since disappeared.

Byrne was livid at this additional evidence of government misconduct. He told the defense team he would listen again to their argument for dismissal.

In the White House, Nixon seethed. "We have the rocky situation where the sonofabitching thief is made a national hero and is going to get off on a mistrial," he told an aide. "And the *New York Times* gets a Pulitzer Prize for stealing documents. . . . They're trying to get at us with *thieves*. What in the name of God have we come to?"

The courtroom was packed on the afternoon of May 11. Extra chairs had been set up along the wall, and a crowd of people unable to get seats stood in the hall, craning their necks to see in. The jury was not present, and Judge Byrne had given reporters permission to fill the jury box.

Ellsberg had on his usual conservative suit, but Russo, as if expecting something special, was sporting a blue shirt with a bright red and white striped tie.

That morning, Judge Byrne had listened to arguments for and against ending the trial. Now, his face flushed, stumbling over his opening sentences, he began to read from a legal pad.

"Commencing on April 26, the government has made an extraordinary series of disclosures regarding the conduct of several governmental agencies regarding the defendants in this case. It is my responsibility to assess the effect of this conduct upon the rights of the defendants."

Byrne summarized the revelations, including details of the Plumbers' activities. "We may have been given only a glimpse of what this special unit did regarding this case," he read, "but what we know is more than disquieting."

This case, said the judge, raised serious issues, issues he would have liked to present to a jury. But the government's transgressions could no longer be ignored.

"Bizarre events have incurably infected the prosecution of this case," Byrne continued.

A rumble of voices came from the spectators' benches.

"I am of the opinion, in the present status of the case, that the only remedy available—"

The voices grew louder. People stood. A few jumped onto the benches.

"—is that this trial be terminated and the defendants' motion for dismissal be granted."

The place erupted in cheers. Daniel Ellsberg reached his arms toward Patricia. She ran into his embrace.

"We did it!" she shouted. "We did it!"

The crowd in the hall shoved the doors open and charged in, everyone clapping and whistling, hugging, and crying. One of Ellsberg's lawyers pulled out a fat cigar and lit up under the "No Smoking" sign on the wall.

Judge Byrne said, "Thank you very much, gentlemen, for your efforts," his voice drowned out by the bedlam in the courtroom. He walked out the door behind his bench.

Reporters started calling out questions to Ellsberg—Was he happy with the ruling?

"Yes, yes," he said, "we're very happy."

"There'll be parties tonight!" Patricia added.

As the prosecutors slipped out, a reporter shouted: "What's your reaction?"

"No comment," said one of the government lawyers.

"Is there an appeal possible?"

"No. It's over. It's dead."

The victory celebration started moving toward the doors, carrying the Ellsbergs along in the flow. An even bigger crowd waited outside on the courtroom steps and on the sidewalk below—more supporters, more reporters aiming microphones and cameras.

There was a tremendous roar as the courthouse doors opened. Daniel and Patricia, arm in arm, stepped into the sunlight.

May 11, 1973. Daniel and Patricia Ellsberg outside the federal courthouse in Los Angeles, after charges against Ellsberg were dismissed.

PAINFUL TRUTH

"AREN'T YOU JUST AS GLAD it's all over, though?" Richard Nixon asked an aide the next day.

"I think it's good to have it over."

"This guy ain't going to be the big hero," Nixon added.

Daniel Ellsberg would be in the spotlight a little longer, though. After a night of celebration, Ellsberg and Russo answered questions at a packed press conference the next morning. Russo told reporters he was going to turn his attention to the effort to impeach President Nixon. Ellsberg agreed with the goal of impeachment. "But I personally have thought enough about Richard Nixon," he said, "and I hope never to think about him again."

Asked his opinion of what the trial had accomplished, Ellsberg gave an answer that applied to everything he'd done—everything he'd risked—since his decision to begin copying the Pentagon Papers.

"Telling the truth," he said, "the very painful truth."

He ended by saying that he was looking forward to resuming a quiet life of researching and writing, with much less attention from the press. "It's been a good relationship we've had over the last several years," he joked, "but it's over now. I'm going back to my wife."

Two weeks later, Everett Alvarez, James Stockdale, and hundreds of former POWs sat in an auditorium at the State Department. They had been invited to Washington, D.C., for a celebratory dinner at the White House later that evening. Nixon welcomed the men, thanked them for their heroic service—and couldn't resist getting in a shot at Daniel Ellsberg.

"And let me say, I think it is time in this country to quit making national heroes out of those who steal secrets and publish them in the newspapers."

The men jumped up and cheered.

The clip made the TV news the next morning. "It's not easy to be fully relaxed," Ellsberg told a journalist, "while watching the president make that kind of attack on you."

But if Nixon had any more plans in store for Ellsberg, he never got the chance to enact them. Dealing with the ever-expanding Watergate scandal was taking all his time. At Senate hearings, John Dean testified that he had talked with the president more than thirty times about details of the cover-up. The assistant who had set up Nixon's secret recording system also testified, describing in detail how it worked. Both Congress and Watergate prosecutors asked Nixon for the tapes. He refused to hand them over.

Not a moment of peace resulted from Nixon's "peace with honor."

The North Vietnamese immediately began moving more troops and weapons from North to South. "If the Communists dare put a foot in our zones, we will kill them," President Thieu told the people of South Vietnam. The violence erupted again, with both sides going on the attack. Communist forces began gaining ground.

Nixon and Kissinger wanted to resume the American bombing. Watergate tied their hands. In June, both the House and Senate approved bills to block all funds for U.S. military activities in Vietnam. Nixon was too politically weak to veto the bill.

"With every passing day, Watergate was circumscribing our freedom of action," Kissinger, the one person unscathed by scandal, later said. "We were losing the ability to make credible commitments, for we could no longer guarantee congressional approval."

Ellsberg, a self-described "Watergate junkie," watched the drama speed toward its climax. He had risked everything to help end the American war in Vietnam. What struck him now was the realization that, in a winding and utterly unpredictable way, he might have accomplished his goal. "Nixon's effort to get me was the foundation of Watergate," Ellsberg reasoned. "And without Watergate, I think Nixon might have been able to keep up the bombing of Vietnam indefinitely."

313

Henry Kissinger tended to agree. "If it were not for domestic difficulties, we would have bombed them," he said in September. "This is now impossible."

★ ★ ★

On the night of August 8, 1974, Richard Nixon sat at his desk in the Oval Office. Around him, crews adjusted lights and cameras, setting up for the president's final broadcast.

The Supreme Court had ruled unanimously that Nixon must turn over his White House recordings. The tape of Nixon and his staff plotting to use the CIA to block the FBI's investigation of the Watergate break-in proved to be the smoking gun prosecutors were looking for. Here was irrefutable proof that Nixon had personally orchestrated the cover-up.

Nixon's approval rating plunged to 26 percent. The House Judiciary Committee voted 27–11 in favor of impeachment. The full House was preparing to vote on impeachment, and Nixon was going to lose. That's when he decided to take a step no American president had ever taken.

A few minutes after nine o'clock, the light on the camera facing Nixon's desk glowed red. He was on the air.

"Good evening," Nixon began. "This is the thirty-seventh time I have spoken to you from this office, where so many decisions have been made that shaped the history of this nation."

He told Americans that his preference was to complete the term to which he'd been elected, but that he longer had enough support to continue. "Therefore," he announced, "I shall resign the presidency effective at noon tomorrow. By taking this action,

August 9, 1974. Nixon addresses his staff before leaving the White House for the last time.

I hope that I will have hastened the start of that process of healing which is so desperately needed in America."

After the speech, Kissinger and Nixon walked together toward the president's living quarters. In a subdued voice, Kissinger said that history would one day rank Nixon among the great presidents.

"That depends, Henry, on who writes the history."

Nixon officially resigned the next day. His vice president, Gerald Ford, was sworn in as president. Nixon thanked the White House staff, and said goodbye to Ford.

"Good luck, Mr. President," Nixon said, shaking Ford's hand.

"Thank you, Mr. President."

Outside, under a low gray sky, Richard, Pat, and Tricia Nixon walked along a red carpet to a waiting helicopter. Nixon climbed the steps, turned, smiled, and raised his arms in a final salute. The

315

blades of the helicopter began to whirl. As they rose into the air, the family looked down at the city. Gerald Ford and the White House staff stood on the lawn, still waving.

Nixon leaned back in his seat and closed his eyes.

THE WHITE HOUSE
WASHINGTON

August 9, 1974

Dear Mr. Secretary:

I hereby resign the Office of President of the United States.

Sincerely,

Richard Nixon

11:35 AM

The Honorable Henry A. Kissinger
The Secretary of State
Washington, D. C. 20520

HK

Richard Nixon's letter resigning the presidency of the United States.

★ ★ ★

On the morning of April 29, 1975, Philip Caputo was awakened by the sounds of falling bombs. Ten years before, Caputo had been one of the first marines to see combat in Vietnam. Now thirty-three, with a wife and two sons, he was back in Vietnam, this time as a journalist, covering the final battle for Saigon. It would all be over soon, that much was clear.

North Vietnamese units were shelling the city from just two miles away. Fires raged and the roads out of Saigon were jammed with refugees and water buffaloes pulling overloaded carts and crying children searching for parents and retreating South Vietnamese soldiers.

There was another explosion. The walls of Caputo's hotel room trembled.

"They've just passed the word," announced a fellow reporter, his ear to a radio. "That's it. It's one-hundred percent evacuation. It's bye-bye everybody."

Anticipating the worst, American authorities had set up evacuation points for its citizens. Caputo moved quickly through the chaotic streets to one of these spots and crowded onto one of several waiting buses, packing in with about seventy other journalists and U.S. embassy officials. With shells exploding all around, the bus sped to a military airbase and stopped in front of a complex that had once been General Westmoreland's headquarters. A bomb slammed into the runway as they ran for the nearest building.

Marine transport helicopters swooped down, landing on the nearby tennis courts.

"Let's go!" a sergeant hollered, "Drop all your luggage. No room for that. Move! Move! Move!"

Caputo let his suitcase fall and ran onto the tennis courts. Crouching marines, their machine guns aimed outward, guarded the landing zone as about sixty people shoved onto each helicopter. Caputo got a spot and felt the chopper climbing quickly to get above the range of enemy rockets. "My mind shot back a decade," he later recalled, "to that day we had marched into Vietnam, swaggering, confident, and full of idealism."

A total of 58,193 Americans died in Vietnam. Over 300,000 were wounded. The number of Vietnamese soldiers and civilians killed

U.S. personnel leave Saigon under North Vietnamese fire.

since 1964 was estimated to be at least two million. The United States had dropped a total of eight million tons of bombs on Vietnam, Laos, and Cambodia—more than three times the total dropped by American planes during World War II. Thousands of unexploded bombs and mines would continue to kill and maim civilians in the years ahead.

Lyndon Johnson said, "I'm not going to be the first American president to lose a war."

Richard Nixon said, "I will not be the first president of the United States to lose a war."

In a way, each accomplished his goal. On April 30, 1975, when North Vietnamese troops crashed through the gates of the presidential palace in Saigon and raised their flag above the city, Lyndon Johnson lay in a Texas cemetery. Nixon was home in California, in disgrace. It fell to Gerald Ford to inform the American people that the country had just lost its first war.

"The evacuation has been completed," Ford told the nation. "This action closes a chapter in the American experience."

EPILOGUE
HISTORY REPEATS

The world has changed in many ways since Daniel Ellsberg gave the Pentagon Papers to the *New York Times* in 1971. The Cold War is over, and fear of communist expansion has been replaced by the menace of international terrorism. Relations between the United States and Vietnam are now friendly. The documents that took Ellsberg weeks to photocopy would fill a fraction of the space on a ten-dollar flash drive.

But big questions raised by Ellsberg's story are alive and well. Governments must keep some information secret in order to function—but how much secrecy is too much? When, if ever, are citizens justified in leaking information the government has deemed secret? Suppose a citizen leaks information that exposes government wrongdoing, but breaks the law in doing so. Should that person be dragged into court or hailed as a hero?

In January 2013, an American documentary filmmaker named

As Snowden anticipated, American law enforcement agencies were eager to arrest the leaker and haul him home to face charges of violating the Espionage Act. The press started calling him "the most wanted man in the world." Snowden jumped on a plane to Moscow and was granted asylum by the Russian government, putting him out of reach of U.S. authorities.

In the United States, debate raged. Was Snowden a hero for blowing the whistle on a perilous threat to the basic liberties guaranteed to all Americans? Was he a villain for stealing secrets and undermining the government's ability to protect the public?

President Barak Obama's position was clear: he considered Snowden a dangerous criminal. "If any individual who objects to government policy can take it in their own hands to publicly disclose classified information," Obama charged, "then we will not be able to keep our people safe, or conduct foreign policy." Secretary of State John Kerry, who more than forty years before had been the first Vietnam War veteran to testify before Congress against the war, put it more bluntly. "Edward Snowden is a coward, he is a traitor, and he has betrayed his country."

To many Americans, this was starting to sound very familiar.

"What Edward Snowden did wasn't the first time an American has leaked secret government data," CNN news anchor Don Lemon told his audience on June 9, 2013. Forty-two years earlier, Lemon explained, another government insider had set off a firestorm by leaking secret documents to the press. "Daniel Ellsberg joins me now live from Berkeley, California."

Ellsberg appeared on the screen. His hair was white, his face lined, his blue eyes sharp and focused. At the end of his trial four

323

decades earlier, he had told reporters he intended to live a fairly quiet life from that point on—quiet, at least, in comparison to the tumultuous Pentagon Papers years. He had done that. He and Patricia had settled in Berkeley and worked together in the peace and anti-nuclear weapons movements. By Ellsberg's own calculations, he was arrested at protests at least twenty-five times. At eighty-two, he was as engaged in politics and as opinionated as ever.

Lemon began by asking Ellsberg's opinion of Snowden.

"I think he's done an enormous service," Ellsberg said, "incalculable service—it can't be overestimated—to this democracy."

"You say you like what he has done. But he has broken the law."

"I would have done just what he has done," Ellsberg shot back. "I would have broken that law."

Fighting high winds, sabotage, and engine failure, a group of trailblazing pilots soar to new heights in the first women's air race across America.

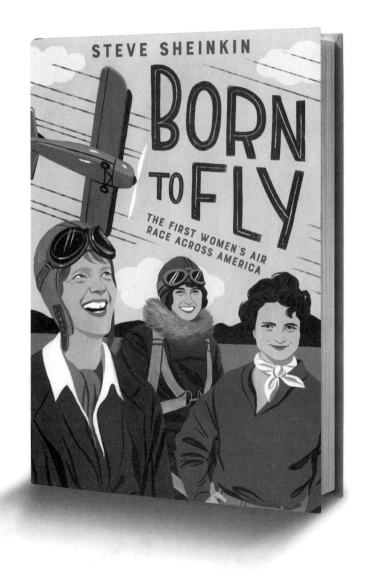

TURN THE PAGE FOR A SNEAK PEEK . . .

BORN TO FLY

They were the kinds of kids who jumped off the roofs of buildings.

Louise McPhetridge did it when she was just seven—climbed to the roof of her family's barn in Bentonville, Arkansas, opened a giant umbrella, and leapt. Not the best idea, maybe, but she *did* aim for a haystack, and wasn't badly hurt.

And besides, she had a perfectly good reason. She *knew* she was born to fly.

Ruth Elder balanced on top of a shed in Anniston, Alabama. She was about twelve. She called to her pony. It came charging. Anxious girls and boys gazed up as Ruth bent her knees, waited, waited—and sprang from the shed, landing with a smack on the back of the galloping horse.

Marvel Crosson was thirteen when she attempted her first flight. She and her younger brother, Joe, had been walking home from school that day in Sterling, Colorado, when they noticed people streaming into the county fairgrounds. Marvel and Joe had no money to get in. They found a hole in the fairground fence and peeked through.

There on the grass, right in front of their eyes, was a flying machine. Or was it?

This was 1913, just ten years after the Wright brothers made the world's first powered flight. Airplanes were still very much a work in progress. Most Americans had never even seen one. The thing on the field looked like a chair with flimsy fly's wings. Behind the seat was a chugging motor and a giant fan.

A man sat in the seat. He shouted something. The motor roared louder. The fan blades spun. The rickety contraption bounced down the field, gaining speed, and then, somehow, *incredibly*, defied gravity and lifted into the air. Marvel had to remind herself to breathe.

As the plane flew low buzzing circles over the crowd, Joe, who was ten, started jumping up and down and hollering, "I'm going to be an aviator! I'm going to be an aviator!"

With its propeller behind the pilot's seat, this early aircraft design was called a "pusher." And yes, it actually took off.

Marvel didn't shout or jump. She didn't say a word. She just quietly made a decision—flying was the only thing she would ever want to do.

Starting now.

Back at the family home, she grabbed an umbrella—not quite wings, but the closest thing she could find—and she and Joe scrambled to the roof of the garage. She opened the umbrella and inched to the edge of the roof and was about to take off when her mother sprinted out of the house, yelping and waving her arms.

The flight was canceled. Or, to be more precise, postponed.

Amelia Earhart didn't jump off a roof. Not exactly.

When she was about eight, she realized the top of the shed in the yard of her family's Kansas City, Kansas, home was the perfect starting spot for a roller coaster. She and her sister, Muriel—Amelia called her Pidge—hammered two-by-fours into tracks and leaned the ride against the roof. They greased the tracks with lard from the icebox and found a wooden crate to use as a car.

Amelia insisted on going first. She carried the crate to the roof and crammed herself in, knees against chest. Pidge and their friend Ralphie stood on the top rung of a ladder, holding the car in place.

"Let me go!"

The crate shot forward, much faster than expected. The track broke with a thunderous *crack*, catapulting car and rider into the air. Amelia soared across the yard, slammed into the grass, and tumbled to a stop.

Alarmed adults ran out from nearby houses.

Amelia leaped up, her dress torn, bleeding from her lip, eyes flaming with joy.

"Oh Pidge," she shouted, "it's just like flying!"

Amelia Earhart may as well have been speaking for all the pilots in this story. The goal was always to get in the air.

After thousands of years of gazing with envy at birds in the sky, humans could suddenly climb into a plane and fly. This is a story about young women who wanted in on the action. They were in a hurry to know how planes worked and to learn how to fly them. They were eager to test themselves against each other, to push planes faster and higher, to smash each other's records in the sky. These are the pilots who would compete in the spectacular Women's Air Derby of 1929, the first women's cross-country air race—and the most controversial air race the country had ever seen.

Air racing was among America's most popular sports in the 1920s, and cross-country races were the Super Bowls of their time. Aviation was new and incredibly dangerous, so when daring pilots set out to race unreliable planes over mountains and across deserts, it made for thrilling drama. These multi-day races featured fierce rivalries, back-and-forth battles for the lead, violent storms, and mechanical failures in the air. There were *always* crashes in these races. In almost every race, at least one pilot was killed.

The first Women's Air Derby would be no exception.

The twenty pilots who would meet in the derby came from all over the country, each with her own story. But they had a lot in common. Besides jumping off roofs.

All were born in the last few years of the nineteenth century or the first few years of the twentieth. They were girls who loved tools and mechanical things, rough sports and risky adventures. They were the kinds of kids who got called "daredevils" and "tomboys." Ruth Elder was typical of the group. She didn't mind being different. She *did* mind that her school wouldn't let her try out for football.

When Marvel Crosson's parents spent their life savings on a new automobile, Marvel took the entire engine apart. She wanted to figure out how it worked—and make it go faster. Mr. Crosson walked into the garage and was horrified to find his children, Marvel and Joe, sitting on the floor surrounded by tiny pieces of his prized possession. The kids put the car back together. It wasn't any faster, but it ran.

At age eleven, four years after her umbrella flight, Louise McPhetridge upgraded to a hot-air balloon. She and some boys from the neighborhood cut canvas from a porch awning, tied it with ropes into the shape of a big balloon, and heated the air inside with oil lamps.

It was time to fly. The boys were nervous.

"It's not so awful big," a kid named Richard said of their invention. "We better let Lou go up."

Lou wouldn't have it any other way. She climbed onto the roof of a shed with the entire contraption strapped to her back and was all set for a test flight when Richard's mother looked out an upstairs window of her house and saw a girl with an oddly bloated backpack about to leap into the sky.

It was another canceled flight.

The winter after her roller-coaster experiment, Amelia Earhart got a new sled. And a stern warning: The correct way for girls to ride a sled was sitting up. Lying on your belly was faster, but not ladylike.

Amelia promptly climbed a steep and icy street, dropped belly-down onto her sled, and pushed off.

She was flying down the hill when a horse pulling a loaded cart stepped out from a side street and stood directly in her path. There was no time to turn, barely time to scream, before the sled sped *between* the horse's front and back legs, *under* its massive belly, and on down the street.

Lucky she hadn't been sitting up like a good girl. To Amelia, that was the lesson.

Her grandmother took a different view. "You don't realize," she lectured, "that when I was a small girl, I did nothing more strenuous than roll my hoop in the public square."

Amelia made an effort. For a few days, she walked calmly through her grandmother's front gate, instead of jumping over the fence.

Too boring. She went back to jumping.

As she'd later explain, "Some elders have to be shocked for everyone's good now and then."

That's something else these future fliers had in common—they were constantly being told to behave more like "proper girls." They were the kinds of kids who defied the command and went right on being themselves.

At her family's home in Southern California, Florence Lowe, another future derby pilot, rode horses when she was supposed to be inside sipping tea. She tracked mud and manure through the formal living room, then used her frilly dresses to clean her riding boots. At school, she challenged the boys to spitting contests. Horrified, the Lowes shipped their daughter to a series of boarding schools, each stricter than the last, but harsh discipline and stiff uniforms proved no match for Florence. One day she brought her horse, Dobbins, into her dorm room. The principal called her to his office and demanded an explanation.

"Poor Dobbins," she said with a straight face, "he must have been so lonesome that he came upstairs to look for me."

They were kids who fell in love with planes at first sight. They were girls who were told that flying was not for them.

Evelyn Trout's first vision of flight was similar to Marvel's. Evelyn—known to friends as Bobbi—was twelve, walking home from school in Hamilton, Canada, where she was staying with relatives. She heard the sound of an engine. An engine in the sky. The grinding noise got louder and louder. She looked up, shading her eyes with her hand, and there it was.

"An airplane!"

She watched, frozen in place, until the plane slipped over the trees and out of sight. Bobbi sprinted home. She had to tell *someone*. She found her aunt Edna in the basement, arms full of jars of preserved vegetables.

"I loved school," Amelia Earhart recalled, "though I never qualified as teacher's pet."

Marvel Crosson—looking ready to leap.

Bobbi Trout (second from left) with high school friends.

Florence Lowe, teen rebel.

Never one to take it slow, Louise McPhetridge left home for college at sixteen.

"Someday I'll be up there!" Bobbi whooped. "Someday I'm going to fly an airplane!"

Aunt Edna smiled at her niece. The kid had always marched to her own drummer. At five years old, she'd announced she was done with dolls and wanted tools instead for Christmas. But flying airplanes? That was taking it too far.

Edna said, "Young ladies of good families do not fly airplanes."

All the pilots in this story heard some version of that lecture.

These girls grew up at a time when life for women in the United States was very different from today. Until 1920, when the pilots were kids or teens, women in most states were not even allowed to *vote*. That finally changed with the ratification of the Nineteenth Amendment to the Constitution—but opportunities for American women were still severely limited.

In high school, Amelia Earhart started collecting articles about women working in fields she found interesting: medicine, law, engineering, film. These jobs were so completely dominated by men, the few women who broke into them made the news. As Amelia knew, women who wanted careers were expected to stick to traditionally female fields: teaching, nursing, social work. Important work, but what if that wasn't what you wanted to do? What if your heart was set on the cutting-edge world of aviation?

The generations of women who had fought for and won the right to vote had faced resentment, angry opposition, even the threat of physical harm. This harsh and very recent history was painfully clear to the pioneering pilots of the Women's Air Derby.

"In those days," Marvel Crosson later explained, "flying was regarded as dangerous for men and impossible for women."

RACING TO THE SKY

Marvel. That was her real name.

Her mother, Elizabeth Crosson, had read a novel called *Marvel* while pregnant and liked the sound of the name. And maybe she knew, when she first saw her baby girl, that the kid would live up to it.

An athletic teen, with bright eyes and curly black hair, Marvel devoured every book and article she could find on aviation. She talked endlessly about flying, about getting her own plane one day. But she'd never actually been on a flight.

In the summer of 1919, after she graduated high school, Marvel and her family set off on a road trip to California. In San Diego, she and Joe dropped their parents off at yet another historical site, then slipped away to *their* idea of a tourist attraction—Dutch Flats airfield.

It was a glimpse of heaven.

"There were planes everywhere!" Marvel remembered. "Pilots going about their business just as though it was the most natural thing in the world."

A pilot walked up and offered them a ride for five dollars each.

"We've only got two-fifty," Marvel said.

They were in luck. Business was slow.

"Hop in," the man said. "Both of you."

It was a little, open-cockpit plane with two seats, one behind the other. The pilot jumped into the back seat. Marvel and Joe put on borrowed goggles and crammed into the front. The pilot gunned the engine, darted down the grass airstrip, and rose into the air so quickly Marvel's chin slammed into her chest.

Marvel, like so many of the pilots in this story, would later *try* to describe the thrill of her first flight, the full-body sensation of soaring in an open cockpit, the pure freedom of it, the blast of air in her face, the views of earth from above, the music of the vibrating metal wires between the wings.

The plane circled one thousand feet above the field for ten minutes. To Marvel, it was ten seconds.

Back on the ground, Marvel and Joe walked in a daze to the car. They sat a long while in silence.

Finally, Joe turned to his sister and said what she'd already been thinking.

"Marvel, that settles it. We've got to have a plane!"

There were some practical problems with the plan. First, planes were expensive. She and Joe had no money. That was solvable. They'd get jobs and save. It would just take time.

Also, the family lived in rural Colorado. There were no airfields nearby. Nowhere to take flying lessons. The solution, they decided, was to persuade their parents to move with them to sunny San Diego. All the way home, and for a solid year after, they gave their parents what Marvel called "the California treatment." It eventually worked.

Marvel got a job in a camera store in San Diego. Joe found work as a car mechanic. They saved every penny. One day, when Marvel was getting ready to leave for work, Joe came rushing in. He had big news but wouldn't say what it was, only that she had to take the afternoon off and come with him.

He explained as they sped across town—a customer at his garage had been talking about flying. He said he'd heard of an airplane for sale, a little navy trainer left over from World War I. The guy who'd owned it had died in a crash. In a different plane, that is.

Joe parked at a waterfront warehouse, and they jumped out. The man at the garage had been right. There was an airplane. Sort of. Technically, there was a stack of wooden crates with airplane parts packed inside.

After a bit of bargaining, the owner's widow agreed to sell for $150—a little over $2,000 in today's money. Together, Marvel and Joe had just enough. They wedged the crates into their car, raced home, hauled everything to the yard behind their house, and started to put their airplane together.

"When Mother and Father saw what we had done, there was quite a revolution," Marvel later recalled. "In addition to messing up the backyard, they were sure that we both were planning to get killed."

By this point, though, the Crosson parents had abandoned hope that their children would lose interest in flying. Marvel knew everything would be okay when she overheard her dad say to her mom, "Well, if anything is going to happen to those kids, it'll happen anyhow. Let them alone—they're happy!"

★

WORKS CITED

For anyone researching a book attempting to cover Daniel Ellsberg, the Pentagon Papers, the Vietnam War, and Watergate, there is a nearly endless supply of sources to read, to watch, and to listen to. Adding to the wealth of published material is the fact that many of the participants are still alive. I was extremely fortunate to have the opportunity to speak several times with Daniel Ellsberg, as well as with Patricia Ellsberg and other key figures. Below are the sources used for the quotations, stories, and facts used in this book. Many of the sources—most tantalizingly the Johnson and Nixon White House recordings—are available to anyone online.

Books and Magazines

Alvarez, Everett, Jr. and Anthony S. Pitch. *Chained Eagle: The True Heroic Story of Eight and One Half Years as a POW by the First American Shot down over North Vietnam*. New York: Donald I. Fine, Inc., 1989.

Ambrose, Stephen E. *Nixon: The Triumph of a Politician, 1962–1972*. New York: Simon and Schuster, 1989.

Appy, Christian G. *Patriots: The Vietnam War Remembered from All Sides*. New York: Viking, 2003.

Arnold, Martin. "Daniel Ellsberg at the Trial of Anthony J. Russo." *Esquire*, January 1974.

Bagdikian, Ben H. *Double Vision: Reflections on My Heritage, Life, and Profession*. Boston: Beacon Press, 1995.

Bamford, James. "The Most Wanted Man in the World." *Wired*, August 2014.

Bates, Milton J., ed. *Reporting Vietnam: American Journalism 1959–1975*. New York: Library of America, 1998.

Berman, Larry. *No Peace, No Honor: Nixon, Kissinger, and Betrayal in Vietnam*. New York: The Free Press, 2001.

Beschloss, Michael. *Reaching for Glory: Lyndon Johnson's Secret White House Tapes, 1964–1965*. New York: Simon & Schuster, 2001.

Beschloss, Michael. *Taking Charge: The Johnson White House Tapes, 1963–1964*. New York: Simon & Schuster, 1997.

Caputo, Philip. *A Rumor of War.* New York: Henry Holt and Company, 1977.

Caputo, Philip. *10,000 Days of Thunder: A History of the Vietnam War.* New York: Atheneum Books for Young Readers, 2005.

Caputo, Philip. *13 Seconds: A Look Back at the Kent State Shootings.* New York: Chamberlain Bros., 2005.

Cassidy, John. "Why Edward Snowden Is a Hero." *The New Yorker,* June 10, 2013.

Chanoff, David and Doan Van Toai. *Vietnam: A Portrait of Its People at War.* London: I. B. Tauris & Co., 2009.

Chennault, Anna. *The Education of Anna.* New York: Times Books, 1980.

Cooper, Charles. *Cheers and Tears: A Marine's Story of Combat in Peace and War.* Reno, NV: Wesley Press, 2006.

Dallek, Robert. *Flawed Giant: Lyndon Johnson and His Times, 1961–1973.* New York: Oxford University Press, 1998.

Dallek, Robert. *Lyndon B. Johnson: Portrait of a President.* New York: Oxford University Press, 2004.

Dallek, Robert. *Nixon and Kissinger: Partners in Power.* New York: HarperCollins Publishers, 2007.

Doyle, Edward, Samuel Lipsman, and the editors of Boston Publishing Company. *The Vietnam Experience: Setting the Stage.* Boston: Boston Publishing Company, 1981.

Duiker, William J. *Ho Chi Mihn.* New York: Hyperion, 2000.

Edmondson, Madeleine and Alden Duer Cohen. *The Women of Watergate.* New York: Stein and Day, 1975.

Ehrlichman, John. *Witness to Power: The Nixon Years.* New York: Simon and Schuster, 1982.

Ellsberg, Daniel. *Papers on the War.* New York: Simon and Schuster, 1972.

Ellsberg, Daniel. *Risk, Ambiguity, and Decision.* Ph.D. thesis, 1961.

Ellsberg, Daniel. *Secrets: A Memoir of Vietnam and the Pentagon Papers.* New York: Viking, 2002.

Esper, George and the Associated Press. *The Eyewitness History of the Vietnam War, 1961–1975.* New York: Ballantine Books, 1983.

Fall, Bernard, B., ed. *Ho Chi Minh: On Revolution: Selected Writings, 1920–1966.* New York: Frederick A. Praeger Publishers, 1967.

Foley, Michael S. *Confronting the War Machine.* Chapel Hill: University of North Carolina Press, 2003.

Frankel, Max. *The Times of My Life and My Life with* The Times. New York: Random House, 1999.

Gibbons, William. *The U.S. Government and the Vietnam War, Vol. 2.* Prepared for the U.S. Senate Committee on Foreign Relations by the Congressional Research Service. Washington, D.C.: U.S. Government Printing Office, 1985.

Gilbert, Marc Jason and William Head. *The Tet Offensive.* Westport, CT: Praeger, 1996.

Goodale, James C. *Fighting for the Press: The Inside Story of the Pentagon Papers and Other Battles.* New York: CUNY Journalism Press, 2013.

Goulden, Joseph C. *Truth Is the First Casualty: The Gulf of Tonkin Affair—Illusion and Reality.* Chicago: Rand McNally & Company, 1969.

Halberstam, David. *The Best and the Brightest.* New York: Ballantine Books, 1969.

Haldeman, H. R. *The Ends of Power.* New York: Times Books, 1978.

Haldeman, H. R. *The Haldeman Diaries: Inside the Nixon White House.* New York: G. P. Putnam's Sons, 1994.

Harding, Luke. *The Snowden Files: The Inside Story of the World's Most Wanted Man.* New York: Vintage Books, 2014.

Hendrickson, Paul. *The Living and the Dead: Robert McNamara and Five Lives of a Lost War.* New York: Vintage Books, 1997.

Herring, George C., ed. *The Pentagon Papers: Abridged Version.* New York: McGraw-Hill, 1993.

Hersh, Seymour M. *The Price of Power: Kissinger in the Nixon White House.* New York: Summit Books, 1983.

Hunt, Howard E. *Undercover: Memoirs of an American Secret Agent.* New York: G. P. Putnam's Sons, 1974.

Hunt, Michael H. *Lyndon Johnson's War: America's Cold War Crusade in Vietnam, 1945–1968.* New York: Hill and Wang, 1996.

Isaacson, Walter. *Kissinger: A Biography.* New York: Simon & Schuster, 1992.

Johnson, Claudia T. *Lady Bird Johnson, A White House Diary.* New York: Holt, Rinehart and Winston, 1970.

Johnson, Lyndon Baines. *The Vantage Point: Perspectives on the Presidency, 1963–1969.* New York: Holt, Rinehart and Winston, 1971.

Kahin, George. *Intervention: How America Became Involved in Vietnam.* New York: Alfred A. Knopf, 1986.

Karnow, Stanley. *Vietnam: A History.* New York: Penguin Books, 1983.

Kearns, Doris. *Lyndon Johnson & the American Dream.* New York: Harper & Row Publishers, 1976.

Kesby, Rebecca. "North Vietnam, 1972: The Christmas Bombing of Hanoi." *BBC News* magazine, December 14, 2012.

Kissinger, Henry. *Ending the Vietnam War.* New York: Simon & Schuster, 2003.

Krogh, Egil. "Bud, with Matthew Krogh." *Integrity: Good People, Bad Choices and Life Lessons from the White House.* New York: Public Affairs, 2007.

Kutler, Stanley. I., ed. *Abuse of Power: The New Nixon Tapes.* New York: The Free Press, 1997.

Liddy, G. Gordon. *Will: The Autobiography of G. Gordon Liddy.* New York: St. Martin's Press, 1980.

Logevall, Fredrik. *Choosing War: The Lost Chance for Peace and the Escalation of War in Vietnam.* Berkeley: University of California Press, 1999.

McCain, John, with Mark Salter. *Faith of My Fathers: A Family Memoir.* New York: Random House, 1999.

McGinniss, Joe. "The Ordeal of Daniel Ellsberg." *Playboy,* October, 1972.

McMaster, H. R. *Dereliction of Duty: Lyndon Johnson, Robert McNamara, the Joint Chiefs of Staff, and the Lies that Led to Vietnam.* New York: HarperCollins, 1997.

Mann, Robert. *A Grand Delusion: America's Descent into Vietnam.* New York: Basic Books, 2001.

Moise, Edwin E. *Tonkin Gulf and the Escalation of the Vietnam War.* Chapel Hill: University of North Carolina Press, 1996.

Moran, Jordan. "The First Domino: Nixon and the Pentagon Papers." Presidential Recordings Program, Miller Center of Public Affairs, University of Virginia.

Moskin, Robert. "Ellsberg Talks." *Look,* October 5, 1971, 31–42.

Nixon, Richard M. *RN: the Memoirs of Richard Nixon.* New York: Simon & Schuster, 1978.

Oberdorfer, Dan. *Tet: The Story of a Battle and Its Historic Aftermath.* Garden City, NY: Doubleday & Company, 1971.

Patti, Archimedes L. A. *Why Viet Nam? Prelude to America's Albatross.* Berkeley: University of California Press, 1980.

Perry, Mark. *Four Stars.* Boston: Houghton Mifflin Company, 1989.

Prados, John. *The White House Tapes: Eavesdropping on the President.* New York: The New Press, 2003.

Prados, John and Margaret Pratt Porter, eds. *Inside the Pentagon Papers.* Lawrence: University of Kansas Press, 2004.

Reeves, Richard. *President Nixon: Alone in the White House.* New York: Simon & Schuster, 2001.

Reporting Vietnam: American Journalism, 1959–1975. Introduction by Ward Just. New York: The Library of America, 1998.

Risner, Robinson. *The Passing of the Night: My Seven Years as a Prisoner of the North Vietnamese.* New York: Random House, 1973.

"Robert S. McNamara, Architect of a Futile War, Dies at 93," *New York Times*, July 6, 2009.

Rudenstine, David. *The Day the Presses Stopped: A History of the Pentagon Papers Case*. Berkeley: University of California Press, 1996.

Russo, Anthony. "Inside the RAND Corporation and Out: My Story." *Ramparts*, April 1972, 45–55.

Salisbury, Harrison E. *Behind the Lines-Hanoi: December 23, 1966–January 7, 1967*. New York: Harper & Row Publishers, 1967.

Salisbury, Harrison E. *Without Fear or Favor: The New York Times and Its Times*. New York: Times Books, 1980.

Schell, Jonathan. *The Military Half: An Account of Destruction in Quang Ngai and Quang Tin*. New York: Vintage Books, 1968.

Schrag, Peter. *Test of Loyalty: Daniel Ellsberg and the Rituals of Secret Government*. New York: Simon & Schuster, 1974.

Sheehan, Neil. *A Bright Shining Lie: John Paul Vann and America in Vietnam*. New York: Random House, 1988.

Sheehan, Neil, Hedrick Smith, E. W. Kenworthy, and Fox Butterfield. *The Pentagon Papers: The Secret History of the Vietnam War as Published by the New York Times*. New York: Bantam Books, 1971.

Stockdale, Jim and Sybil. *In Love and War: The Story of a Family's Ordeal and Sacrifice during the Vietnam Years*. New York: Harper & Row Publishers, 1984.

Summers, Anthony. *The Arrogance of Power: The Secret World of Richard Nixon*. New York: Viking, 2000.

"The Suspect: A Hawk Who Turned Dove," *Newsweek*, June 28, 1971.

Taylor, David. "The Lyndon Johnson Tapes: Richard Nixon's 'Treason.'" *BBC News* magazine, March 22, 2013.

Toobin, Jeffrey. "Edward Snowden Is No Hero," *The New Yorker*, June 10, 2013.

Turner, Karen Gottschang with Phan Thanh Hao. *Even the Women Must Fight: Memories of War from North Vietnam*. New York: John Wiley & Sons, 1998.

Ungar, Sanford. *The Papers and the Papers: An Account of the Legal and Political Battle over the Pentagon Papers*. New York: Columbia University Press, 1972.

Weisberg Stuart E. *Barney Frank: The Story of America's Only Left-handed, Gay, Jewish Congressman*. Amherst, MA: University of Massachusetts Press, 2009.

Wells, Tom. *The War Within: America's Battle over Vietnam*. Berkeley: University of California Press, 1994.

Wells, Tom. *Wild Man: The Life and Times of Daniel Ellsberg*. New York: Palgrave, 2001.

Wenner, Jann. *The Rolling Stone Interview: Dan Ellsberg*. San Francisco, CA: *Rolling Stone*, 1973.

Westmoreland, General William C. *A Soldier Reports*. Garden City, NY: Doubleday & Company, Inc., 1976.

Willbanks, James H. *The Tet Offensive: A Concise History*. New York: Columbia University Press, 2007.

Woods, Randall B. *LBJ: Architect of American Ambition*. New York: The Free Press, 2006.

Zinn, Howard. *A People's History of the United States, 1492–Present, 25th Anniversary Edition*. New York: HarperCollins, 1999.

Newspapers

"2 Defendants Say Trial Told 'Painful Truth,'" *New York Times*, May 13, 1973.

"3 Top Nixon Aides, Kleindienst Out; President Accepts Full Responsibility," *Washington Post*, May 1, 1973.

"After the Pentagon Papers: A Month in the New Life of Daniel Ellsberg," *New York Times*, December 12, 1971.

"Air of Expectancy, Then Tears, Shouts, Embraces," *New York Times*, May 12, 1973.

"And One Copy for Ellsberg," *Washington Post*, September 28, 1971.

"Berrigan, Baez, Ellsberg Speak," *Los Angeles Times*, January 8, 1973.

"Champagne Party: 'I'm So Happy for You,' Juror Tells Ellsberg," *Los Angeles Times*, May 13, 1973.

"Court Step Likely," *New York Times*, June 15, 1971.

"Cuban Says He and Two Others Broke into Psychiatrist's Office," *New York Times*, May 10, 1973.

"Daniel Ellsberg of M.I.T. Marries Patricia Marx," *New York Times*, August 9, 1971.

"Daniel Ellsberg's Closest Friend: His Wife, Patricia," *New York Times*, August 30, 1972.

"Daniel Ellsberg's Talk with Walter Cronkite," *Boston Globe*, June 24, 1971.

"Defense Opens Its Case at the Pentagon Papers Trial," *New York Times*, February 28, 1973.

"Defense Secretary, Architect of U.S. Involvement in Vietnam Robert McNamara Dies," *Washington Post*, July 7, 2009.

"Edward Snowden, NSA Files Source: 'If They Want to Get You, in Time They Will,'" *The Guardian*, June 9, 2013.

"Edward Snowden: The Whistleblower behind the NSA Surveillance Revelations," *The Guardian*, June 9, 2013.

"Ehrlichman Tied to Ellsberg Case," *New York Times*, May 2, 1973.

"Ellsberg Admits Leak, Freed on Bond," *Boston Globe*, June 29, 1971.

"Ellsberg Begins Testimony in L.A. Pentagon Papers Trial," *Los Angeles Times*, April 11, 1973.

"Ellsberg Case: Defendants Freed, Government Convicted," *New York Times*, May 13, 1973.

"Ellsberg Case Dismissed," *Los Angeles Times*, May 11, 1973.

"Ellsberg Denies Charges," *New York Times*, December 31, 1971.

"Ellsberg Denies Guilt, Will Fight," *New York Times*, August 17, 1971.

"Ellsberg Enters Plea of Innocent," *Boston Globe*, August 17, 1971.

"Ellsberg First Person to Face Trial for News Leak," *Boston Globe*, June 29, 1971.

"Ellsberg Found a Mood 'Almost of Conspiracy' in Government," *Boston Globe*, June 20, 1971.

"Ellsberg: From Hawk to Dove," *New York Times*, June 27, 1971.

"Ellsberg: How He Prepped to Go Public," *Boston Globe*, July 4, 1971.

"Ellsberg Judge Dismisses Counts," *Washington Post*, May 12, 1973.

"Ellsberg Jury Completed in Dramatic Court Scene," *New York Times*, January 13, 1973.

"Ellsberg Says War Papers Taught Him: Distrust Authority," *Boston Globe*, October 14, 1971.

"Ellsberg Talks with Cavett," *Boston Globe*, July 22, 1971.

"Ellsberg Tells of Shift in Views," *New York Times*, April 12, 1973.

"Ellsberg Tells Why His Views Changed," *Los Angeles Times*, April 12, 1973.

"Ellsberg: The Case for the Defense," *New York Times*, April 15, 1973.

"Ellsberg Trial, All Its Ironies Intact, Grinds Toward a Beginning," *Boston Globe*, June 11, 1972.

"Ex-Pentagon Aide Phones Message," *New York Times*, June 19, 1971.

"Ex-POWs Start the Transition," *Los Angeles Times*, February 19, 1973.

"FBI Hunting Ellsberg Clues," *Boston Globe*, July 25, 1971.

"FBI Report of Ellsberg Bugging Disrupts Trial," *Los Angeles Times*, May 10, 1973.

"Gravel Read, Stopped, Dried His Tears," *Washington Star*, July 1, 1971.

"How Laura Poitras Helped Snowden Spill His Secrets," *New York Times Magazine*, August 13, 2013.

"Judge in Pentagon Papers Trial," *New York Times*, January 17, 1973.

"Judge Rules Ellsberg Trial Must Continue," *Los Angeles Times*, May 1, 1973.

"Kin Identify U.S. Pilot in N. Viet Nam Film," *Boston Globe*, November 12, 1964.

"Krogh Quits, Claims Guilt in Burglary of Ellsberg's Doctor," *Los Angeles Times*, May 9, 1973.

"Last Two Guilty in Watergate Plot," *Washington Post*, January 31, 1973.

"New Trial Barred," *New York Times*, May 12, 1973.

"NSA Leaker Snowden Made the Right Call," *Washington Post*, July 7, 2013.

"Only Few Memorable Moments Enliven Pattern of Tedium at the Ellsberg Trial," *New York Times*, February 20, 1973.

"Secret Papers Figure Feted by U.S. Workers," *Washington Post*, September 24, 1971.

"Senators in Shouting Match over Ellsberg Testimony," *Washington Post*, May 17, 1973.

"Supreme Court, 6–3, Upholds Newspapers on Publication of Pentagon Report," *New York Times*, July 1, 1971.

"The Busy Life of Daniel Ellsberg," *Boston Globe*, December 19, 1971.

"The Case for the Prosecution," *New York Times*, February 25, 1973.

"The Plumbers," *New York Times*, July 22, 1973.

"The World of the Ellsberg Trial," *New York Times*, February 5, 1973.

"This Was the Right Way to End It, Ellsberg Says," *Washington Post*, May 12, 1973.

"Trial Will Go On," *New York Times*, April 12, 1973.

"Tricia Nixon Takes Vows in Garden at White House," *New York Times*, June 13, 1971.

"U.S. Sees Ellsberg Issue as Simple Case of Theft," *New York Times*, January 18, 1973.

"Vietnam Archive: Study Tells How Johnson Secretly Opened Way to Ground War," *New York Times*, June 15, 1971.

Websites, Films, Recordings, and Other Sources

"Conversations with History: Daniel Ellsberg." University of California Television. University of California Television (UCTV).

Hearts and Minds, documentary film by Peter Davis, 1974.

Hughes, Ken. "A Rough Guide to Richard Nixon's Conspiracy Theories," Miller Center of Public Affairs, University of Virginia. Online exhibit at millercenter.org/presidentialclassroom/exhibits/a-rough-guide-to-richard-nixons-conspiracy-theories

Hughes, Ken. "Nixon's Biggest Crime Was Far, Far Worse than Watergate." Miller

Center of Public Affairs, University of Virginia, online article, June 18, 2012. millercenter.org/ridingthetiger/nixons-biggest-crime

Lyndon Johnson Recordings: LBJ Presidential Library: www.lbjlib.utexas.edu /johnson/archives.hom/dictabelt.hom/content.asp

Miller Center at the University of Virginia: millercenter.org/scripps/archive /presidentialrecordings/johnson

"Neil Sheehan Interview," Conversations with History, Institute of International Studies. University of California, Berkeley, 1996.

Neil Sheehan Interview: Academy of Achievement online video: www .achievement.org/autodoc/page/she1int-1

Neil Sheehan Papers. Library of Congress, Boxes 27, 57, 63–66, 121.

Our Nixon, CNN Flims, documentary film by Brian Frye and Penny Lane, 2013.

Richard Nixon Recordings: Nixon Presidential Library and Museum: www .nixonlibrary.gov/forresearchers/find/tapes/index.php

The website nixontapes.org: nixontapes.org/index.html

Patricia Marx Interviews. WNYC archives. Online at www.wnyc.org/series/ archives-and-preservation/

Pentagon Papers. Complete copy of documents online at: www.archives.gov /research/pentagon-papers/

Pentagon Papers. Related documents and recordings: The National Security Archive. The George Washington University, Washington, D.C.: www2.gwu .edu/~nsarchiv/NSAEBB/NSAEBB48/

Pentagon Papers. Trial documents are online at the Famous Trials exhibit. University of Missouri, Kansas City: law2.umkc.edu/faculty/projects/ftrials/ellsberg /ellsberghome.html

"Pentagon Papers Leaker Daniel Ellsberg Praises Snowden, Manning," NPR News, August 3, 2013.

The Most Dangerous Man in America: Daniel Ellsberg and the Pentagon Papers, documentary film by Judith Ehrlich and Rick Goldsmith, 2009.

Author Interviews

Daniel Ellsberg: many email and phone conversations, August 2013–October 2014.

Patricia Ellsberg: September 30 and October 14, 2014.

Robert Ellsberg: September 23, 2014.

Randy Kehler: August 7, 2014.

SOURCE NOTES

Prologue: Feasibility Study

1 Details of Hunt and Liddy scouting Fielding's office are found in: Liddy, *Will*, 224–227; Hunt, *Undercover*, 164–166; Wells, *Wild Man*, 9–10.

2 "Daniel Ellsberg is the most dangerous": Ellsberg, *Secrets*, 434; Hirsh, *Price of Power*, 385.

3 "Señora, somos doctors": Hunt, *Undercover*, 166.

3 "Did you have time": Hunt, *Undercover*, 166.

Cold Warrior

7 "Kind of a nerd" and other childhood details are from: Wells, *Wild Man*, 53–60; Ellsberg, *Secrets*, 24–25.

8 "I was terrible": Wells, *Wild Man*, 63.

8 "I had become": Ellsberg, *Secrets*, 24.

9 "I didn't seem the type": Ellsberg, *Secrets*, 26.

10 "To act reasonably": Ellsberg, *Risk, Ambiguity, and Decision*, 1.

10–12 Ellsberg's meeting with McNaughton, including quote "Vietnam is one crisis after another": Ellsberg, *Secrets*, 35–36.

12 Background information on Vietnam and "I'm not very organized" quote found in: Prados, *Inside the Pentagon Papers*, 31.

12 For details of rising tension in Gulf of Tonkin: Moise, *Tonkin Gulf*, 74–106; and McNamara, *In Retrospect*, 130–132.

13 Details of first day at the Pentagon are from Ellsberg, *Secrets*, 7–10, and from author interview with Daniel Ellsberg.

13 "My very first day": documentary film, *The Most Dangerous Man in America*, by Judith Ehrlich and Rick Goldsmith.

Day One

14 "Am under continuous torpedo attack": Ellsberg, *Secrets*, 7.

15 "We're going to really strike": Wells, *Wild Man*, 203.

15–16 McNamara background and "smartest man" quote: *New York Times*, July 6, 2009; *Washington Post*, July 7, 2009.

16 "Yes, Bob": Phone conversation, LBJ tapes, Aug. 4, 1964.

17 Stockdale's flight above Gulf of Tonkin, including his quotes in: Stockdale, *In Love and War*, 15–21.

18 "What in the hell has been going on": Stockdale, *In Love and War*, 22.

18 Herrick's "Review of action" cable is from: McNamara, *In Retrospect*, 133.

20 Stockdale's own doubts are described in: Stockdale, *In Love and War*, 23.

20 McNamara describes meeting with LBJ and top staff in: McNamara, *In Retrospect*, 133.

20 "All right. Let's go": Goulden, *Truth*, 35.

21 "I wish the hell": Goulden, *Truth*, 151.

21 "The latest dope": McNamara, *In Retrospect*, 134.

22 "Do we know for a fact": Mann, *Grand Delusion*, 351.

22 "For all I know": Goulden, *Truth*, 160.

22 Everett Alvarez describes his preflight jitters and takeoff in: Alvarez, *Chained Eagle*, 20–21.

Hostile Action

24 Ellsberg describes scene in McNaughton's office in: Ellsberg, *Secrets*, 11–12.

24 "My fellow Americans": Lyndon Johnson, televised address to the nation, August 4, 1964. Available online at Miller Center [millercenter.org/president/speeches/detail/3998]

25 Alvarez describes his mission and shoot-down in: Alvarez, *Chained Eagle*, 22–26.

27 "The attacks were deliberate": Dallek, *Flawed Giant,* 153.

28 "Congress approves and supports": Joint Resolution of Congress, August 7, 1964. Available online at avalon.law.yale.edu/20th_century/tonkin-g.asp

28 Wayne Morse gets late-night call in: Karnow, *Vietnam: A History*, 391.

29 "Hell, Wayne": Goulden, *Truth*, 49.

29 "I am unalterably opposed": Mann, *Grand Delusion*, 359.

29 "Our Navy played absolutely no part": Mann, *Grand Delusion*, 360.

30 "Our national honor": Dallek, *Flawed Giant*, 273.

30 Ellsberg describes his reaction to the Gulf Resolution in: Ellsberg, *Secrets*, 12–16.

31 "I really looked down": Prados, *Inside the Pentagon Papers*, 44.

31 "We were all cold warriors": Prados, *Inside the Pentagon Papers*, 37.

Welcome Americans

32 Ho Chi Minh background is described in: Karnow, *Vietnam*, 130–138.

33 Henry Prunier's experience in Vietnam is described in: Appy, *Patriots*, 38–39.

34 Ho's declaration of independence is described by Archimedes Patti, an OSS agent present at the event, in: Patti, *Why Viet Nam?* 249–252.

35 Truman's response to Ho's declaration in: Patti, *Why Viet Nam?* 379–382.

35 "Your rifles": Ellsberg, *Secrets*, 26.

36 Conditions in North and South Vietnam after Geneva Accords are described in: Karnow, *Vietnam*, 239–241.

36 "You have a row of dominoes": Appy, *Patriots*, 46.

37 "Lyndon Johnson is not going down": Logevall, *Choosing War*, 77.

Wider War

38 Ellsberg describes his job and daily routine in: Ellsberg, *Secrets*, 37–40; and from author interview with Daniel Ellsberg.

38 Details of Ellsberg's family life, including divorce, are described in: Ellsberg, *Secrets*, 34; Wells, *Wild Man*, 175, 189.

38 "He was sad": Wells, *Wild Man*, 207.

39 "All this was exciting": Ellsberg, *Secrets*, 46.

40 McNaughton nearly fires Ellsberg in: *Secrets*, 40.

40 "You will stay here" and details of Alvarez's first months as a POW are described in: Alvarez, *Chained Eagle*, 64–79.

41 "We know there's going to be a war": Alvarez, *Chained Eagle*, 110.

41 "We are not about": Hunt, *Lyndon Johnson's War*, 83.

41 The "Johnson Treatment" is described in every LBJ biography, including: Dallek, *Lyndon B. Johnson*, 86–88.

42 "I don't think it's worth": Dallek, *Flawed Giant*, 145.

42 Goldwater calling Johnson "soft": Dallek, *Flawed Giant*, 141.

42 Goldwater threatens to use atomic bombs in: Randall, *LBJ*, 513.

42 "We seek no wider war": Dallek, *Flawed Giant*, 146.

43 "We all knew that": Ehrlich and Goldsmith, *Most Dangerous Man* film.

43 "On the day the electorate": Ellsberg, *Secrets*, 51.

43 "The time has come" and details of the meeting with Johnson: Karnow, *Vietnam*, 427; McNamara, *In Retrospect*, 167.

44 "I feel like a hitchhiker": Karnow, *Vietnam*, 412.

44 Ellsberg describes his memories of seeing films of World War II bombings in: Ellsberg, *Secrets*, 22–23.

45 "An order from McNamara": Ellsberg, *Secrets*, 68.

Patricia

46 "I need blood": Ellsberg describes this scene in: Ellsberg, *Secrets*, 68–70; and in the Erlich and Goldsmith documentary film, *The Most Dangerous Man in America.*

47 "That night's work": Ellsberg, *Secrets*, 72.

47 "Now we're off to bombing": Beschloss, *Reaching for Glory*, 194.

48 "We seek no wider war": Mann, *Grand Delusion*, 407.

48 "The brutal fact": Dallek, *Flawed Giant*, 255.

49 "I guess we've got": Beschloss, *Reaching for Glory*, 211.

49 "Oh my god!": Ellsberg, *Secrets*, 73.

49 Marines arrive at Da Nang: Esper, *Eyewitness History*, 53.

51 Caputo's first impressions are described in: Caputo, *A Rumor of War*, 53–56.

51 Patricia Marx background information is found in: Wells, *Wild Man*, 215–217; Edmondson, *Women of Watergate*, 105–106. Archives of her radio show, *Patricia Marx Interviews*, are available at WNYC [archives].

51 "Stay away from him": Marx tells this story in: Erlich and Goldsmith, *The Most Dangerous Man in America,* a documentary.

52 "I thought Dan was interesting": Wells, *Wild Man*, 220.

52 "I opened the door": Wells, *Wild Man*, 221.

52 "I saw that she had": Ellsberg, *Secrets*, 75.

52 "I have tomorrow off": Ellsberg describes asking Marx for a date in: Ellsberg, *Secrets*, 75; and in the film, *The Most Dangerous Man in America.*

54 *"I hope this is not going"*: Ellsberg describes the war protest in: Ellsberg, *Secrets*, 76; and in the film, *The Most Dangerous Man in America.*

54 "How can you be going": Marx tells this story in the film, *The Most Dangerous Man in America.*

54 "Despite the fact": PBS press tour for the film, *The Most Dangerous Man in America.* www.youtube.com/watch?v=Kpvwx762aSk

55 "By the next morning": Ellsberg, *Secrets*, 77.

55 "I was falling in love": Ellsberg, *Secrets*, 138.

Limited Operations

56 "The U.S. Marine Force will not": Ellsberg, *Secrets*, 73.

56 Caputo describes his first patrol in: Caputo, *A Rumor of War*, 76–94.

59 Deteriorating conditions in South Vietnam are described in: Karnow, *Vietnam*, 437.

59 "If I were Ho": Dallek, *Flawed Giant*, 261.

60 "You don't come here": Logevall, *Choosing War*, 371.

60 "Are we sure to win": Wells, *Wild Man*, 206.

61 Ellsberg describes McNaughton's bookcase and secret binder in: Ellsberg, *Secrets*, 79–80.

61 "I want to be": Patricia Ellsberg, interview with the author

61 "The conflict in Southeast Asia": McNamara, *In Retrospect*, 187.

62 "Of the thousands of cables": McNamara, *In Retrospect*, 187.

62 "The decision you face now": Ellsberg, *Secrets*, 82.

63 "Their staying power": Karnow, *Vietnam*, 439.

63 "Cut our losses and withdraw": McNamara's options detailed in: Kearns, *Lyndon Johnson*, 280.

63 "He had no stomach": Dallek, *Flawed Giant*, 249.

64 "I knew from the start": Johnson describes his sleepless nights and fears in: Kearns, *Lyndon Johnson*, 251.

Diving Board

65 "It was too much for me": Ellsberg describes this scene in: Ellsberg, *Secrets*, 81–82.

66 "*How had McNaughton*": Ellsberg, *Secrets*, 84.

67 "I asked Secretary McNamara": Kahin, *Intervention*, 371–374; includes selections from the transcript of Johnson's July 22 meeting.

69 "We did not choose": Lyndon Johnson televised address to the nation, July 28, 1965.

69 "What? Has he changed": Ellsberg, *Secrets*, 95.

70 The reaction of top military leaders to Johnson's announcement is described in: Perry, *Four Stars*, 156.

70 "We felt that it would be desirable": Ellsberg, *Secrets*, 96.

70 Ellsberg's new office, diminished role in the Pentagon is described in; Wells, *Wild Man*, 224.

71 "If you can't live": Conversations with History: Daniel Ellsberg, University of California Television.

71 Ellsberg describes the appearance of the German poet in: Ellsberg, *Secrets*, 98; I also asked him about it in one of our interviews, and he told me the story, adding a few details that, at Patricia's request, he had not included in his book. Patricia Ellsberg filled in further detail during a separate interview.

Kill Ratio

72 "I was death's bookkeeper": Caputo, *A Rumor of War*, 169.

72 "How recent are those figures": Caputo describes this scene in: Caputo, *A Rumor of War*, 171–172.

73 "If he's dead and Vietnamese": Caputo, *A Rumor of War*, 229.

73 "If that general's going": Caputo, *A Rumor of War*, 176.

74 "Come on in, Major": Cooper describes his visit to the White House in: Appy, *Patriots*, 122–123.

76 "You're safest in a single": Ellsberg describes his long drives with Vann in: Ellsberg, *Papers on the War*, 145–154.

77 Interactions with Vietnamese children: Ellsberg, *Secrets*, 134; Ellsberg, *Papers on the War*, 138.

77 "I remember my children": Ellsberg, *Papers on the War*, 138.

79 "There's little doubt": Ellsberg, *Papers on the War*, 152.

Escalation

80 Stockdale describes his shoot-down and trip to prison in: Stockdale, *In Love and War*, 102–113.

82 "Not that I was ready": Wells, *Wild Man*, 263.

82 "I was impressed": Ellsberg, *Secrets*, 139.

83 "It wasn't totally clear": This and the following two Patricia Marx quotes in: Wells, *Wild Man*, 264.

84 "A military solution": McNamara describes meeting with Johnson and growing skepticism about the war in: McNamara, *In Retrospect*, 224.

84 Krulak's report and meeting with McNamara described in: Sheehan, *A Bright Shining Lie,* 630–632; Hendrickson, *The Living and the Dead*, 232.

85 Johnson wrestling with decision about troops is described in: Dallek, *Flawed Giant*, 343, 359.

85 For a description of the draft up to and including early years of Vietnam War: Foley, *Confronting the War Machine*, 35–39; Caputo: *10,000 Days*, 88.

86 "I had a personal desire": *New York Times*, December 12, 1971.

86 Ellsberg describes the scene with the girl finding her doll in: Ellsberg, *Secrets*, 128.

Break-Up

88 "We had made a desert": Ellsberg describes this flight and his conversation with the pilot in: Ellsberg, *Secrets*, 135–136.

90 McNamara's conclusion in: Hendrickson, *The Living and the Dead*, 235.

90 "No amount of bombing": Karnow, *Vietnam*, 233.

90 CIA report described and Johnson's response in: Perry, *Four Stars*, 159.

91 "I looked at those kids": *New York Times*, December 12, 1971.

91 "What's going to happen": Patricia Marx's interview with Neil Sheehan. This and many other of Marx's WNYC interviews online at www.wnyc.org/story /neil-sheehan/

93 "How *can* you": Ellsberg describes this argument in: Ellsberg, *Secrets*, 140; both Ellsberg and Marx comment on the fight in: Ehrlich and Goldsmith, *The Most Dangerous Man in America*.

93 "I thought she was unreasonable": Moskin, "Ellsberg Talks," 40.

Making Progress

94 "Komer here is saying": Ellsberg describes his conversation in the plane with McNamara in: Ellsberg, *Secrets*, 141; and in Ehrlich and Goldsmith, *The Most Dangerous Man in America*.

95 "Gentlemen, I've just come back": Ellsberg, *Secrets*, 142. You can see film of McNamara delivering this line in: Ehrlich and Goldsmith, *The Most Dangerous Man in America*.

95 "*I hope I'm never*": Ehrlich and Goldsmith, *The Most Dangerous Man in America*.

95 McNamara describes his eventful visit to Harvard in: McNamara, *In Retrospect*, 254–256.

97 "How many innocent women": The student who led McNamara to safety was Barney Frank, later the first openly gay member of Congress. He describes the day in: Weisberg, *The Story*, 61–63.

98 "For the first time": McNamara, *In Retrospect*, 256.

98 "I have only a few years left": Visit with the elderly couple described in: Ellsberg, *Papers on the War*, 185–186.

100 "I would make myself": Wells, *Wild Man*, 266.

100 "I'm thirty-six": Wells, *Wild Man*, 266.

Search and Destroy

101 "You'll be mortared tonight": Ellsberg, *Secrets*, 145.

102 Ellsberg describes the mortar attack and shell landing near his bed in: Ellsberg, *Secrets*, 146–147.

102 Ellsberg describes his first experiences in combat in: Moskin, "Ellsberg Talks," 33; and in Ellsberg, *Secrets*, 152–155.

104 Additional details of life for infantrymen in Vietnam are from: Caputo, *10,000 Days*, 6–7.

105 Firefight on January 1, 1967, is described in: Ellsberg, *Secrets*, 155–160.

109 "Sergeant, do you ever feel": Ellsberg, *Secrets*, 160; and Ehrlich and Goldsmith, *The Most Dangerous Man in America*.

Lasting Impression

110 Ellsberg describes his final march in Vietnam in: Ellsberg, *Secrets*, 161–167.

112 Ellsberg's bout with hepatitis is described in: Wells, *Wild Man*, 267; Ellsberg, *Secrets*, 174.

114 The car accident is described in: Wells, *Wild Man*, 70–72; Ellsberg tells the story in: Ehrlich and Goldsmith, *The Most Dangerous Man in America*.

115 "I think it probably left an impression": Ehrlich and Goldsmith, *The Most Dangerous Man in America*.

Credibility Gap

119 "You will write apology": Alvarez describes interrogations and torture in Alvarez, *Chained Eagle*, 158–162. Many of the pilots held in North Vietnamese prison camps later wrote memoirs, and all describe being tortured and abused. Stockdale details his experiences in: Stockdale, *In Love and War*; McCain describes his in: McCain, *Faith of My Fathers*.

120 Tap code shortcuts are described in: Stockdale, *In Love and War*, 160.

120 April 15 protests are described in: Wells, *The War Within*, 133–134.

121 Protests hitting home with top officials is described in: Wells, *The War Within*, 105–108.

121 "I'm not going to be": Dallek, *Flawed Giant*, 500.

121 "This war could go": Dallek, *Flawed Giant*, 459.

122 "When we add divisions": Karnow, *Vietnam*, 518.

122 "That military genius": Wells, *The War Within*, 219.

122 Johnson describes his decision to approve escalation: Johnson, *The Vantage Point*, 370.

122 "We are very sure": Dallek, *Flawed Giant*, 472.

122 Marx's anger with Ellsberg and "Bug off" line: Wells, *Wild Man*, 270.

123 "Dan, it looks very good": Ellsberg, *Secrets*, 184; Halberstam, *Best and Brightest*, 637.

123 "I was mad": Ellsberg, *Secrets*, 183.

124 "I don't think we can have": Bundy conversation described in: Ellsberg, *Secrets*, 183.

124 "We had failed": McNamara, *In Retrospect*, 280.

124 "Tell your researchers": McNamara, *In Retrospect.* 280.

124 Early work on the Pentagon Papers, including Ellsberg's small role is described in: Ellsberg, *Secrets*, 186–187.

125 "They could hang people": Halberstam, *Best and Brightest*, 633.

The Power of Leaks

126 "An emotional basket case": Wells, *The War Within*, 198.

126 "The goddamned Air Force": Wells, *The War Within*, 198.

126 "He does it all the time": Wells, *The War Within*, 198.

126 McNamara's break with Johnson and move to the World Bank is described in: Karnow, *Vietnam*, 524–525.

126 "I do not know to this day": McNamara, *In Retrospect*, 311.

126 "I have never been more": Wells, *The War Within*, 222.

127 "A new phase is now starting": Willbanks, *Tet Offensive*, 197.

128 Preparations for Tet attacks are described in: Oberdorfer, *Tet*, 4–5.

128 "They're coming in!": Oberdorfer, *Tet*, 8.

128 Additional details of attack on the U.S. embassy are in: Willbanks, *Tet Offensive*, 34–35; Oberdorfer, *Tet*, 6–16.

128 "Looks like some trouble": Oberdorfer, *Tet*, 18.

129 Overview of Tet Offensive is described in: Caputo, *10,000 Days*, 74.

130 "The enemy's well-laid plans": Willbanks, *Tet Offensive*, 201.

130 "The reporters could hardly believe": Willbanks, *Tet Offensive*, 35.

130 "What the hell is going on": Randall, *LBJ*, 825.

131 "I wanted to be free": Ellsberg, *Secrets*, 181.

131 "I used to take a shower": Ellsberg's new life and beach shack are described in: Wells, *Wild Man*, 272.

132 "We couldn't break him": Gilbert, *The Tet Offensive*, 19.

132 "We face a situation": Westmoreland, *A Soldier Reports*, 352.

132 Ellsberg learns of secret troop request in: Ellsberg, *Secrets*, 202.

133 *New York Times* breaks troop request in: *New York Times*, March 10, 1969.

133 "As I observed the effect": Ellsberg, *Secrets*, 204.

Low Point

134 "But once a decision": LBJ describes reaction to the leak in: Johnson, *The Vantage Point*, 403.

134 "A majority of people": Kearns, *Lyndon Johnson*, 337.

135–136 Johnson's speech on March 31, 1969, including "I shall not seek": Kearns, *Lyndon Johnson*, 348.

136 "We have just toppled": Ellsberg, *Secrets*, 211.

136 Ellsberg describes hearing of the Martin Luther King, Jr. and the Robert F. Kennedy assassinations in: Ellsberg, *Secrets*, 220–221.

137 "If in November" and Nixon's promises of "peace with honor": Summers, *The Arrogance of Power*, 293.

138 "Things were spinning": Caputo describes his firsthand view of the Chicago riots in: *13 Seconds*, 10–12.

139 "Most of my energy went": Ellsberg describes this personal low point in: *Secrets*, 224.

139 "I'm going to seek peace": Dallek, *Flawed Giant*, 579.

139 "It wasn't a big contribution": Ellsberg, *Secrets*, 225.

140 "The bombing halt undercut": Nixon, *RN*, 328.

140 "Anna, I'm speaking": Dallek, *Nixon and Kissinger*, 74. The episode of Nixon undercutting peace talks is also documented in: Berman, *No Peace, No Honor*; and Ambrose, *Nixon: The Triumph of a Politician*, among other sources.

141 "I am regularly in touch": Berman, *No Peace*, 33.

141 "The prospects for peace": Ambrose, *Nixon*, 212.

141 "This is treason": Mann, *Grand Delusion*, 621.

141 "It would rock the world": Berman, *No Peace*, 34.

142 "I want to talk to you": President Johnson conversation with Senator Everett Dirksen, November 2, 1968. Recording of this conversation online at the LBJ Presidential Library: www.lbjlib.utexas.edu/johnson/archives.hom/Dictabelt.hom/highlights/may68jan69.shtm

Madman Theory

143 The entire (and incredible) Nixon-Johnson phone conversation of November 3, 1968, is online at LBJ Presidential Library: www.lbjlib.utexas.edu/johnson/archives.hom/Dictabelt.hom/highlights/may68jan69.shtm

144 "The materials are so explosive": Berman, *No Peace*, 33.

145 "I play it gloves off": Kutler, *Abuse of Power*, 9.

145 "I hope it's right" and details of final day of the campaign are described in: Nixon, *RN*, 330–331.

145 Nixon describes waiting for returns, finding out he won in: Nixon, *RN*, 333–334.

147 "Richard Nixon is not fit": Ellsberg, *Secrets*, 228.

147 Ellsberg's impressions of Kissinger and working for him are described in: Ellsberg, *Secrets*, 230–232.

148 "Dan, you don't have a 'win' option": Ellsberg, *Secrets*, 234.

148 Nixon's social awkwardness is discussed in: Dallek, *Nixon and Kissinger*, 90–92.

149 Johnson recalls the awkward scene in the White House Red Room in: Johnson, *The Vantage Point*, 563.

149 "I reflected on how inadequate": Johnson, *The Vantage Point*, 565.

150 Nixon's first night in White House with family: Nixon, *RN*, 366.

"I call it the madman theory": Hersh, *Price of Power*, 53; Haldeman reported this conversation in his memoir: Haldeman, *The Ends of Power*, 122.

The Pentagon Papers

151 "A very odd man": Dallek, *Nixon and Kissinger*, 91.

152 "Gentlemen, we have reached": Nixon, *RN*, 381.

152 Situation in Vietnam as Nixon takes over is described in: Ambrose, *Nixon*, 241.

152 "But we have to look at": Nixon, *RN*, 381.

152 "My administration was only": Nixon, *RN*, 382.

152 Nixon's duel reporting system on Cambodia bombing is discussed in: Karnow, *Vietnam*, 607.

152 Ellsberg gets a copy of Pentagon Papers in: Ellsberg, *Secrets*, 243.

153 "The same old spark": Wells, *Wild Man*, 309; "It was exciting": author interview with Ellsberg.

154 "Outrageous": scene described in: Reeves, *President Nixon*, 75.

154 "Find out who leaked": Dallek, *Nixon and Kissinger*, 122.

154 "It's right": Ellsberg, *Secrets*, 260.

154 "I couldn't make anyone": Hersh, *Price of Power*, 326; Ellsberg, *Secrets*, 331.

155 Ellsberg describes his visit to Ohio University and reflections that the visit inspired in: Ellsberg, *Secrets*, 247–248.

156 "Let me put a question": Ellsberg, *Secrets*, 248.

156 Ellsberg describes the painful process of reading the Pentagon Papers in Ellsberg, *Secrets*, 250–257.

157 "What I had in my safe": Ellsberg, *Secrets*, 289.

Whole Vote

159 "The same sets of alternatives": Rudenstine, *The Day the Presses Stopped*, 40.

159 "Only atomic bombs": Sheehan, *The Pentagon Papers*, 571.

159 "No American president": Moskin, "Ellsberg Talks," 34.

160 "A worthy effort gone wrong": Ellsberg, *Secrets*, 256.

160 "It wasn't that we were": Ellsberg, *Secrets*, 257.

160 Nixon's early strategy in Vietnam: Ambrose, *Nixon*, 277–278; Nixon, *RN*, 390–392.

161 "But at the same time": Nixon, *RN*, 396.

161 "I refuse to believe" and plans for the "savage blow": Hersh, *Price of Power*, 126; Ambrose, *Nixon*, 299.

161 "I will not be the first": Ambrose, *Nixon*, 300.

162 *"Cast your whole vote"*: Ellsberg describes this pivotal scene in: Ellsberg, *Secrets*, 263–269. Randy Kehler shared his recollections of the event with me in an interview in 2014. The text of Thoreau's "Civil Disobedience" is available online at: xroads.virginia.edu/~HYPER2/thoreau/civil.html

163 "Yesterday our friend Bob": this scene is described in: Ellsberg, *Secrets*, 271–272; author interview with Randy Kehler.

Night Work

165 "I want to come over": Wells, *Wild Man*, 321.

166 Russo describes his background and firing from Rand: Russo, "Inside the RAND Corporation," 45–55.

166 "Dan, you should leak that": Ehrlich and Goldsmith, *The Most Dangerous Man in America* film.

166 "You know the study": This conversation is described in: Ellsberg, *Secrets*, 295; recalled by Russo in Ehrlich and Goldsmith, *The Most Dangerous Man in America*.

167 Ellsberg's exit from Rand with the first batch of documents is described in: Ellsberg, *Secrets*, 299–300.

168 "I wanted to help": Wells, *Wild Man*, 322.

168 The scene at Lynda Sinay's office during the first night of copying is described in: Ellsberg, *Secrets*, 301–302; and by both Ellsberg and Russo in Ehrlich and Goldsmith, *The Most Dangerous Man in America*.

170 "In a month or so": Ellsberg, *Secrets*, 303.

170 "Within a couple of weeks": Ellsberg, *Secrets*, 305.

171 Scene with Robert Ellsberg at the restaurant is described in: Ellsberg, *Secrets*, 306.

171 "I had a sense of being included": Wells, *Wild Man*, 329.

172 "Your alarm's gone off again": Ellsberg describes this scene in: Ehrlich and Goldsmith, *The Most Dangerous Man in America*.

172 "I learned how to work a Xerox": Wells, *Wild Man*, 329.

Troublemaker

173 "I went ballistic": Wells, *Wild Man*, 330.

173 "I need to talk to you right away": Cummings-Ellsberg confrontation in: Wells, *Wild Man*, 331–332.

175 "Don't get rattled": Antiwar demonstrations and Nixon's response are described in: Ambrose, *Nixon*, 304; Nixon, *RN*, 402–403.

175 "I knew that after all the protests": Wells, *The War Within*, 377.

175 Mary Ellsberg describes her night of photocopying in: Wells, *Wild Man*, 332–334.

176 "I asked her that night": Ellsberg, *Secrets*, 329.

176 Russo's innovation and "Instant declassification": Ellsberg, *Secrets*, 308.

177 "It was a touchy situation": Ellsberg, *Secrets*, 324.

177 Ellsberg and Marx leave for DC together, with Papers in: Ellsberg, *Secrets*, 324.

177 "Let us all understand": Nixon's famous "silent majority" speech is described and excerpted in: Dallek, *Nixon and Kissinger*, 164–165. Transcript at: www.nixonlibrary.gov/forkids/speechesforkids/silentmajority.php

178 "I had the public support I needed": Nixon, *RN*, 410.

179 "He was articulate": Wells, *Wild Man*, 351; Ellsberg describes Fulbright meeting in: Ellsberg, *Secrets*, 326–328.

179 "Now we were agreeing": Wells, *Wild Man*, 309.

179 "She still wasn't sure": author interview with Ellsberg.

179 "He's a troublemaker": PBS press tour for the film, *The Most Dangerous Man in America*.

Behind the Mask

180 Alvarez describes visit to Museum of the Revolution in: Alvarez, *Chained Eagle*, 218.

181 Kissinger-Tho talks in Paris are described in: Berman, *No Peace*, 65–67.

182 "We had to think about initiatives": Hersh, *Price of Power*, 170.

182 Cummings calls with news of FBI visit in: Ellsberg, *Secrets*, 333.

182 "Have you been talking": Wells, *Wild Man*, 334.

183 Cummings explains how the FBI heard of Ellsberg's photocopying in: Wells, *Wild Man*, 334–335.

183 "It's too bad it has to end": Ellsberg, *Secrets*, 334.

183 "If I had to choose": contemplating Forster quote: Wells, *Wild Man*, 345.

184 "It's possible that the campuses": Ambrose, *Nixon*, 344.

184 "To protect our men": Nixon quotes from his Cambodia speech in: Nixon, *RN*, 451.

185 Caputo describes trip to Kent State and scene there in: Caputo, *13 Seconds*, 21–24.

186 "To answer stones and bad language": Caputo, *13 Seconds*, 25.

186 "Those few days after Kent State": Nixon, *RN*, 457.

186 Campus protests are described in: Ambrose, *Nixon*, 351. Kissinger describes protesters at his apartment in: Kissinger, *Ending the Vietnam War*, 170.

186 "The purpose was to keep": Krogh, *Integrity*, 109.

187 "He's very disturbed": Dallek, *Nixon and Kissinger*, 202.

187 "Searchlight is on the lawn": Krogh describes this scene in: Krogh, *Integrity*, 105–106.

188 "I know that probably most of you": Soon after Nixon's late-night visit to the Lincoln Memorial, he dictated a detailed memo about the experience, which is excerpted in: Nixon, *RN*, 461–466.

189 Krogh arrived to witness the scene at the Capitol, which he records in: Krogh, *Integrity*, 115.

Bridges Burned

190 The Ellsberg-Marx wedding is described in: "Daniel Ellsberg of M.I.T. Marries Patricia Marx," *New York Times*, August 9, 1970.

190 Ellsberg describes his meeting with Kissinger in: Ellsberg, *Secrets*, 346–348.

192 "That wasn't the way you talked": Ellsberg, *Secrets*, 348.

192 The Ellsbergs' Cambridge apartment is described in: Wells, *Wild Man*, 373; and in: "After the Pentagon Papers," *New York Times*, December 12, 1971.

193 "I want to do it": Ellsberg, *Secrets*, 362.

193 "I'm sorry, I can't do it": Ellsberg, *Secrets*, 363.

194 Russo's helicopter plan is described in: Salisbury, *Without Fear or Favor*, 79.

194 "These senators don't seem" and Patricia Ellsberg's reaction to reading the Papers in: Ellsberg, *Secrets*, 363–364.

194 Kissinger-Ellsberg confrontation at M.I.T. is described in: Ellsberg, *Secrets*, 352–353; Kissinger would later describe this scene to Nixon in: Nixon White House recordings, June 17, 1971.

196 "You know, boys, it's a good thing": Ambrose, *Nixon*, 423; history of presidential recordings: Prados, *The White House Tapes*, 1–12.

196 "Mr. President, you'll never remember": Prados, *The White House Tapes*, 13.

197 "Absolutely not": Dallek, *Nixon and Kissinger*, 248.

197 "bulldog tenacity," and Sheehan's reputation in: Salisbury, *Without Fear or Favor*, 17–18.

197 Ellsberg describes spending night at Sheehan's in: Ellsberg, *Secrets*, 368.

War Room

198 "We can't get into something": Salisbury, *Without Fear or Favor*, 80. Salisbury, a colleague of Sheehan at the *Times*, provides a detailed inside account of the Pentagon Papers story from the newspaper's point of view.

198 "You have my permission": Salisbury, *Without Fear or Favor*, 83.

198 "You've been talking": Ellsberg, *Secrets*, 371.

199 "As soon as I got together": Wenner, "The Rolling Stone Interview," 33.

199 The scene in Spencer's apartment is described in: Ellsberg, *Secrets*, 372–373.

200 "If this is the quality": Ungar, *The Papers and the Papers*, 88.

200 "Well, we've got to get enough": Nixon White House recording, March 19, 1971.

201 The Treadway Motor Inn scene is described in: Salisbury, *Without Fear or Favor*, 35; Rudenstine, *The Day the Presses Stopped*, 52–53.

202 "What the hell is going on": Frankel, *The Times of My Life*, 325.

202 Ellsberg out of the loop: Salisbury, *Without Fear or Favor*, 134.

203 "the greatest story": Salisbury, *Without Fear or Favor*, 93.

203 "Have you heard about": Goodale describes the meeting with *Times* bosses in detail in: Goodale, *Fighting for the Press*, 45–47.

204 "Everyone has to remember": for another account of this meeting, including this quote, see: Salisbury, *Without Fear or Favor*, 118–123.

A Matter of Patriotism

205 Ellsberg's visit to Kehler at La Tuna was described to me in an interview with Randy Kehler.

207 "Each day someone has to die": John Kerry's testimony before the U.S.

Senate Committee on Foreign Relations, April 22, 1971. Online at: www.c-span video.org/program/181065-1

207 "Man, am I glad": Prados, *Inside the Pentagon Papers*, 63. Room 1106 is also described in: Salisbury, *Without Fear or Favor*, 165.

208 "It's a matter of patriotism": Salisbury, *Without Fear or Favor*, 171.

208 "I have to stop you right now": Ellsberg, *Secrets*, 383.

209 "That study you showed me": Ellsberg, *Secrets*, 385.

209 "He hasn't given me any warning": Ellsberg, *Secrets*, 386.

210 "Let it be four thirty": Salisbury, *Without Fear or Favor*, 6.

211 "I would prefer to have it in the Rose Garden": Nixon describes the day of Tricia's wedding in: Nixon, *RN*, 504–507; more in: Ambrose, *Nixon*, 445.

211 Ron Ziegler gets a message from *New York Daily News*: Salisbury, *Without Fear or Favor*, 207.

212 "I owe him this": Salisbury, *Without Fear or Favor*, 214.

212 Howard Zinn describes his night with the Ellsbergs in: Wells, *Wild Man*, 410–411.

213 "Well at least I'm standing": Haldeman, *The Haldeman Diaries*, 299.

213–214 *Times* headlines: *New York Times*, June 13, 1971.

214 "I may be going out of town": Wells, *Wild Man*, 413.

Slow Build

217 Nixon's morning and initial reaction are described in: Salisbury, *Without Fear or Favor*, 232.

217 "We must be exceedingly careful": Wells, *Wild Man*, 459.

217 "The key for us": Prados, *Inside the Pentagon Papers*, 78.

218 Goodale's reaction is described in: Goodale, *Fighting for the Press*, 1.

218 "The story is a bust": Salisbury, *Without Fear or Favor*, 215.

218 "Oh my God. It has hit": this and reactions of Carol Cummings and Robert Ellsberg in: Wells, *Wild Man*, 415.

219 "This has got to have been": Wells, *Wild Man*, 414.

219 The reaction at Rand is described in: Wells, *Wild Man*, 416–417.

219 "It is unconscionable": Nixon White House recordings, June 13, 1971. Transcript and recording online at: whitehousetapes.net/transcript/nixon/005 -059

220 "A Consensus To Bomb": *New York Times*, June 14, 1971.

220 "If the police come": Salisbury, *Without Fear or Favor*, 238.

221 "I tell you Bob": Prados, *Inside the Pentagon Papers*, 79.

221 "Unfortunately for Henry": Prados, *Inside the Pentagon Papers*, 78.

221 "Don't give 'em anything": Goodale, *Fighting for the Press*, 73.

221 "You mean to prosecute the *Times*": Nixon White House recording, June 14, 1971.

222 "What is your advice on that *Times* thing": Nixon White House recording, June 14, 1971.

222 "Patricia and I listened": Ellsberg, *Secrets*, 387.

222 "Something must be going on": Goodale, *Fighting for the Press*, 74.

223 "The material published in the *New York Times*": the text of Mitchell's telegram is printed in: Salisbury, *Without Fear or Favor*, 240.

223 "You can't stop publishing": Goodale, *Fighting for the Press*, 74.

224 "What does Louis say": scene on the 14th floor is described in Salisbury, *Without Fear or Favor*, 243–244; Goodale, *Fighting for the Press*, 74–76.

Mr. Boston

225 "Go ahead": Salisbury, *Without Fear or Favor*, 243–244.

225 Goodale's late night calls are described in: Goodale, *Fighting for the Press*, 77.

226 "Mitchell Seeks to Halt Series on Vietnam": *New York Times*, June 15, 1971.

226 "We're convinced you're the source": "The Suspect: A Hawk Who Turned Dove," *Newsweek*, June 28, 1971, 16.

226 "It wasn't any one page": Ellsberg, *Secrets*, 389.

226 "This is a very bad situation": Nixon White House recording, June 15, 1971.

228 Goodale describes finding lawyers to take the case as well as the scene in the courtroom in: Goodale, *Fighting for the Press*, 78–82.

228 "But there has never been a publication": Goodale, *Fighting for the Press*, 83.

228 "The judge wants us to stop": Goodale, *Fighting for the Press*, 84.

229 "Call Mr. Boston": Bagdikian, *Reflections*, 3. Bagdikian provides a detailed account of his role in the Pentagon Papers story in this memoir.

229 "An old friend has an important" and conversation with Ellsberg: Bagdikian, *Reflections*, 4–5.

230 "Judge, at Request of U.S.": *New York Times*, June 16, 1971.

230 "If we don't publish": Ungar, *The Papers and the Papers*, 134.

230 "Do you have back trouble": Bagdikian, *Reflections*, 7.

231 Bagdikian describes picking up the boxes and meeting Ellsberg in the motel in: Bagdikian, *Reflections*, 7–12.

232 "We can't go back": Ehrlich and Goldsmith, *The Most Dangerous Man in America*.

Underground

233 Marina's lemonade stand as described in: Prados, *Inside the Pentagon Papers*, 69.

233 Scene inside Bradlee's home, including Graham's "go ahead" is described in: Salisbury, *Without Fear or Favor*, 293; Prados, *Inside the Pentagon Papers*, 68–70.

234 "Curse that son of a bitch": Nixon White House recordings, June 17, 1971. Transcript and recording at: whitehousetapes.net/transcript/nixon/525-001

235 "By the end of the meeting": Dallek, *Nixon and Kissinger*, 312.

235 "I want him exposed": Prados, *Inside the Pentagon Papers*, 84.

235 "Documents Reveal U.S. Effort in '54": *Washington Post*, June 18, 1971.

236 "I'm sure you will understand": Ungar, *The Papers and the Papers*, 153.

236 Gravel describes his meeting with Bagdikian in: Ehrlich and Goldsmith, *The Most Dangerous Man in America*.

236 "The security of the nation": Gurfein's famous statement excerpted in: Salisbury, *Without Fear or Favor*, 312.

237 "I tried to stay one step ahead": Ungar, *The Papers and the Papers*, 191. Ellsberg describes his time as a fugitive in: Ellsberg, *Secrets*, 393–408.

238 "Daniel gave up everything": Ellsberg, *Secrets*, 398.

238 "The whereabouts of Daniel Ellsberg": *Boston Globe*, June 20, 1971.

238 Tom Oliphant and the *Boston Globe*'s role in the story are described in: Ungar, *The Papers and the Papers*, 178–180; and Wells, *Wild Man*, 427–429.

239 "Secret Pentagon Documents Bare JFK Role": *Boston Globe*, June 22, 1971.

240 "Well, Tom, I see you're in the act": Ungar, *The Papers and the Papers*, 180.

240 "I showed up at the courthouse": Russo, "Inside the RAND Corporation," 54.

240 Lynda Sinay's arrest is described in: Wells, *Wild Man*, 449.

241 "Where is Dan": *Wild Man*, 441.

241 Gordon Manning describes his dealings with Ellsberg's team in: Wells, *Wild Man*, 436–437.

Arrest

243 "Mr. Cronkite": Cronkite tells this story in: Wells, *Wild Man*, 438–439.

244 "During the controversy": A transcript of the interview can be found in: *Boston Globe*, June 24, 1971.

245 Other papers publish on June 24: Rudenstine, *The Day the Presses Stopped*, 249.

246 "I can't do that": Ellsberg indicted and talks to lawyer: Ellsberg, *Secrets*, 404–405.

246 "After the last two glorious weeks": Ellsberg, *Secrets*, 405.

247 "It was like going from Yankee Stadium": Goodale describes Supreme Court scene in: Goodale, *Fighting for the Press*, 159–163.

248 "Wouldn't we then—the federal courts": Salisbury, *Without Fear or Favor*, 332.

248 "I think I've done a good job" and arrest scene in: *Boston Globe*, June 29, 1971; *Washington Post*, June 29, 1971; Ehrlich and Goldsmith, *The Most Dangerous Man in America*.

Fame

250 "I have in my possession the Pentagon Papers": Ungar, *The Papers and the Papers*, 259–262; Gravel tells his story in: Prados, *Inside the Pentagon Papers*, 72–74; he is also featured in: Ehrlich and Goldsmith, *The Most Dangerous Man in America*.

251 "In revealing the workings": Ungar, *The Papers and the Papers*, 244.

251 Reactions at newspapers are described in: Ungar, *The Papers and the Papers*, 250.

251 "Daniel Ellsberg is the most dangerous": Ellsberg, *Secrets*, 434; Hirsh, *Price of Power*, 385.

252 "We've got to get him": Nixon White House recordings, June 30, 1971.

253 "I really need a son of a bitch": Nixon White House recordings, July 1, 1971.

253 "Thanks to the drama": Ellsberg, *Secrets*, 413.

254 "Mr. Ellsberg has been hailed": Ehrlich and Goldsmith, *The Most Dangerous Man in America*.

254 "We've just been informed": Wells, *Wild Man*, 506.

254 "It was a tremendous boost": Wells, *Wild Man*, 507.

254 "You have done a great duty" and other letters to Ellsberg in: *New York Times*, December 12, 1971.

254 "I was typhoid Mary": Ehrlich and Goldsmith, *The Most Dangerous Man in America*.

254 "Hang him from the highest" and other reactions at Rand: Wells, *Wild Man*, 453.

255 "close to treason": Wells, *Wild Man*, 458; Cavett mentions the Benedict Arnold comparison in his interview with Ellsberg, transcript in: *Boston Globe*, July 22, 1971.

255 Patricia Ellsberg describes her father's reaction and her response in: Wells, *Wild Man*, 451–452.

255 "As I read, Ehrlichman told me": Krogh describes this fateful day in: Krogh, *Integrity*, 14–18.

256 "I certainly wasn't in the habit": Krogh, *Integrity*, 30.

The Plumbers

257 Krogh meets Liddy and describes early days of the Plumbers in: Krogh, *Integrity*, 35–41; Liddy gives his version in: Liddy, *Will*, 145–149; Hunt gives his version in: Hunt, *Undercover*, 146–148.

257 "I could kill a man": Wells, *Wild Man*, 16.

258 "A short, dapper man": Krogh, *Integrity*, 39.

258 "A mood of manic resolve": Krogh, *Integrity*, 41.

259 "Unstable, self-righteous": Wells, *Wild Man*, 16.

259 "The picture that emerged": Wells, *Wild Man*, 17.

259 "The more Liddy and I discussed": Hunt, *Undercover*, 163.

259 "black bag job": Liddy, *Will*, 158.

259 Krogh describes the memo and Ehrlichman's response in: Krogh, *Integrity*, 67.

260 Hunt and Liddy meet "Steve" in: Liddy, *Will*, 162; Hunt, *Undercover*, 164.

261 "I am not guilty": *New York Times*, August 17, 1971.

261 "It was almost like he glowed": Wells, *Wild Man*, 509.

262 FBI investigating Ellsbergs is described in: *New York Times*, August 30, 1972.

262 "They asked me a whole lot": Wells, *Wild Man*, 475; additional details of investigation are on pages 478–481.

263 "Psychologically, it's not so bothersome": *New York Times*, August 30, 1972.

264 "First your guys give me": Hunt, *Undercover*, 165.

264 "Very few of the pictures": Krogh, *Integrity*, 71.

265 Final approval of project and money from Colson are described in: Krogh, *Integrity*, 72; Liddy, *Will*, 164.

265 "Now for God's sake": Liddy, *Will*, 165; Hunt, *Undercover*, 168.

Bag Job

266 "All was as it should be": Hunt, *Undercover*, 169.

267 "Well, we'd like to get": scene is described in: Wells, *Wild Man*, 19.

267 Liddy helping the team break-in is described in: Liddy, *Will*, 167–168; Barker gives his version of events in: Wells, *Wild Man*, 19–21.

270 "George, this is Edward": Hunt, *Undercover*, 170.

270 "What's happened" and heading with Liddy for the building: Hunt, *Undercover*, 171; Liddy, *Will*, 168.

271 "I bet Krogh's pissing": Hunt, *Undercover*, 172.

271 "Eduardo, there was nothing": Hunt, *Undercover*, 172.

272 "Do you think there is an Ellsberg": Hunt, *Undercover*, 174.

273 "Would you really have used it": Liddy, *Will*, 169.

273 "Get them away from there": Ehrlichman, *Witness to Power*, 400; Krogh, *Integrity*, 75.

273 "The White House Plumbers": Appy, *Patriots*, 439.

273 "A botched break-in": Krogh, *Integrity*, 77.

Consequences

274 "I wasn't discouraged": Liddy, *Will*, 170.

274 "We'll make waiters out of them": Wells, *Wild Man*, 509; Liddy discusses the LSD plan in: Liddy, *Will*, 170–171.

275 "Brothers and sisters": the scene and Ellsberg's talk are reported in: "Secret Papers Figure Feted by U.S. Workers," *Washington Post*, September 24, 1971.

275 Ellsberg to LA, visiting Russo: "The Busy Life of Daniel Ellsberg," *Boston Globe*, December 19, 1971. This is a particularly interesting article because the writer, Anthony Lucas, spent several weeks with Ellsberg during this stressful time.

276 "I realized how many": "After the Pentagon Papers: A Month in the New Life of Daniel Ellsberg," by Anthony Lucas, *New York Times*, December 12, 1971.

276 New charges added to indictment: Wells, *Wild Man*, 528–529.

276 "Dan and I are charged": Russo, "Inside the RAND Corporation," *Ramparts* magazine, April 1972, 55.

277 "Both Haldeman and Henry": Nixon, *RN*, 589.

277 "That's why we've got to": Dallek, *Nixon and Kissinger*, 371.

277 "I still think we ought to": Nixon White House recordings, April 25, 1972.

278 "This period was one of the most intense": Ellsberg, Patricia, "Got to be True," article on her website.

278 "If heads are knocked": Wells, *Wild Man*, 492.

278 "Our mission is to hit him": Schrag, *Test of Loyalty*, 124.

278 Capitol protest and assault are described in: Wells, *Wild Man*, 496–500.

279 Plumbers scout Watergate in: Liddy, *Will*, 220.

280 "I remember feeling": Ellsberg, *Secrets*, 419.

280 "For this I'm going to do": Wells, *Wild Man*, 514.

Preposterous

281 "a comedy of errors": Nixon White House recordings, June 23, 1972. This meeting also includes the infamous "smoking gun" conversation; transcript and recording online at: www.nixonlibrary.gov/forresearchers/find/tapes /watergate/trial/transcripts.php

281 Early attempts at Watergate: Hunt, *Undercover*, 222–225; for a great source on key players and timeline of Watergate see: http://www.washingtonpost .com/watergate/

282 "Gordon, I know you like scotch": Liddy, *Will*, 318.

283 "There's flashlights": Liddy, *Will*, 335–336; Hunt, *Undercover*, 241–243.

284 "Is that you": Liddy, *Will*, 338.

284 "Ground Combat Role Nears": headlines and Nixon's reaction are described in: Nixon, *RN*, 625–626; Ambrose, *Nixon*, 560.

286 "The White House has had no involvement": Ambrose, *Nixon*, 567.

286 "Is it Liddy": Nixon White House recordings, June 23, 1972.

287 Ellsberg preparing for trial is described in: "The World of the Ellsberg Trial," *New York Times*, February 5, 1973.

287 "Louis Marx presently refuses": "Daniel Ellsberg's Closest Friend: His Wife, Patricia," *New York Times*, August 30, 1972.

288 "That's great. So I'm home free": Ellsberg, *Secrets*, 431.

Peace with Honor?

289 "Henry, you tell those sons of bitches": Ambrose, *Nixon*, 592.

289 Breakthrough in peace talks is described in: Hersh, *Price of Power*, 561.

290 "The most important thing": Hersh, *Price of Power*, 563.

291 "The South Vietnamese people": Berman, *No Peace*, 167.

291 "I wanted to punch Kissinger": Berman, *No Peace*, 164.

292 Nixon describes painful tooth incident in: Nixon, *RN*, 715.

292 "I am at a loss to explain": Nixon, *RN*, 717.

292 "I repeat my personal assurances": Berman, *No Peace*, 187.

293 "Both North and South Vietnam": Kissinger-Tho showdown is described in: Berman, *No Peace*, 189.

293 "We have no choice": Hersh, *Price of Power*, 618.

293 "Atta boy": bombing described by prisoners in: Alvarez, *Chained Eagle*, 248–250; Stockdale, *In Love and War*, 431.

294 "Despair. Horror": Wenner, "The Rolling Stone Interview," 10.

294 "savage and senseless": Karnow, *Vietnam*, 667; "War by tantrum": Nixon, *RN*, 738.

294 "Perhaps no more than 400 to 500": Hersh, *Price of Power*, 625.

295 "If both sides now return": Hersh, *Price of Power*, 627.

295 "It was not my responsibility": Hersh, *Price of Power*, 632.

295 "You have tarnished": Dallek, *Nixon and Kissinger*, 452.

295 "You have my assurance": Karnow, *Vietnam*, 672.

296 Judge Byrne and the courtroom are described by Peter Schrag, who covered the trial, in: Schrag, *Test of Loyalty*, 174, 225; Wells, *Wild Man*, 538.

296 "The odds are in favor": Moskin, "Ellsberg Talks," *Look* magazine, 42.

297 "Send over whatever agent": Dallek, *Flawed Giant*, 622.

297 "I have asked for this radio": Nixon Address to the Nation, January 23, 1973. Online at: www.presidency.ucsb.edu/ws/?pid=3808

298 "I came away": Berman, *No Peace*, 261.

298 Liddy, McCord conviction is described in: "Last Two Guilty in Watergate Plot," *Washington Post*, January 31, 1973.

Bizarre Events

299 "There it is": Alvarez, *Chained Eagle*, 256–259.

301 "When things are going well": "Only Few Memorable Moments Enliven Pattern of Tedium at the Ellsberg Trial," *New York Times*, February 20, 1973.

301 "Any American who knew what we did": Schrag, *Test of Loyalty*, 318.

302 Ellsberg on the stand: Schrag, *Test of Loyalty*, 319–324.

302 "If at any time": Ehrlichman, *Witness to Power*, 375; Schrag, *Test of Loyalty*, 333.

304 "I know about that": Ehrlichman, *Witness to Power*, 405.

304 "This is to inform you": Schrag, *Test of Loyalty*, 329.

305 "Mr. Ellsberg, I don't need to reveal": Ellsberg, *Secrets*, 449; "Trial Will Go On," *New York Times*, April 28, 1973.

305 "I wish I could say": Schrag, *Test of Loyalty*, 331.

305 "Today, in one of the most difficult": Nixon Address to the Nation, April 30, 1973.

306 "The White House, by initiating this meeting": "Judge Rules Ellsberg Trial Must Continue," *Los Angeles Times*, May 1, 1973.

306 "The conduct of the President": Schrag, *Test of Loyalty*, 342.

307 Ellsberg visits saloon: Schrag, *Test of Loyalty*, 345.

307 "We have the rocky situation": Nixon White House recordings, May 11, 1973.

308 "Commencing on April 26": dismissal scene described in: Schrag, *Test of Loyalty*, 352–356; Wells, *Wild Man*, 556; Ellsberg, *Secrets*, 455–456; "This Was The Right Way to End it, Ellsberg Says," *Washington Post*, May 12, 1973.

Painful Truth

311 "Aren't you just as glad": Nixon White House recordings, May 12, 1973.

311 "But I personally have thought enough": press conference covered in: "Two Defendants Say Trail Told 'Painful Truth,'" *New York Times*, May 13, 1973.

312 "And let me say": Nixon's "Remarks at a Reception for Returned Prisoners of War," online at www.presidency.ucsb.edu/ws/?pid=3856; Ellsberg describes his reaction in: Wenner, "The Rolling Stone Interview," 15.

313 "If the Communists dare put": Berman, *No Peace*, 243.

313 "With every passing day": Hersh, *Price of Power*, 637.

313 "Watergate junkie": Wells, *Wild Man*, 558.

313 "Nixon's effort to get me": Appy, *Patriots*, 436.

314 "If it were not for domestic": Berman, *No Peace*, 261.

314 "This is the thirty-seventh time": Nixon Address to the Nation, August 8, 1974; Nixon gives his recollections of the scene in Nixon, *RN*, 1083.

315 "That depends, Henry": Nixon, *RN*, 1084.

315 "Good luck, Mr. President": Nixon, *RN*, 1089.

317 Caputo's description of the American evacuation in: Caputo, *A Rumor of War*, 338–346.

318 Casualty figures are described in: Appy, *Patriots*, 163–164; for detailed breakdowns see: www.archives.gov/research/military/vietnam-war/casualty-statistics.html#category

319 "The evacuation has been completed": Berman, *No Peace*, 272.

Epilogue: History Repeats

320 For a moment-by-moment account of Snowden's initial contacts with Poitras and Greenwald, see: Harding, *The Snowden Files*, 62–79.

320 Another very detailed account: "How Laura Poitras Helped Snowden Spill His Secrets," *New York Times Magazine*, August 13, 2013.

322 "I do not want to live in a world": Watch Snowden's first interview from Hong Kong hotel room at: www.theguardian.com/world/video/2013/jun/09/nsa-whistleblower-edward-snowden-interview-video

322 For both sides of the Snowden hero vs. traitor debate, see "Why Edward Snowden Is a Hero" and "Edward Snowden Is No Hero," *The New Yorker,* June 10, 2013.

322 "If any individual who objects": Remarks by the president, January 17, 2014. www.whitehouse.gov/the-press-office/2014/01/17/remarks-president -review-signals-intelligence

323 "Edward Snowden is a coward": Bamford, "The Most Wanted Man in the World," *Wired,* August 2014.

323 For Ellsberg's opinion, in his words: "NSA Leaker Snowden Made the Right Call," *Washington Post,* July 7, 2013.

323 Don Lemon's introduction and interview with Ellsberg: CNN, June 9, 2013. www.cnn.com/video/?/video/bestoftv/2013/06/10/exp-pentagon-papers -whistleblower-on-nsa.cnn

ACKNOWLEDGMENTS

Many thanks to Daniel Ellsberg for taking the time to talk with me several times during the research and writing of this book. Ellsberg has written extensively about his life and granted hundreds of interviews, but our conversations produced a handful of details and clarifications that I would not have wanted to do without. Thanks also to Patricia Ellsberg, Robert Ellsberg, and Randy Kehler for answering questions and sharing recollections.

Rick Goldsmith, co-director and producer of the documentary *The Most Dangerous Man in America*, helped me get in touch with Ellsberg— and made a must-see film on this story, which was a big boost to my research. Thanks to Sarah Pirtle for putting me in touch with Randy Kehler; and to Andy Lanset, director of the archives at New York Public Radio, for helping me find recordings of Patricia Marx's radio interviews; and to the staff of the Library of Congress for making available the Neil Sheehan Papers. Thanks again to the Saratoga Springs Public Library, for the endless supply of books and a quiet place to read them.

As she has been on past projects, Deirdre Langeland was as much a collaborator as an editor on this book. We went back and forth on everything from big structural issues to individual word choices, and as always she encouraged (forced) me to redo the opening about ten times. Thank you for that, really. Thanks as always to Anne Diebel for her amazing design work, and to Claire Dorsett for finding some mighty obscure photos and guiding us down the homestretch. Thanks also to Simon Boughton and everyone at Roaring Brook/Macmillan for backing this book idea, and to Susan Cohen and the Writers House team for making it all happen.

I'm running out of ways to explain how important my wife, Rachel, is to this whole process, but here's one specific example. Long before there was anything to read, she helped settle many of the toughest questions about what to put in and what to cut. When she says, "You gotta keep that," her word is final. Thank you, Rachel.

PHOTO CREDITS

INDEX

Numbers in **bold** indicate pages with illustrations

for, 161, 207, 319; madman theory for ending war, 150, 152; marriage of daughter, 211–212, 213–214; opinions about, 147, 151; out-of-control presidency, first step of, 273; peace with honor agreement, 289–291, 297–298; protests against war during presidency of, 174–175, **174**, 184–189, **185**, **188**; publication of Papers, reaction to, 217, 219–220, 221–222; recording of conversations by, 195–197, 312–313, 314; resignation of, 314–316, **315**, **316**; social events, feelings about, 148; television attack on Ellsberg, 312; undermining of peace talks by, 140–145, 297; Vietnamization policy, 177–178, 181–182, 184, 200–201

North Vietnam: allies of, 11, 49; attacks on by South Vietnam, 28–29, 30–31; bombing of, 43–45, 75–76, 277–278, 279–280, **280**, 289, 292–295, 313–314; collaboration with Viet Cong, 42; communist government in, 11; creation of after war with France, 36–37; financial aid offer from Johnson, 59; map of, **19**; mining harbors in, 75–76, 279; missile firing at radar station of, 11–12; staying power of and commitment to long fight, 62–63, 68; torpedo boat base in, attack on, 20–22, 25–27; torpedo firing at *Maddox* by, 12

P

Pentagon, 12–13, 24, 27, 38–40, 66, 70
Pentagon Papers: betrayal and release of, 183–184; Congressional subcommittee session to insert Papers into public record, 250–251; copies of, 152; copying of, 165–174, 175–176, 198–199, 301; copying of, FBI investigation about, 182–183, 192–193; copying of by Sheehan, 201–202; copy to Zinn, 210;

discrepancies between truth and government messages about war, 125; distribution to newspapers around country, 240, 245–247, **247**; Ellsberg access to, 152–153, 156–157; Ellsberg attitude toward release of, 248–249, 253–254, 275–276, 311–312; Ellsberg role in, 124–125; Espionage Act and release of, 204, 208–209, 223, 246; Fulbright option to release, 177, 178–179, 182; idea behind writing, 98, 124–125; importance of release of, 194; Kissinger disinterest in, 191–192; leak of, FBI investigation about, 232, 240–241, 256; leak of, speculation about Ellsberg link to, 222, 226, 232; length of, 156; lesson from, 244–245; Marx reading of, 194; McGovern option to release, 193; McNamara role in, 124–125; *Post* option to release, 229–232, 233–234; publication of, legal ruling on, 236–237, 246, 247–248, 251, **252**; publication of by *Globe*, **239**; publication of by *Post*, 233–234, 235–236; publication of by *Times*, 209–211, 212, 213, 214, 220, 223–226; reaction to publication of, 217–220, 221–222; secrecy about, 124–125, 152–153; Sheehan option to release, 197–198, 199–204; source of leak of, 218–219, 222, 226; stopping publication of, legal order for, 226–228, **227**, 230, 237, 240; stopping publication of, Mitchell efforts for, 221–224, 226, 239–240, 245–246; stopping publication of, request for, 235–236

Plumbers, 258. *See also* Special Investigations Unit
Poitras, Laura, 320–322
Prisoners of war and Hao Lo prison: Alvarez experience, 40–41, 81; bombing of, 293–294; dinner at White House after return to US, 312; Hanoi